WESTCLOX

Electric

Jim Linz

This beautiful display piece is free to our dealers with a purchase of 12 or more Westclox during Westclox Week. This display is in three colors—red, blue and gray. It is so constructed that a flasher unit can be used.

Schiffer Publishing Ltd

4880 Lower Valley Road, Atglen, PA 19310 USA

No. 47131   No. 47133   No. 47135

Library of Congress Cataloging-in-Publication Data

Linz, Jim
  Westclox: electric / by Jim Linz.
    p. cm.
  ISBN: 0-7643-1910-8 (pbk.)
  1. Westclox (Firm) 2. Clocks and watches, Electric--United
States--History. 3. Clock and watch making--United States--
History. I. Title
TS544 .L58 2004
681.1'16-dc22

                    2003021284

Designed by Joseph M. Riggio Jr.
Type set in Van Dijk/Humanist 521 BT

ISBN: 0-7643-1910-8
Printed in China
1 2 3 4

Published by Schiffer Publishing Ltd.
4880 Lower Valley Road
Atglen, PA 19310
Phone: (610) 593-1777; Fax: (610) 593-2002
E-mail: Info@schifferbooks.com
Please visit our web site catalog at **www.schifferbooks.com**
We are always looking for people to write books on new and
related subjects. If you have an idea for a book please contact
us at the above address.

This book may be purchased from the publisher.
Include $3.95 for shipping.
Please try your bookstore first.
You may write for a free catalog.

In Europe, Schiffer books are distributed by
Bushwood Books
6 Marksbury Ave.
Kew Gardens
Surrey TW9 4JF England
Phone: 44 (0)20-8392-8585
Fax: 44 (0)20-8392-9876
E-mail: Bushwd@aol.com
Free postage in the UK. Europe: air mail at cost

Acknowledgments

This book would not have been possible without the cooperation of the Library and Research Center of the National Association of Watch and Clock Collectors. The Library contains extensive records on Westclox including trade catalogs, advertisements, service manuals, photographs, and copies of *Tick Talk*. These records provided the foundation for my research and are extensively pictured throughout this book both in photographs of individual clocks and watches taken from catalogs and *Tick Talk* and in photographs of Westclox plants and their employees. Special thanks to Beth Bisbano, former Research Director, and Sharon Gordon, Librarian, for their assistance.

The Westclox History pages at Bill Stoddard's website—clockhistory.com—also proved invaluable in the preparation of this book. The website contains a wealth of information about the company and its products and is also a good reference for those seeking to restore a Big Ben. Personal communication from Bill Stoddard supplemented the information gleaned from his website.

In addition,

–Chris Bailey of the American Clock and Watch Museum has been invaluable in my overall research on Art Deco era clocks. Hopefully, that research will lead to future volumes covering additional manufacturers.

–Sara Hassan made available a number of clocks from her collection.

–Bill Meehan shared the results of his own extensive research on Art Deco era clocks, giving me a head-start toward this and future efforts.

–Lee Werling advised me of the existence of the collection of *Tick Talk*'s at the NAWCC Library and of their rich research potential.

–Bob Merchant assisted in sorting through magazines and wholesale jewelry catalogs to locate advertisements and other pertinent information.

Contents

Part One: Overview
Chapter 1: Introduction

Westclox was not a pioneer in the development of either household electric clocks or electric automobile clocks. In fact, it entered both markets through acquisition.

First, it acquired the Sterling Clock Company of Meriden, Connecticut, an early leader in the production of electric automobile clocks. Soon after acquiring the company in 1928 it moved the entire operation to its Peru-La Salle plant. Sterling continued to operate under its own name for several years after being acquired but was gradually fully absorbed into the Westclox line.

Next, the Hamilton-Sangamo Clock Company, an early pioneer in electric clock making, was acquired. It was a Sangamo electric movement that powered Westclox's first electric clocks, the Models 820 and 840 Big Ben Electrics introduced in 1931.

During the 1930s and 1940s, Westclox continued to introduce new models, some with manual—spin-to-start—movements and others with self-starting synchronous movements developed by Westclox engineers. Although its first electric clocks used Sangamo movements, Westclox engineers had begun developing their own electric movements several years earlier, filing a series of patent applications for synchronous clock motors starting in 1926.

Despite its late start, Westclox became an industry leader in the production of electric clocks during the 1950s and 1960s, due in large part to such innovations as the Drowse® alarm and Magic Touch® alarm. Westclox also became a pioneer in the development of battery-operated clocks and, in the late 1960s and 1970s, the development of quartz watches and clocks.

> "What name do you think of first when you think of an alarm clock?"
>
> Eighty-seven percent said "Big Ben" or "Westclox" in surveys conducted by eight leading publications before and after World War II.
>
> (Reported in *Tick Talk*, July 1950)

The former Westclox Administration Building in Peru-La Salle, Illinois.

Closeup of the decorative brickwork along the top of the Administration Building.

Design Determines Value

Westclox, like other manufacturers, placed the same clock movement in a variety of cases to establish a product line that would appeal to a range of aesthetic tastes. Values, then, depend more on the strength of the design than on the "innards" of the case.

Westclox, like General Electric and Telechron, depended primarily on its in-house design staff to develop new case designs. In the 1930s and 1940s, the task fell primarily to Max Schlenker, both an engineer and designer. Rather than interpreting the work of eras gone by, Schlenker broke new ground with his designs, almost exclusively interpretations of the evolving Art Deco style. His designs were supplemented by designs by Paul Darrot, Design Chief for parent company General Time, and other Westclox staff.

The primary exception to the use of in-house design personnel was the use of famed industrial designer Henry Dreyfuss to design Big Ben, Baby Ben, Ben Electric, and Pocket Ben. In this author's opinion, the Dreyfuss designs are bland and unimaginative compared to those of Schlenker and Darrot.

As the Westclox product line rapidly expanded in the 1950s and 1960s, the dependence on the in-house design staff continued. Several impressive Mid-Century Modern designs were generated. With the current interest in Mid-Century Modern, such clocks are among the most collectible Westclox.

Westclox also introduced several children's novelty clocks during the late 1950s and 1960s. Because of their novel designs, some of these clocks are highly desirable to collectors.

A Tale of Two Cities

The production of electric clocks began at the Peru-La Salle factory in 1931 and continued at that location until 1954 at which time it was moved to the newly constructed General Time plant in Athens, Georgia. The Athens plant produced electric clocks for both the Westclox and Seth Thomas Divisions of General Time.

The Peru-La Salle plant continued in operation until 1980, at which time it was closed and remaining production moved to other locations. The Athens plant remained in operation until General Time filed for bankruptcy in 2001.

Untitled Poem Commemorating the Closure of the Peru-La Salle Plant

Here we are, having our last fling.
Eating & drinking, pretending nothing is happening.
Talley gave us a quick notice, like putting the keys in the door,
Some of us saw it coming, others almost hit the floor.
We'll remember the years we put in for Westclox,
There were wristwatches, pocket watches, you name it, all kinds of clocks.
Wagner gave most of us our very first start,
He had the pick of the litter.
The people put in many years, so they are feeling a little bitter.
Remember when we had ping-pong & bowling as our daily sport,
And remember the *Tick Talks* as our monthly report.
And Quarter Century dinners we enjoyed many years.
Taking all that away left us with a few tears.
Westclox selling out to Talley, that we didn't mind at all,
We all had our jobs we were still on the ball.
Talley in turn left us in a little rutt.
He took away all the clocks, THAT! Was a <u>kick</u> in the butt.
He gave us fuze work, the Government wanted us to make,
Talley in turn passed away, then came the big shake.
The Government took over, and we thought things were going well,
March 31ˢᵗ they're closing the door,
And telling us all to go to hell.
We've worked together for years, Many couldn't see eye to eye,
And yet at this time of parting, we hate to say goodbye.
Before we part, we'll wish each other good luck.
With a little faith and believing, Talley will open its doors,
So people can make another buck.

Rosie
March 5, 1980

Tick Talk

This book traces the history of the Western Clock Company through the pages of *Tick Talk*, the award winning employee magazine launched in May 1913 to promote worker-company relations. In addition to news of new product introductions and advertising, *Tick Talk* informed employees of new benefits, upcoming vacations, and changes in work hours. It constantly stressed the importance of safety, both at the plant and away from work. *Tick Talk* also served as the company's social column, with employees from each department contributing "news" about that department. In addition to weddings, births, and deaths, the columns included gossip about who was dating whom, who had a new car, etc.

Tick Talk spelled out in images of Westclox employees. (Photo: *Tick Talk*, May 5, 1924)

Tick Talk

For its first ten years, *Tick Talk* was edited by W.S. Ashby. In 1926, L.B. Richards assumed responsibility for editing *Tick Talk* in addition to his duties as advertising manager. Reynolds, who joined Westclox in 1914, spent the eleven years immediately preceding his selection as advertising manager as a sales representative in Ohio. He retired in 1966. W.C. Andrews succeeded him as editor of *Tick Talk*.

W.S. Ashby, *Tick Talk* editor, 1916-1926. (Photo: *Tick Talk*, February 20, 1926)

L.B. "Richie" Richards, *Tick Talk* Editor, 1926-1966. (Photo: *Tick Talk*, July 1926)

Photographs of employees, their families, and extended families were often included. Often, pictures of eligible bachelors would be accompanied by the caption "Treat for the Ladies." Similarly single "girls" would merit special attention.

Tick Talk provided extensive coverage of recreational activities, particularly the bowling league that used lanes constructed in the basement of one the factory buildings. Tick Talk also included humor—Tickle Talk—as well as poems, letters from satisfied customers, and news of "Westclockers" serving in the military.

A separate dealer edition of Tick Talk was prepared for jewelers and other retailers until the late 1920s. This edition contained news of new product introductions, tips on preparing effective show windows, announcements of advertising campaigns and competitions, and tips for the jewelers on how to take cases apart and make basic repairs.

Tick Talk was named one of the ten best employees' publications by the National Safety Council in 1927-1929 and continued to gain special recognition into the 1960s. In 1967, the magazine format was replaced by a tabloid newspaper format.

Interspersed throughout this book are photographs and stories from the pages of Tick Talk to give the reader a sense of the company and its employees as well as its products. Also included is a sampling of Tick Talk's special Christmas covers.

In 1929, Tick Talk was named one of the ten best employee magazines for the third straight year in a contest sponsored by the National Safety Council. The only company newsletters placing ahead of Tick Talk were the Kodak Magazine of the Eastman Kodak Company and The Rouser produced by the Clark Manufacturing Company.

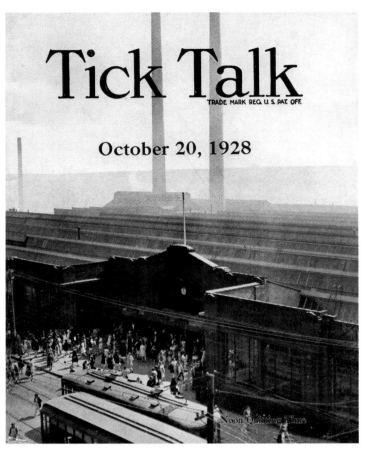

"Noon Quitting Time" in front of the Westclox plant in Peru, Illinois, as portrayed on the cover of the October 28, 1928, Tick Talk.

Sales Displays

An important part of Westclox's sales strategy was the window display. A wide range of colorful displays, many with stunning Art Nouveau and Art Deco designs, were provided free to dealers to help them create effective Westclox window displays. Special contests were conducted to encourage dealers to devote an entire window to the display of Westclox. Because most of the displays were created for special promotions, jewelers and other retailers generally used and then discarded the displays. As a result, examples of Westclox advertising displays seldom surface.

This volume captures many of the displays, presenting over 200 examples gleaned from the pages of Tick Talk and Westclox catalogs. Because of their rarity, early advertising displays are likely to command significantly higher prices that most clocks.

A Westclox advertising card, approximately 1-1/2" x 3". (Photo: Whitaker Collection, NAWCC)

Tick Talk
TRADE MARK REG. U. S. PAT. OFF.

June 20 & July 5, 1931

Tick Talk takes off for summer vacation. (Photo: *Tick Talk*, June 20 & July 5, 1931)

Westclox Ventures into New Product Lines

In the late 1960s, Westclox introduced a new line of weather instruments including thermometers, barometers, and hygrometers. After Talley Industries acquired General Time in a hostile takeover in 1968, the Westclox name was applied to a variety of other electronic products including smoke detectors, burglar alarms, and cassette recorders. There does not currently appear to be strong collector interest in any of these products.

But My Clock's Not Included

In preparing this volume, every attempt was made to include all models introduced through 1970. Using *Tick Talk* and product catalogs, both dates of introduction and major design changes were captured. Sadly, neither the collection of *Tick Talk*'s nor catalogs was complete. Particularly lacking in research on electric clocks are catalogs from the early 1950s. In addition, models developed by Westclox's Canadian and British plants are excluded. As a result, there are inevitably a few models that slipped through the cracks. If you have such a model, please contact the author so that it can be included in a future update.

Jim Linz
PO Box 221011
Chantilly, VA 20153-1011
Jimlinz@documenteddesign.com

Prior to the 1930 introduction of the first Westclox electric, the Western Clock Company established itself as a world leader in the production of spring wound alarm clocks. This 1930 Westclox ad in a wholesale jewelry catalog shows off the "big four"—Big Ben, Baby Ben, Sleep-Meter, and America. (Photo: Leonard Krower & Son, Inc. catalog, 1930)

Chapter 2: An Overview of Westclox and General Time

United Clock Company

Westclox's roots can be traced to the thriving Connecticut clock making industry of the late nineteenth century. For it was in Waterbury, Connecticut, that Charles Stahlberg developed the production process that was to revolutionize clock making.

In 1884, Stahlberg left his employ at the Waterbury Clock Company (now a part of the Timex Corporation) and, together with three other men from Waterbury, Connecticut—William Paton, Henry Davis, and a Mr. Dolph—moved to Peru, Illinois, with plans to establish a clock factory to produce reliable, low-priced clocks based on Stahlberg's new process for molding multiple parts together using molten metal.

Peru businessman F.W. Matthiessen, Sr. would prove instrumental in securing needed financial backing for the new venture and would ultimately gain control of the company. Matthiessen was one of the founders of the Matthiessen and Hegeler Zinc Company, among the world's largest zinc producers.

The relationship between Stahlberg and Matthiessen began over a small order Stahlberg placed for four pounds of zinc. As Stahlberg explained his planned use of the zinc in the production of a revolutionary new clock movement, Matthiessen's interest grew. Soon Matthiessen was organizing Peru businessmen to lend financial support to Stahlberg and his new United Clock Company. The company began operations in 1884 from the back of what was then Brylski's Department Store.

With financial backing from local businessmen recruited by F.W. Matthiessen, the United Clock Company began construction of a three-story plant. The original plant, a mere 100 feet long and 40 feet wide, was later torn down and replaced.

As the building neared completion, Joe Klein joined the firm and began making patterns and tools for installation in the new clock factory. Once installation of the new shafting and machinery was complete, production slowly increased from one clock to twenty clocks per day.

By the time the new firm was incorporated as the United Clock Corporation on December 23, 1885, production reached fifty clocks per day and the number of employees increased to twenty. The day's production was loaded on a pushcart and sold at local stores or given away as premiums.

F.W. Matthiessen, a La Salle zinc manufacturer who acquired the defunct United Clock Company and renamed the company the Western Clock Manufacturing Company. (Photo: *Tick Talk*, August 1952)

Western Clock Manufacturing Company

As the company's sales floundered, however, most of the investors grew restless and the small company filed for bankruptcy in 1887. After a second bankruptcy filing, F.W. Matthiessen bought out the other investors, acquiring the plant and its equipment for about two cents on the dollar. He quickly renamed the firm the Western Clock Manufacturing Company and set out to pursue Stahlberg's dream even as Stahlberg left town to pursue other dreams.

Matthiessen quickly replaced the existing management, bringing in Ernst Roth as the new General Manager. It was Roth, a Matthiessen relative, who would reshape the fortunes of the company by hiring George Kern to develop and design a new type of alarm clock—Big Ben.

Although Matthiessen brought in new management, he steadfastly held to Stahlberg's revolutionary method of clock construction despite the concerns of many in the clock industry.

The firm continued to struggle for several years. Even as others in the clock industry expressed continuing doubt about the Western Clock Manufacturing Company's revolutionary production methods, the firm's management remained committed to those methods.

For several years, Matthiessen put money into the plant to cover losses. Eventually sales increased to the point that the firm became profitable. During its first five years, employment gradually increased, reaching eighty-one in 1890. The next decade found a tripling of employment to 245 in 1900. By 1910—the year Big Ben was formally introduced to the public—employment quadrupled, reaching 896.

In 1902, the company issued its first known catalog. The catalog included twenty-one clocks and one pocket watch. In addition to a number of nickel-plated brass alarm clocks with top bell, the Western Clock Manufacturing Company offered a cast iron alarm with hidden alarm bell, several ornate ormolu gold-plated models, and five models in imported porcelain cases.

By the time the next catalog was issued in 1907, over seventy-five models were being offered, including a number with impressive Art Nouveau styling. Although the company offered a number of alarm models, the bulk of its efforts were devoted to the production of ornate table clocks. Still, the company's model selection was modest compared to such giants of the industry as Seth Thomas, Waterbury, and New Haven. In addition to finished clocks, the company offered movements in a variety of styles and sizes to enable purchasers to add a Western movement to a clock case of their own design and manufacture.

The successful introduction of Big Ben in 1910 would, however, have a phenomenal effect on the company, leading to a reversal in the trend of increased model offerings and a general move away from the production of table clocks to a strong emphasis on alarm clocks. As sales of Big Ben grew, most other models were dropped during the teens. A 1915 dealer's price list contains only forty-five clock models plus two pocket watches. The completeness of the list is suspect, however, because neither Big Ben nor

Baby Ben is included. The 1919 edition of *First Aid for Injured Westclox*, however, also contains a much reduced product line, illustrating none of the ornate cast iron frame models.

Ernst Roth (Photo: *Tick Talk*, February 20, 1923)

The year 1925 proved to be pivotal for the Western Clock Company as a new motor generating set was installed in the Westclox engine room to supply alternating current. The firm's electric furnaces, used to harden and anneal springs and temper various dies, tools, and clock parts, ran at maximum efficiency on alternating current. Many power plants across the country, such as that serving the La Salle/Peru area, however, were still transmitting direct current at the time.

Plans for the construction of a new five-story addition to the Westclox warehouse were announced in the August 20, 1925, *Tick Talk*. The new building, just west of the existing five-story building, is an exact duplicate of the original building, with the exception of a different placement of the windows. The building added 64,500 square feet of space.

Plans for construction of a new four-story building were announced in the July 20, 1929, *Tick Talk*. The new building, constructed at the corner of East Fifth and Buffalo Streets, added 24,750 feet of floor space. Prior to the construction of this building, all factory buildings had been single-story. Only the five-story warehouse and old Office Building had been more than one-story. The high cost of real estate and the great distance electric trucks must travel between departments were cited as the reasons for the multi-floor factory building.

The Westclox plant was expanded in 1890 through the addition of a wing at the west end of the plant. (Photo: 1956 Westclox open house program)

View of the Westclox plant and workers, February 17, 1905. At the time, the Western Clock Company had a staff of 410. (Photo: *Tick Talk*, August 1952)

The Westclox office staff circa 1911. (Photo: *Tick Talk*, April 20, 1931)

These two photos show the expansion of the Westclox factory between 1920 and 1931. The top picture is a view of the plant from the Rock Island Railroad tracks in 1920. By 1931, the hillside had been dug away and in its place the first two units of the new 5-story factory building had been completed. (Photo: *Tick Talk*, April 5, 1931)

Artist's conception of the new Administration Building in La Salle, Illinois. (Photo: *Tick Talk*, May 1923)

Acquisition of Sterling Clock Company

The Western Clock Company entered the field of electric automobile clocks through the acquisition of the Sterling Clock Company in the late 1920s. Originally located in New York City, the Sterling Clock Company moved to Meriden, Connecticut, in December 1926, taking a three-year lease on the former Parker factory on West Main Street. Less than two years later, in October 1928, Westclox announced the closure of the Meriden plant and the transfer of the Sterling equipment to the La Salle factory.

For several years, the Sterling Clock Company continued to operate as a separate company engaged in selling electric automobile clocks, albeit out of the same factory as the Western Clock Company. On March 1, 1933, however, the Western Clock Company took over the sale of Sterling Electric Automobile Clocks. Employees of the Sterling Clock Company were transferred to the Western Clock Company and assigned to the newly established Sterling Clock Division of the Sales Department.

Formation of General Time

Plans to merge the Western Clock Company and the Seth Thomas Clock Company were announced in the November 5, 1930, *Tick Talk*. Stockholders of the two companies approved the merger at a November 12, 1930, meeting. The plans called for creation of a holding company—General Time Instruments Corporation—to own and control the stock of both firms. Each company continued to operate under its present name and management and each was represented on the Board of the holding company. At the time of the merger, the Western Clock Company was the largest alarm clock manufacturer in the world and Seth Thomas was a leading maker of higher priced timepieces. Although Seth Thomas' principal product at the time was chiming mantle clocks, the company also produced a wide variety of other clocks for the home and office as well as tower and other commercial clocks.

Although the companies were expected to continue operating independently, economies were expected to result from mutual use of the facilities of each, greater effectiveness was expected to result from joint marketing efforts, and a more complete line of products was expected to result from the capabilities of the combined companies.

General Time Instruments Corporation was shortened to General Time Corporation in 1949.

Westclox Employees by Year

1890—23
1900—256
1910—875
1920—1999
1930—2642
1940—3533
1950—4000+

The front of the Westclox factory in La Salle, Illinois, graces the cover of the June 1949 *Tick Talk*.

General Time Expands Through Acquisition

Tick Talk's April 20, 1931, issue carried news of General Time's purchase of pioneering electric clock manufacturer Hamilton-Sangamo. The Hamilton-Sangamo Corporation had been formed in the Spring of 1929 as a joint venture of the Hamilton Watch Company of Lancaster, Pennsylvania, and Springfield, Illinois, and the Sangamo Electric Company of Springfield to take over the marketing of Sangamo electric clocks produced in the Sangamo plant.

It was through a license to produce the Sangamo synchronous movement that Westclox entered the electric clock field in 1931 with the introduction of the Big Ben electric.

Tick Talk noted that the clocks produced by Hamilton-Sangamo are more in keeping with those produced by General Times' Seth Thomas division and that it was expected that the manufacture and sale of Sangamo clocks would be handled through Seth Thomas.

In 1935, General Time purchased the Stromberg Time Corporation of Chicago, a maker of time-recording machines for industry, including time stamps, in- and out-recorders, job recorders, and similar devices. It became the Stromberg Division and operations quickly moved from Chicago to the Seth Thomas factory in Thomaston, Connecticut.

General Time sold its Stromberg Time recorder business to the MITE Corporation in March 1966.

In late 1936, the Western Clock Company was renamed the Westclox Division of the General Time Instruments Corporation. Employees were told in the December 1931 *Tick Talk* that

the change would have little or no effect on plant operations. The change was made in response to recently enacted laws placing heavy burdens on certain inter-corporate transactions.

Big Ben Goes To War

General Time began supporting the defense effort in 1939, almost two years before Japan attacked Pearl Harbor and the United States entered the conflict. Almost immediately after the declaration of war, all General Time plants were quickly turned to full wartime production. Three times the Westclox Division received the Army-Navy "E" award for its exceptional performance. The Peru-La Salle plant manufactured hundreds of thousands of mechanical time fuzes for bombs, rockets, and shells.

Production of war materials at the Peru-La Salle plant increased almost immediately after the December 7, 1941, attack and, on July 31, 1942, all production of timepieces stopped. *Tick Talk* noted that:

[w]ith the cessation of clock and watch production, Westclockers, many of whom had worked on one specialized job for 30 and 40 years, had to take new work producing strange instruments of war. Machines were hard to get. Shift work, with all it headaches and readjustments in one's daily life, had to be put in effect.

One of the biggest problems of the period was the constantly changing demands of the War Department to meet the ever-changing requirements of our armed forces. Sometimes these changes struck without any advance notice, requiring the wholesale moving of workers in the plant.

Material was always a problem … and along with problems of this nature was the task of keeping the plant functioning smoothly and finding new workers to take the place of the almost 700 young men and women who left us to enter the service.

Westclox produced a wide array of small parts and devices for the war effort. For example, it produced 7.5 million fuzes of all types.

Cover to the program commemorating Westclox's receipt of the Army-Navy "E" during World War II.

Westclox received the Army Navy "E" for their work in support of the war effort during World War II. (Photo: Whitaker Collection, NAWCC)

Westclox Becomes Unionized

The roots of unionization at Westclox can be traced back to the wartime transformation of the Westclox factory from clock making to fuse making and to the controversy established by Westclox's attempts to protect the jobs and pay of highly skilled workers shifted into less-skilled and lower-paying positions. This resulted in some workers earning more than others for performing the same tasks. This disparity led to the first labor agreement between Westclox and the International Association of Machinists, signed May 15, 1943. Among the provisions of the first contract was a provision that "women shall receive the same rate of pay as men where they do work of comparable quantity and quality in similar occupations…" The provision had minimal effect, however, because few women at the time were performing the same tasks as male employees.

Acquisition of Haydon Manufacturing

Soon after the end of World War II, General Time acquired the Haydon Manufacturing Company of Torrington, Connecticut. Haydon manufactured industrial timing equipment—things

Westclox Fuzes Used in Bombing Japan

The March 1945 *Tick Talk* notes that fuzes produced in Westclox's La Salle plant played a vital role in the new incendiary bombs dropped on Tokyo. The M-69 bombs, about 19-inches long and weighing six pounds each, were filled with what was called gasoline jell. Its contents burned as long as ten minutes at temperatures above 3000 degrees Fahrenheit.

The bombs were dropped in clusters weighing 100 and 500 pounds, with fourteen bombs in the small cluster and thirty-eight bombs in the large cluster.

The cover to the September 1945 *Tick Talk* reflects Westclox's wartime role.

like timing motors, clock movements, and timers for washing machines, dryers, electric ranges, and X-ray timers. The Torrington plant covered 90,000 square feet of floor space and employed about 600 people in 1954.

In January 1952, General Time purchased a factory in Goshen, Indiana. Initially, the Goshen plant was used entirely to produce war materials to support the Korean Conflict. The Goshen plant had about 65,000 square feet of space and over 200 employees.

New Clock Plant Constructed in Athens, Georgia

In November 1953, General Time announced that it would build a new plant in Athens, Georgia. In explaining the decision to build the new plant, General Time President Donald J. Hawthorne told the Athens Chamber of Commerce that:

>...we are building a plant here to make Westclox electric household clocks. In La Salle we have used up the available labor supply—here in Athens and the surrounding communities you have people looking for jobs. At Westclox, because of the variety of products, it has been difficult to devote the necessary engineering and production time to proper development of electric clocks. In Athens, with nothing to worry about except electric clocks, we should be able to place our Westclox electrics in the same position, marketwise, that our spring clocks are in today.

The first phase of the Athens plant included approximately 110,000 square feet of floor space. Initial employment was about 500 people. The Athens plant was formally dedicated November 3, 1954. It began operations assembling both Westclox and Seth Thomas electric clocks.

The main entrance to General Time's Athens, Georgia, plant. (Photo: *Tick Talk*, September 1957).

The initial cost of the land, buildings, machinery, and equipment for the Athens plant was about $2.5 million.

In 1954, General Time's many divisions produced more than 50,000 clocks, watches, and timing devices daily.

New Government Products Division Established

In June 1964, General Time announced the establishment of a new Government Products Division to consolidate its operations in the military and aerospace field. The new division, with headquarters in Stamford, Connecticut, consolidated activities carried out by General Time's Advanced Electronics Group, the company's Skokie, Illinois, laboratory, Barth Engineering and Manufacturing Company, and the military products section of the Stromberg Division. The Westclox Division was to continue to handle its defense work independently, but was to coordinate its activities with the Government Products Division. In 1964, defense work accounted for about fifteen percent of General Time sales.

Westclox Operations in Other Countries

Westclox was a pioneer in opening new markets. Its products became known in Australia, Canada, Great Britain, South Africa, the Far East, and many other lands.

The Western Clock Company established its first Canadian sales office in Toronto in 1912. As the demand for Westclox products increased, the company decided to operate a factory in Canada to produce clocks for the Canadian market. The Western Clock Company, Limited, of Canada, was incorporated in 1919 as a subsidiary of the Peru-La Salle plant. A small factory building in Peterborough, Ontario, approximately 100 miles northeast of Toronto was purchased in 1920 and operations were begun with a workforce of twenty employees.

Initially, the plant was used primarily for assembly of parts manufactured by the La Salle-Peru plant but, as production increased, the Canadian plant began to manufacture its own parts and started looking for larger quarters.

In 1922, thirty acres were purchased on the outskirts of Peterborough and construction of a new plant commenced. Additional buildings were periodically added, and, by 1953, the factory had a total of 150,000 square feet of floor space. By 1954, the Canadian plant employed over 700 people, manufacturing almost all products in the Westclox line.

During the late 1930s General Time contemplated overseas expansion but the outbreak of World War II put those plans on hold. General Time formed Westclox Limited, a United Kingdom subsidiary in 1939, but operations were halted almost immediately because of the outbreak of World War II.

Overseas expansion was again pursued shortly after the end of World War II with plans to construct manufacturing facilities in Great Britain being announced in the September 1946 *Tick Talk*. Plans called for the new factory to produce both clocks and watches using parts produced by the La Salle, Illinois, and Peterborough, Canada, factories.

Architect's rendering of the "new" Westclox factory in Peterborough, Ontario.
The building was designed by Bernard H. Prack. (Photo: *Tick Talk*, June 20, 1922)

Westclox's Canadian plant. Construction of the plant began in 1922. By 1956, the
plant had been expanded to 150,000 square feet. (Photo: *Tick Talk*, August 1956)

At the time Westclox initiated plans to construct a plant in Great Britain, German manufacturers were reported to be providing most of Britain's timepiece requirements, according to *Tick Talk*. German dominance of the British market prior to the outbreak of World War II seems unlikely, however, as there was a flourishing British clock manufacturing industry dominated by companies such as Smith's and Metamec.

Westclox began preparation for British operations in 1946 by training workers in an old building on the banks of Loch Lomond. In 1948, a new 50,000 square foot factory was completed. The factory, with an initial workforce of twenty-five, began producing four inch alarm clocks, the first model being the "Good Morning."

By 1953, the factory in Dumbarton, Scotland, had grown to 100,000 square feet and 650 employees and was operating at capacity. As labor costs were substantially lower than in the United States and Canada, much of the export market formerly served from the U.S. and Canadian plants was shifted to the Dumbarton plant. Markets served by the Dumbarton factory included Norway, Africa, parts of Asia, New Zealand, and Australia.

Two years after announcing plans for the Scottish plant, General Time, in 1948, began to manufacture Westclox alarms in Sao Paulo, Brazil. By 1954 the Brazilian facility, established to get around money and import restrictions that had driven Westclox out of a formerly lucrative market, employed about 800 people.

At the same time it announced the establishment of the Scottish plant, General Time announced creation of Westclox Proprietary, Limited in Melbourne, Australia. The manufacture of Westclox in Australia would, however, prove short-lived. Closure of the manufacturing facilities established in Melbourne was announced in the September 1953 *Tick Talk*. In its six years of operation the Australian subsidiary manufactured approximately two million clocks.

In announcing the closing, General Time said that changes in the market and economic conditions in Australia no longer warranted the continuation of manufacturing operations in Australia. Following the closure, other divisions of the corporation supplied the Australian market.

Westclox's plant in Strathleven, Dumbarton, Scotland produced clocks for the British market. The plant was "on the grounds of a once famous estate" but a short distance from the "bonnie banks" of Loch Lomond. (Photo: *Tick Talk*, April 1950)

In 1954, General Time operated four plants in the United States, one in Canada, one in Scotland, and had a small assembly operation in Brazil. It employed more than 6,000 people. In 1953, sales exceeded $50 million.

In terms of size, the La Salle, Illinois, Westclox plant was by far the largest operated by General Time. Over 4,200 employees were spread out in buildings covering over 750,000 square feet.

General Time Officers—
A Family Affair

When F.W. Matthiessen retired, he was succeeded by Ernst G. Roth, a relative. Following Roth's sudden death on October 2, 1924, the Western Clock Company continued to be largely a family run business. F.W. Matthiessen, Jr., son of the founder, was elected Chairman of the Board of Directors in February 1925. He was first elected to the Board in 1918. Unlike his father, however, F.W. Matthiessen moved away from Peru-La Salle, living on a large ranch in Triunfo, California.

At the same time F.W., Jr. was elected Chairman of the Board, Ralph H. Matthiessen, grandson of founder F.W., was elected President of the Western Clock Company. First elected to the Board in 1920, R.H. Matthiessen lived in New York where he founded and operated the Motor Haulage Company, a delivery service in downtown New York.

In 1943, Arnold J. Wilson became President of General Time. Wilson, a native of La Salle, was a member of one of La Salle's oldest families and began his career with Westclox, serving as General Manager from 1932 to 1940. He became Executive Vice-President of General Time in 1940, relocating to the corporate headquarters in New York at that time. In addition to his work for General Time, Wilson served as the Chairman of the Board of the La Salle National Bank and Eureka Building Association. He also served as a director of the Hygienic Institute of Peru-La Salle-Oglesby.

Wilson served as President of General Time until his retirement on pension in 1953. He remained on the Board of Directors following his retirement and continued to contribute to the company as a consultant.

Following Wilson's retirement, another longtime Westclox employee—Donald J. Hawthorne—became President of General Time. Hawthorne was raised in Peru and joined the Western Clock Company in 1925. After supervising the operations of the Canadian plant for several years, he became Westclox Works Manager in 1932 and, in 1938, Westclox General Manager. He was added to the General Time Board of Directors in 1939, but remained in Peru-La Salle until 1948, first as Westclox General Manager until 1944 and then as vice president of General Time. He became executive vice president in 1948, at which time he relocated to New York.

Donald J. Hawthorne became President of General Time in April 1953. (Photo: *Tick Talk*, April 1953)

Henry E. Hackman, former Western Clock Company General Manager and Vice President. Hackman joined the Westclox office staff in 1890 when total employment was only eighty-one. He became Chairman of the Board of Directors in 1932. (Photo: *Tick Talk*, July 1, 1937)

Arnold J. Wilson, President of General Time, 1943 to 1953. (Photo: *Tick Talk*, April 1953)

In the first twenty-five years after its founding in 1931, General Time had three presidents. Pictured left to right are Ralph H. Matthiessen, 1931-1944; Arnold J. Wilson, 1944-1953; Donald J. Hawthorne. (Photo: *Tick Talk*, June-July 1956)

Westclox Becomes A Leader In Employee Benefits

During the first forty years of the twentieth century, the Western Clock Company established itself as an innovator and leader in the establishment of employee benefits in areas such as reduced working hours, disability and unemployment compensation, retirement, and health care. It was frequently recognized by business journals for its leadership.

Work Hours Shortened—Westclox periodically reduced work hours at the Peru-La Salle plant. Between 1889 and 1903, the workweek was 60 hours. Although the workweek was officially reduced to 57 hours between 1903 and 1909, the plant often ran until 9 p.m. when demand was high. In 1909 the workweek was reduced to 54 hours followed by a further reduction to 50 hours in 1918. Only two years later, it was reduced to 47 hours, and then, in 1927, to 47.5 hours. In 1930, Saturday hours were eliminated, creating the 40-hour workweek.

Vacation Pay—In 1920, Westclox added paid vacations to its benefit package, becoming one of the nation's first employers to provide such a benefit. That year, 423 Westclockers qualified for either one or two weeks paid vacation, depending on their length of service. By 1937, this number had grown to 2,474, approximately eighty-two percent of the Westclox workforce. Those with five or more years of service received two weeks paid vacation, while those with two to five years service received a one week paid vacation.

Annuity Plan—The Western Clock Company established a voluntary Income and Pension Plan for its employees in 1924, the first group annuity plan. Under the plan, employees and the employer share the cost. In the 1932 issue of *Forbes*, Le Roy A. Lincoln, Vice President of the Metropolitan Life Insurance Company, praised the Western Clock Company for its foresight stating that:

> It is a high compliment to the intelligence and foresight of the management of that company [Western Clock Company] that, despite the subsequent great spread and development of group annuity plans, no essential changes have been found necessary in its original plan. Many of the principles being used today had their origin in that plan.

Life Insurance—In 1917, life insurance coverage was added for all employees who had worked for the company for six months. Payments ranged from $300 to $2,000 depending on length of service.

Sickness Benefit Plan—Westclox established a Sickness Benefit Plan in 1926, providing benefits to Income and Pension Plan members who were ill or disabled for more than a week. The following table shows the number of Income and Pension Plan members by year, 1926-1932, followed by the number receiving sickness benefits. In 1932, one Westclocker received sickness benefits for twenty-three weeks; another for seventeen weeks. The entire cost of the Sickness Benefit Plan was paid by the company.

1926—1723—151
1927—1905—147
1928—2120—203
1929—2092—156
1930—2186—92
1931—2241—71
1932—1674—72

In 1949, the Sickness Benefit Plan was still being provided to Westclockers as a free benefit, paid for entirely by the company. All employees enrolled in the Income and Pension Plan were eligible for benefits. Maximum benefits were determined by length of service:

25 years and over—39 weeks
20-24 years—34 weeks
15-19 years—30 weeks
10-14 years—26 weeks
5-9 years—13 weeks
2-4 years—7 weeks

Employees who were absent from work due to sickness or occupational illness were eligible to receive benefits, at half pay.

An employee who had drawn the maximum benefits within twelve consecutive months was required to actively work for at least six months before again being eligible for benefits. The total weeks for which an employee could draw benefits over his or her entire period of service could not exceed three weeks benefit for each year of service.

Student Loans—In 1928, Westclox began a program of student loans to enable its employees to attend the Elgin Watchmaker College.

Unemployment Benefits—During the height of the Great Depression, the Western Clock Company established an experimental Temporary Unemployment Benefit Plan to ensure stable, permanent employees a minimum of half pay for a period of six months during the winter months when work was expected to be slack. During the period covered by the experiment, more than $30,000 was expended from the fund. The unemployment benefit plan ran from August 30, 1932, to April 22, 1933.

Pre-Pension Plan—In 1932 Westclox established a plan to provide cash payments to workers with ten years or more of service who were dismissed because of lack of work. Payments were tied to worker age and length of service.

Christmas Bonus—Westclox first provided its employees a Christmas Bonus in 1936. All employees with one year's service were given a bonus equal to two weeks pay. Employees with less than a year's service received pro-rated bonuses based on length of service. Bonuses totaled over $115,000 in 1936.

Health Insurance—Westclox established a new Hospital & Surgical Insurance Plan in 1950. Initial Coverage included:

–$7.00 a day for hospital room and board for employees and actual costs up to $7.00 a day for dependents;
–Up to $105 for other hospital charges;
–Up to $150 for operations; and
–$75.00 for maternity benefits ($150 for a Caesarian Section).

The employee's monthly premium ranged from $1.18 for single employees to $3.98 for the employee, spouse, and children.

Maternity Leave—In 1953 Westclox revised its maternity policy to provide health benefits while women were on maternity "leave." Women did not receive pay while on maternity leave.

JUNE   1959   JULY

July was vacation time at Westclox. This scene of boys frolicking in the water made frequent appearances in *Tick Talk*. (Photo: *Tick Talk*, June/July 1959)

The August 1934 *Tick Talk* reported that since the establishment of the pension plan in 1924, thirty-eight Westclockers had retired on pension. Payments to the thirty-eight retirees totaled $16,581.

In 1950, 3,549 Westclockers qualified for vacation pay, with 2,244 receiving two-weeks and 1,305 receiving one week. Those not qualifying for vacation pay were required to take the two weeks off without pay.

"The Western Clock Company has always been in the forefront in progressive labor policies, and barring unforeseen developments, hopes and expects to maintain its position."

Tick Talk, January 5, 1927

Recreational Activities

The Peru-La Salle factory also provided its employees numerous recreational activities. These included establishment of such facilities as:

–A recreation area established across from the factory with baseball diamonds and picnic areas (1918).

–A library (1918). New acquisitions were listed in *Tick Talk*.

–Tennis courts (1919).

–A four-lane bowling alley located in the basement of one of the factory buildings (1923). Bowling leagues were soon formed and league results became a regular feature of *Tick Talk*. The lanes remained open until 1958.

–A player piano placed in the cafeteria (1923). The company sponsored lunch hour dances several days a week.

–An ice rink (1925).

–Tennis courts and horseshoe pits (1928).

–Free garden plots, plowed and furrowed by the company (1931).

The company also supported a number of other employee activities including an orchestra and glee club organized in 1913, a men's basketball team—the Clockers—established in 1907, a military band established in 1917, an Art and Camera Club active during the 1930s, an indoor baseball team in the early 1900s, and the Westclox Entertainers, a theatrical group.

An annual Christmas party was organized for the children and grandchildren of Westclox employees.

Westclox's 1914 indoor baseball team. (Photo: *Tick Talk*, March 1952)

In 1923, Westclox announced plans to install four bowling alleys in the basement of the old store building. The alleys—described as the finest in the country—had automatic pinsetters, shaded lights, and five balls per alley. (*Tick Talk*, February 23, 1923)

The Westclox bowling alleys. Bowling was a popular pastime for Westclox employees and *Tick Talk* reported all the league results. (Photo: *Tick Talk*, May 20, 1924)

The "new" cafeteria at the La Salle/Peru plant. (Photo: *Tick Talk*, September 1949)

Westclox Helps Meet Employees Housing Needs

To help ensure an adequate labor force, the Western Clock Company helped its employees find suitable housing. First, it operated a dormitory for female employees from 1919 to 1928. As male employees enlisted in the military during World War I, the company needed to attract and retain female workers. An important component of this recruitment effort was the availability of low-cost housing for women coming from outside the Peru-La Salle area. In addition to hot and cold running water, the rooms provided a dresser, couches, and large closets. The dormitory was closed June 1, 1928.

Second, it purchased a large tract of land near the factory in 1920 and built homes on the property that were then sold to its employees at cost—typically $3,000 to $4,000. It even offered an installment plan; employees could make payments over a three-year period. Beginning in 1925, employees were allowed to purchase lots in Central Park and build their own homes. By 1927, the company had set up a real estate department to manage Central Park, including both initial sales and resales.

Finally, the Western Clock Company established a second housing development—Grove Residence Park—in 1929. This development was marketed toward Westclox's upper management and other wealthy businessmen. Among its many features were the inclusion of parkland, underground wiring, and restrictive covenants similar to those in place in many present-day housing developments. For example, the covenants forbid homeowners from cutting trees over 5-inches in diameter without prior approval from the Grove Owners Association; did not allow temporary buildings to be maintained on any lot; and did not allow signs larger than 18-inches by 30-inches. Minimum building costs were established and lot owners were required to obtain approval of building plans before construction could begin. Like many developments across the country in the 1930s—including the government-sponsored new town, Greenbelt, Maryland—covenants also excluded Blacks and other non-Caucasians from home ownership.

To make Westclockers better appreciate their hours and working conditions, *Tick Talk* occasionally ran articles describing conditions in other manufacturing plants. For example, the October 28, 1928, *Tick Talk* reported that the following sign was posted by management at a mill in Massachusetts:

The mill will be put in operation 10 minutes before sunrise at all seasons of the year, and the gate will be shut 30 minutes past eight each evening.

Anyone damaging machinery or impeding the progress of work must pay for the losses incurred.

Anyone employed for a specified period of time must make up lost hours before receiving his pay.

Anyone who quits without giving a month's notice forfeits four weeks' wages.

From September till March, 25 minutes will be allowed for breakfast, 30 minutes for dinner, and 25 minutes for supper, and no more.

During the summer months all employees must have their breakfast before going to work.

Houses being developed in La Salle's Central Park development. (Photo: *Tick Talk*, March 5, 1926)

Quarter Century Club

The Western Clock Company established the Quarter Century Club to recognize employees who had worked for Westclox for twenty-five or more years. An annual banquet was held to recognize new members, mark new milestones, such as thirty, forty, and fifty years of service, and welcome back retired members. In 1958, the Quarter Century club had 814 active members—twenty-five percent of the Westclox work force. By 1968, there were 1,008 active members and 403 associate members.

Many workers spent their entire working careers with Westclox. Pictured is John W. Hanson who retired in January 1950 after forty-nine years of service. When he started with Westclox in 1899, Hanson worked ten hours a day, six days a week. Total Westclox staffing at the time was about 250. (Photo: *Tick Talk*, January 1950)

Another of Westclox's long time employees was Frances Lang. Ms. Lang joined the company in 1907 and is shown in this 1950 photo after forty-three years of service. (Photo: *Tick Talk*, March 1950)

As of December 1952, eleven Westclockers had completed fifty years of service. Each employee reaching the fifty-year milestone was given a $1000 Government bond.

As of December 1949, 721 Westclox employees, 18.2 percent of the workforce, had twenty-five or more years of service, including two with over fifty years of service and another seventy-six employees with between forty and fifty years service. (*Tick Talk*, December 1949)

Employee Safety

The *Tick Talk* cover for March 1935 announces the end of Westclox's safety record at over 11 million hours without a lost time accident.

Tick Talk
TRADE MARK REG. U. S. PAT. OFF.

A Lost Time Accident
Breaks Perfect Record at
11,114,599.8 Hours

March :-: 1935

Westclox continually stressed the importance of goggles. (Photo: *Tick Talk*, May 1955)

Another of the frequent reminders to wear safety goggles. (*Tick Talk*, March 1953)

ter how minor, Westclox was able to operate in 1930 without a lost time accident until the final weeks of the year. It accomplished the same feat in 1931, losing its perfect record in December.

That December 1931 lost time accident, however, would prove to be the plant's last for several years. The May 1934 *Tick Talk* brought news that Westclox had made safety history, having operated 7,280,604 man-hours without a disabling injury.

The Editor of the *National Safety News* noted at that time that Westclox had had a strong reputation for safety for at least ten years, saying that "Safety at Westclox antedates the national movement in the United States by several years. It is difficult to trace back the threads of this movement to their source, and to point out definitively any one occasion as being the start of safety work at this plant."

He went on to state that:

> It may be somewhat of a blow to those who consider modern accident prevention work as something distinctly American to learn that this company received its inspiration in Germany. About 1900, before there was any national effort for accident prevention in this country, F.W. Matthiessen, then owner of practically all the stock in the company, visited Germany and observed with interest the safety work that was being done there. He brought the idea back to his own plant.
>
> The germ was planted, but it was decided in those early days that if safety was to have a healthy growth, it must not be imposed from without, but must grow and develop naturally from within.

Westclox ran the record to 11,111,599.8 hours before an accident in March 1935 ended the accident-free streak after more than three years.

"Radium is the most energetic metal in the world... This flow of electrical energy is so active that one cannot expose the unprotected skin directly to its bombardment, since the tissues are completely destroyed by a close contact with it." J. A. Reinhardt writing in the March 20, 1923, *Tick Talk*.

Westclox was a leader in the Safety First movement, at one time holding the nation's longest safety record. *Tick Talk* frequently featured graphic reminders to wear safety goggles as well as other safety tips. It also reprinted many safety cartoons created by the National Safety Council.

Westclox suffered numerous lost time accidents in 1929 and each time *Tick Talk* published the details of the injury and what could have been done to prevent the injury. For example, in August an employee suffered a serious eye injury when a hot chisel slipped from his grip and struck him in the eye. Although the employee had been provided goggles, he was not wearing them at the time. Similarly, a fifth lost time accident was reported in the November *Tick Talk*. In this case an employee suffered a bruise but did not have it treated by the medical department. When the bruise became infected, he was unable to work for ten days.

With an increased emphasis on accident prevention and a visit to the health unit whenever an accident occurred, no mat-

---

"The most outstanding accident prevention record of all time has been achieved by the Western Clock Company which, employing 2,300 people, recently passed the ten million accident-free hour mark... This demonstrates that accidents—in industry at least—are really unnecessary if reasonable diligence, supplemented by adequate mechanical safeguarding, be employed."

T.A. Burke, National Safety Council, February 1935

By the early 1950s, the Westclox safety record was greatly diminished from the achievements of the 1930s, where a single lost time accident in a year was cause for concern. *Tick Talk* featured safety reminders throughout the 1950s. These reminders included tips both on how to stay safe at work and how to avoid accidents while on vacation. In 1956, Westclox had twenty-one lost time accidents. The following year that number was reduced to fifteen, and, in 1958, only seven lost time accidents were reported, prompting the National Safety Council to give Westclox an Award of Merit. The award recognized both the improved safety record and the lower rate of lost time accidents at Westclox compared to those of other comparable industries.

Hail, Hail, the gangs all here,
We're going to boost for safety,
We're going to boost for safety,
Hail, Hail, the gangs all here,
We're going to boost for safety now.

Reprinted from *Tick Talk*, March 26, 1926

Talley Acquires General Time

In 1968, General Time was acquired by Talley Industries in a hostile takeover. Whereas General Time had its roots firmly planted in Peru-La Salle, Talley Industries had no such roots. As its own financial difficulties grew, Talley Industries slowly moved Westclox production out of Peru-La Salle to plants located in other parts of the country and to overseas plants. During its final months in operation, the La Salle-Peru plant's only work was on a government contract. Although the plant closure was scheduled for March 31, 1980, the final closure actually occurred in August 1980.

General Time's corporate offices were moved from New York City to Stamford, Connecticut, in 1966.

Many Factors Contributed to Peru Plant Closure

The 1980 closure of the Peru-La Salle plant was not totally unexpected. Several years earlier, a search had been started for a new plant outside Peru-La Salle and all clock production had been shifted to other plants. At the time of its closure, the plant, which once employed from 3,000 to 4,000 workers had only 600 employees and was working on just one government contract. The closure followed a decision by the House of Representatives to defer work under the contract. Although the loss of the one remaining government contract was the event that triggered the closure, many other factors provide the underlying reasons for the closure.

First, Westclox never developed productive relationships with its labor unions. Unions frequently called strikes at the Peru plant, slowing or shutting down production. A 1975 strike by the Machinists Union appears to have all but sealed the fate of the Peru plant. When the United Steel Workers of America, with more than a thousand Westclox employees, refused to cross the picket lines and report for work, the State of Illinois declared them eligible for unemployment compensation based on a newly enacted law. Although Westclox quickly ended the strike and reached agreement on a new contract with the steelworkers to avert a new strike, it just as quickly shifted production of quartz watches from its Peru plant to one in Davenport, Iowa. More importantly, it announced the search for a new plant site outside Illinois. The primary states considered—Ohio, Florida, Tennessee, and Arkansas—were all right-to-work states.

A Peru community activist offered the assistance of the La Salle-Peru community and the State of Illinois in locating the needed factory space within the community. In response, the Chairman of General Time—C.N. Krewson—essentially told the activist that the community had already been considered and rejected as a potential location. Among the factors Krewson cited in site selection were the state's unemployment compensation and worker's compensation laws.

The following year, General Time announced that it would construct a new manufacturing facility in Huntsville, Alabama, and shift all remaining clock production from the Peru-La Salle factory to that facility upon its completion. In a 1992 interview, former chief stylist Ellworth Danz called the Huntsville plant a "disaster," stating that the company set wages so low that it had trouble retaining employees and thus never developed a skilled workforce. The Huntsville plant was quickly closed and most domestic production shifted to the Athens, Georgia, plant.

The actual decision to close the Peru-La Salle plant followed one final strike call. When female workers—over the objections of their higher paid male co-workers—voted to strike, Talley Industries promptly announced the closure of the Peru-La Salle plant.

A second, and related, factor contributing to closure of the Peru-La Salle plant was the generally pro-labor environment in Illinois compared to other states, particularly those in the South. A clear example of this pro-labor stance was the aforementioned award of unemployment compensation—paid by the company—to non-striking workers refusing to cross picket lines. The new workers compensation law passed by the Illinois legislature in August 1975 was estimated to significantly increase Illinois employers' unemployment taxes over the following two years. Illinois was considered at the time to have among the worst business climates in the country; this was reflected by the loss of 195 companies and over 91,000 jobs between 1967-72.

Neglect of the physical plant also contributed to the decision to close, although it is unclear which came first, the neglect or the decision to close. In a 1992 interview, the former head of Industrial Relations for the Peru plant noted that General Time had allowed the plant to fall into disrepair. He pointed out that the company failed to take advantage of an opportunity to construct and equip a new plant just outside Peru-La Salle at government expense during World War II.

Increased competition from overseas also contributed to the closure of the Peru plant. Domestic clock and watchmakers were at a distinct competitive disadvantage compared to manufacturers in Switzerland, Germany, and the Far East. With labor costs accounting for sixty to seventy percent of the costs of producing clocks and watches, U.S. manufacturers could not compete on an equal footing with foreign competitors with low wage rates and few employee benefits. Manufacturers, like Westclox, in strongly pro-union states where workers had won hard-fought battles for higher wages and costly benefits were particularly affected. A 1949 reciprocal trade agreement between the United States and Switzerland had made it easier for low-priced Swiss clocks and watches to enter the U.S. market.

When the Government declared the U.S. clock-making industry non-essential in terms of military readiness in 1958, it resulted in the reduction of protective tariffs and import quotas, opening the flood gates to foreign competition. When protective tariffs were further reduced in 1962, Westclox quickly opened a new manufacturing plant in Hong Kong. Whereas Westclox had previously used its foreign plants to produce clocks and watches for foreign markets, the new venture in Hong Kong was to produce clocks for import into the U.S. market.

Following the plant closure, the Peru-La Salle factory and office buildings became the property of the Peru Development Land Trust. Space in the buildings is now leased to several companies. In 1992, the factory's deteriorating twin smokestacks were brought down with explosives.

Exit Talley Industries, Exit General Time

In 1988, management from the General Time Division bought the Division, reverting to the name General Time Corporation. The "new" General Time Corporation continued to manufacture both Westclox and Seth Thomas clocks until 2001, at which time it ceased operations and filed for bankruptcy. Rights to the Westclox and Big Ben trademarks were sold to Salton, Inc. Current "Big Ben" models are manufactured in China.

Chapter 3: Advertising and Marketing

Early Marketing Efforts

When the United Clock Company originally opened its doors, marketing essentially consisted of loading the days production on a pushcart and peddling the clocks to local merchants. It wasn't until a young Frenchman named Gaston Le Roy joined the firm that the company began to actively seek new markets and new marketing techniques. Although Le Roy died in World War I before he could fulfill his dream of vast domestic and overseas markets, others carried out his vision. Over the ensuing decades, Westclox aggressively pursued new marketing opportunities, first in the print media and then in the emerging fields of movies, radio, and television. At the same time, however, it provided personal attention to jewelers and other retailers with a force of traveling salesmen and an array of sales helps provided dealers to help bring customers into their shops.

Salesman Bob Fullenwider travels his territory—Iowa—in a Dodge Coupe. Westclox provided Dodges to most of its salesmen in 1924. (Photo: *Tick Talk*, November 4, 1924)

Salesman Bill Paden is shown here in front of one of Westclox's fleet of 1934 Ford Eights. (*Tick Talk*, August 1934)

Gaston Le Roy

Gaston Andre Le Roy d'Etoilles was born in a small town along the English Channel in Northern France. Although he was of noble heritage and educated at Toulon along the Mediterranean, Le Roy nevertheless left France when he turned eighteen, finding employment in New York as a bank messenger and subsequently as a candy maker. It was a friendship with a Western Clock Company stockholder, however, that would bring him to Peru. The stockholder encouraged Le Roy to seek employment with the clock company.

Le Roy quickly headed for Peru-La Salle, talking his way into a job as a clerk. At the time—1902—Le Roy joined the Western Clock Company, most of its clocks were still being sold in the immediate area. Around that time, it was decided that a salesman would travel to nearby towns to encourage merchants to carry the company's products. Although it is not clear whether Le Roy himself made the suggestion, it was Le Roy who filled the first traveling salesman position. Pushing primarily the F.W. alarm, Le Roy's promotional efforts soon resulted in a significant increase in sales.

His efforts proved so successful that his territory was soon expanded to include a weekly visit to Chicago. As Westclox sales territory continued to expand, Le Roy was transferred to New York. He traveled the state for two years promoting Western Clock Company products. By 1906, a number of new models had been developed and Le Roy felt the company needed to develop a new catalog to help promote the new models. At the time, the Western Clock Company's only advertising was prepared by the New York office and placed in export publications.

Le Roy returned to Peru-La Salle to take charge of a newly established printing department. His advertising work, including a new catalog in 1907, was so effective that sales again shot up. But, Le Roy's initial advertising efforts were directed at dealers, not at consumers, appearing primarily in wholesale jewelry catalogs.

With his record of success, Le Roy was called on again to develop a sales plan for the new high-priced alarm clock George Kern had developed. Le Roy spent a year developing a sales campaign. A fundamental portion of the campaign was an appeal directly to consumers through the print media. It is said that Le Roy's plan was so effective that it made Big Ben the best-known alarm clock in the United States. He "endowed it with a personality."

Le Roy developed slogans such as "Don't set your mind. Set Big Ben" for city populations and "Plow deep while sluggards sleep. Big Ben" for farm journals, tailoring the advertising campaign to the readers of the publications in which ads were placed.

Le Roy was also determined to make Big Ben a household name throughout the world. First in Australia in 1913, and then in Europe in 1914, Le Roy set up new sales organizations. While in Europe, Le Roy decided to visit his mother in his native France. Although he had lived in the United States for fourteen years, Le Roy had never filed naturalization papers and was, therefore, still a citizen of France.

No sooner had he arrived in France than it became obvious to Gaston Le Roy that France—and Gaston Le Roy—were headed toward war with Germany. Only two days after returning to France to visit his mother, Gaston Le Roy wrote to friends at Westclox telling them that Germany had declared war and that "I can only say I hope I shall be there until the end." He told his friends in La Salle of the preparations for war and that he had already received orders to report for duty on July 11, 1914.

Although he was a military reservist with no real military training, Gaston Le Roy talked his commanding officer into letting him leave for the first battle of Marne with the regular army troops.

In a postcard to his friends in La Salle-Peru, Le Roy wrote:

> I am on my way to the firing line with the regulars and we are being rushed to the front. I have never been in better health and hope I give a good account of myself. The trains we meet are filled with wounded, French and German. The shrapnel wounds are terrible. The whole thing is ghastly. Best regards to all.

Within days after he mailed the postcard, a simple cablegram arrived at the La Salle Plant. The cablegram, dated October 26, 1914, said simply "LE ROY DIED FOR HIS COUNTRY..."

Magazine and Newspaper Advertisements

A few Big Bens were sold in 1909, but it was not until 1910 that Westclox began to advertise and merchandise him in a big way.

Westclox's first national advertising appeared in the September 24, 1910, *Saturday Evening Post*. Westclox requested and was granted page one for its initial national ad. At first, Westclox ads appeared in the *Saturday Evening Post* every two weeks, always on page one. Several years later, the advertising schedule was changed to a four-week cycle, but the ads remained on page one.

At the time Big Ben was introduced, his price of $2.50 was high for an alarm clock. In developing Big Ben, Westclox management took a calculated risk that the American public would pay a premium price for an alarm with "outstanding quality, good looks, a pleasant and vigorous alarm, easy to read dial, and easy to wind keys." Management was right as Big Ben sales quickly mounted.

This ad, appearing in *Saturday Evening Post*, January 20, 1917, pitches Big Ben to businessmen who must get to work on time. (Photo: *Tick Talk*, January 1917)

This ad, appearing in the *Saturday Evening Post* in November 1916, pitches Big Ben to farmers. (Photo: *Tick Talk*, November 1916)

This advertisement appearing in the February 17, 1917 *Saturday Evening Post* was part of an advertising campaign launched that month. Dealers were provided a free colored window card and, upon request, a lantern slide with the dealer's name and address. (Photo: *Tick Talk*, February 1917)

The October 5, 1928, *Tick Talk* announced a major new advertising campaign to promote the availability of Big Ben DeLuxe, Baby Ben DeLuxe, Ben Hur, and Tiny Tim in old rose, green, and blue for the same price as the standard nickel finish. To show the new models to their best advantage, a series of color advertisements appeared in major magazines and newspapers, beginning with a two-page spread in the September 8, 1928, *Saturday Evening Post*. Full-page ads followed in the September 29, October 27, November 24, and December 22 issues of the *Post*. Color ads were also placed in major women's magazines—*Delineator*, *Good Housekeeping*, *McCall's*, and *Pictorial Review* in October and December. Ads in *Collier's*, *The American Magazine*, newspapers, and farm publications continued to promote the nickel versions.

In March 1964, Westclox launched what was said to be the biggest clock industry newspaper campaign ever run. The campaign involved ads in 208 newspapers with total circulation of thirty-one million. The campaign coincided with the introduction of newly restyled "Bens."

The "Big Book" Details Westclox Advertising in 1926

Said to be among the largest books in the United States, this prop taken to the 1926 Westclox sales convention contains many interesting tidbits of information about the Western Clock Company's 1926 advertising efforts:

—Westclox advertisements were expected to appear on 82,563,412 pages of leading magazines in 1926;

—If those advertisements were pasted on a 30-foot high billboard, that billboard would stretch for 900 miles;

—If all of the magazines containing Westclox ads were placed on a giant scale with the steamer Olympic, which weighs 46,439 tons, on the other side, the weight of the magazines would lift the Olympic out of the Atlantic Ocean.

—If 200 Westclox salesmen set out to call on every reader of magazines carrying Westclox ads during the year, it would take 51 years to complete the job assuming each worked 300 days a year and visited 30 readers a day.

—If every person who reads a magazine carrying a Westclox ad lived in a house with a 25-foot wide lot, there would be sufficient houses to cover both sides of 33 solid streets running from New York to San Francisco.

The 1926 "Big Book" containing information about Westclox advertising. (Photo: *Tick Talk*, August 20, 1926)

Big Ben Goes to the Movies

Beginning in the teens, the Western Clock Company sought opportunities to promote Big Ben through cameo appearances in silent films. *Tick Talk* asked readers to let them know when they spotted Big Ben in a film and frequently featured still photos from the films.

Tick Talk periodically suggested ways for merchants to work in conjunction with a local theater to promote both the film and Big Ben.

Although many silent film stars were pictured with Big Ben during the teens and early 1920s, such celebrity shots largely disappeared in the late 1920s and 1930s just as the Warren Telechron Company was mounting an aggressive campaign featuring film stars.

This advertisement, appearing in the April 6, 1929, *Saturday Evening Post* is representative of Westclox's new approach to advertising—injecting an element of human interest. The ad was presented in four colors in the *Post*, but appeared in black and white in a number of other publications. (*Tick Talk*, April 1929)

This 1919 advertisement for San Francisco's Rialto theatre makes good use of Westclox to promote its current attraction "Better Times" starring the incomparable Zasu Pitts. The ad notes "with apologies to Westclox" and placed the words "now running" on the familiar Westclox tag. The theatre borrowed a number of Westclox alarms to ring in the lobby. (Photo: *Tick Talk*, October 1919)

A sampling of the publications carrying Westclox ads in 1940. (Photo: *Tick Talk*, August 1940)

That's My Baby

Westclox developed a special show card to promote Baby Ben's role in the 1926 Paramount Picture comedy *That's My Baby* starring Douglas MacLean. In the poster, MacLean is shown holding Baby Ben. *Tick Talk* advised jewelers to contact their local Paramount theatre and develop a special marketing program to benefit both the movie and the jeweler.

Jewelers were encouraged to put the special show card, together with other photos from *That's My Baby*, in their show window about a week before the film opened. Several joint ventures between the theatre and jeweler were suggested:

–Obtain discounted admission tickets and provide them free to the first ten persons who buy a Big Ben;

–Arrange with the theater owner to give a special Baby Ben matinee where children bringing in a Baby Ben are admitted free.

–Offer free tickets to the person presenting the oldest Baby Ben and display the oldest clocks with cards showing how long they have been working.

The show card was 11" x 14" and printed in two colors.

Big Ben Stars in Brewster's Millions

Big Ben was more than a prop in Paramount's 1921 film *Brewster's Millions*. Co-star Roscoe "Fatty" Arbuckle plays a clerk who has trouble rising in the morning and repeatedly gets to work late. His problem is solved when three friends, unbeknownst to the others, give Fatty a Big Ben on his birthday. Like a true superhero, Big Ben turns Fatty's life around. Now rising promptly in the morning, Fatty is on the road to fame and fortune.

Scenes from the 1921 silent film "Brewster's Millions" starring Roscoe "Fatty" Arbuckle. (Photo: *Tick Talk*, February 1921)

On the Air With Big Ben

Westclox advertising moved to a new medium—radio—in January 1932 with the launch of "Big Ben Dream Dramas" over seventeen stations of the National Broadcasting Company. The dramas, featuring the Big Ben Chime Alarm, ran twice weekly for thirteen weeks.

The "playlets" told what happens to ordinary people in dreams. Through their dreams, the characters are placed in strange and hazardous adventures. Each dream climaxes with a rescue by the "real hero of the day"—Big Ben Chime Alarm.

The first "Big Ben Dream Drama" featured an elevator operator in a department store. The operator, having trouble with the elevator starter and worried about the crowds expected for a big sale the next day, has a nightmare in which his elevator car becomes a dirigible and takes off through the roof. As the dirigible falls into a tailspin with him at the controls, the Big Ben Chime Alarm gently rescues him.

In the second drama, a banker's nightmare is interrupted when Big Ben takes over.

The radio drama had an immediate impact. Over 100,000 letters and post cards were received during the first month, many asking where they could purchase a Big Ben.

"Dream Dramas" were revived in September 1932, with a series of new dramas running for thirteen weeks. Coverage was expanded to twenty-five stations and the broadcasts moved to Sunday afternoons to reach a wider audience. In addition to the Big Ben Chime Alarm, other members of the Westclox family were weaved into the second series of "Dream Dramas."

"Dream Dramas" returned to the air for another thirteen week run in September 1934 with a revised format. The comedy team of Parker Fennelly and Arthur Allen, formerly known as the Stebbins Boys, created the rural New England characters of Ezra Bates and Luke Tidbury for the new dramas. The new dramas presented a running story line, but each episode was a complete story.

Why Advertise?

"Some people are of the opinion that products could be sold at a lower price if it weren't for the expense of advertising.

"The opposite is the case, for advertising has done much to lower costs.

"If the sales of Westclox timepieces depended upon their merits being advanced by word of mouth, only a limited number would be sold, for after all, word of mouth advertising is a slow process.

"People must learn that a product is available, what it is for, what it will do, and how much it costs. It is advertising's function to tell them.

"Mass production is one of the main reasons that Westclox timepieces, and many of our nation's wonderful household articles, can be sold at prices that bring them within the reach of millions, instead of hundreds.

"Advertising plays an important part in creating a sufficiently large demand to make mass production possible. Mass production does not make a product popular; it is the product's popularity that makes its mass production practical and the price economical, and it is advertising that contributes substantially to that popularity."

Reprinted from *Tick Talk*, January 1950.

Westclox Comes to Television

As television grew in popularity during the 1950s, Westclox began to sponsor both specials and regular programs. For example:

Westclox added the popular TV game show "Name That Tune" to its advertising campaign in April 1959. Contestants on the show, hosted by George De Witt, competed to identify popular songs after listening to brief passages. Westclox bought advertising spots on the program for six weeks, reaching an estimated thirty-two million viewers each week. Different Westclox products were featured on the program each week.

On Sunday April 26, 1959, Westclox sponsored a special star-studded made-for-TV production of "Meet Me in St. Louis." The two-hour remake of the original movie starring Judy Garland, had its own cast of stars—Tab Hunter, Myrna Loy, Ed Wynn, Jeanne Crain, Jane Powell, Walter Pidgeon, and Reta Shaw.

Westclox became co-sponsor of NBC's Tab Hunter Show in September 1960. On the show, Hunter played a young bachelor cartoonist living in a beach house along the California coast with a wealthy playboy friend (played by Richard Erdman). The show revolved around their romantic escapades with a series of beautiful young ladies. Because of the show's popularity, Westclox predicted that its ads would reach fifty percent more viewers than had ever seen Westclox commercials in a single viewing season.

George De Witt, host of "Name That Tune," sponsored by Westclox. (Photo: *Tick Talk*, April 1959)

There's little doubt about Westclox's 1962 sponsorship of the Today show. (Photo: 1962 General Time annual report)

Westclox at Trade Shows and Fairs

Westclox and General Time were frequent exhibitors at both World's Fairs and trade shows including trade shows held in Holland and Japan. Below are a few of the exhibits described in *Tick Talk*.

Century of Progress—Westclox made a prominent appearance at the 1933-34 Chicago "A Century of Progress" World's Fair with a booth in the Textile, Jewelry, and Cosmetics Building. In addition to a display showing the evolution of time using actual time telling instruments from the past such as a sun dial, water clock, burning rope, and hour glass, the Westclox exhibit featured a 3-1/2-foot high replica of the Big Ben Chime Alarm. It was mounted on a revolving 4-foot high pedestal. Visitors could hear Ben Ben's chime by pushing a button.

The 40 inch high Big Ben Chime Alarm weighed approximately 300 pounds. To get the alarm fitting of the giant clock to sound like the smaller model, two regular Big Ben Chime gongs were used. The gongs, with a striking mechanism, were housed in a sound proof box together with a microphone. One gong was used to create the "whispering" alarm and the other to create the "shouting" alarm. The sound of the gongs was carried by the microphone through a radio tube amplifier and then into a loud speaker.

The hands of the clock were driven by a 1/150 horsepower synchronous motor.

Two other replicas—18 inch Big Ben Chime Alarms—were mounted above the arched entrances to the booth. The movements for the three working replicas were made in the Engineering Department.

The exterior of the Westclox booth was a striking combination of black glass and stainless steel.

Present Westclox models were also on display at the World's Fair and retailers throughout the Chicago area were provided special "World's Fair" Big Ben and Baby Ben boxes.

Westclox "freshened up" its booth for the 1934 season, adding plate glass showcases around the booth to improve the display of the Westclox product line and create a better flow to move crowds through the exhibit.

Golden Gate Exposition—General Time created an exhibit at San Francisco's 1939 Golden Gate Exposition. The exhibit, designed by deVaulchier, Blow & Wilmet, Inc., included a giant model of Big Ben with a 6-foot dial. The clock's dial was constructed of two sheets of Polaroid and a disk of acetate, the combination of which produced constantly changing prismatic effects when revolved and illuminated. In addition to the giant Big Ben, the exhibit displayed the products of General Time's Westclox, Seth Thomas, and Stromberg divisions.

The restyled Westclox booth at the 1934 Chicago World's Fair. A plate glass showcase was built around the booth making it possible to display the merchandise to better advantage. Westclox had a rather unique sales policy at the Fair. Whatever sales were made were credited to the purchaser's regular retailer. (Photo: *Tick Talk*, August 1934)

This giant Big Ben was part of the Westclox display at the 1933-34 Chicago World's Fair. (Photo: *Tick Talk*, August 1933)

A Westclox display at a 1958 trade fair in Utrecht, Holland. (Photo: *Tick Talk*, October 1958)

This clock display was used at national trade shows in 1956. (Photo: *Tick Talk*, June 1956)

This 1928 advertisement for the Big Ben De Luxe, Baby Ben De Luxe, Ben Hur, and Pocket Ben appeared in a Bombay, India newspaper. The ad is in Gujarati, one of about 150 languages and dialects in use in India at the time. (Photo: *Tick Talk*, September 5, 1928)

Westclox display created for the "Partners in Production" show held at the Ford Rotunda in Dearborn, Michigan. At the center of the display is a giant Ford auto clock. (Photo: *Tick Talk*, June-July 1956)

Overseas Sales Promotion

By 1938, Westclox were being sold in sixty-eight countries, including South Africa, India, China, and Hong Kong. By 1947, Westclox were being sold in 161 countries outside the United States. About seventy distributors, many of whom had been with Westclox for twenty-five or more years, handle overseas distribution. Westclox shipped its products directly to those distributors who then sent them on in smaller quantities to their customers. Westclox also dealt directly with some foreign customers.

Westclox crated and ready for overseas shipment. (Photo: *Tick Talk*, April 1947)

This fleet of trucks was used to deliver Westclox in Mexico. The slogan translates to "Westclox, Awakes the World." (Photo: *Tick Talk*, November 1952)

Westclox Offers Assistance in Storefront Design

Remember when American products were sold in Japanese markets? It was still happening in 1962 as shown in this Japanese publication. (Photo: 1962 General Time annual report)

Recognizing that the sale of jewelry—and clocks—is dependent on proper display of the merchandise, *Tick Talk*, in its February 1913 issue, had an expert in store front design present suggestions on how to create a modern storefront. The author, publicity manager for the Kawneer Manufacturing Company of Niles, Michigan, emphasized that people go into a jewelry store for one of two reasons. First, they arrive looking for a particular item they know the store carries. Second, they see something in the window and go inside to take a closer look. To help capture those browse-by shoppers, the author suggested that a jewelry store entrance have:

—a generous entrance vestibule so that there is plenty of room for browsing without blocking access to the store;
—a bulkhead 2-1/2- to 3 feet high in order to bring small objects close to the eye of the customer;
—plate glass windows no more than 5-1/2 feet high so that the overhead lights do not dwarf the display; and
—shallow displays no more than 2-1/2- to 3 feet deep both to keep the merchandise in plain view for the customers and to enable staff to quickly retrieve an item from the store window.

The author also included an example of a 17-foot wide storefront constructed of copper, glass, wood, and marble. He noted that the tiled entrance and ornamental lamp announced to every man, woman, and child who passes that "here is a store run by a modern, up-to-date jeweler who keeps abreast of the times…" Jewelers were told that the cost of installing such a front was about $1,450 with costs varying based on the need for structural work.

The *Tick Talk* article concluded by encouraging jewelers to send the height and width of their current store front in order to receive free suggestions on how to create a more effective storefront.

Succeeding issues of *Tick Talk* often featured examples of effective window displays both in the United States and abroad.

In 1931, renewed emphasis on window displays was brought on through the creation of Westclox Week. Developed as a marketing effort to help increase sales during the height of the depression, prizes were provided to retailers submitting photographs of the best store window displays. A special store display was also provided to dealers for use during Westclox Week. Finally, special advertising was run in the *Saturday Evening Post* and other publications promoting the event. This special advertising was estimated to reach over twenty-three million families in the days before the 1938 Westclox Week.

Tick Talk instructed jewelers on how they could create their own displays. Here, it suggests covering a 12" x 15" piece of compo board with white plush velvet or felt and then fastening a group of Pocket Ben boxes to the board with tacks. A Pocket Ben show card is put in the center of the display. (*Tick Talk*, June 1921)

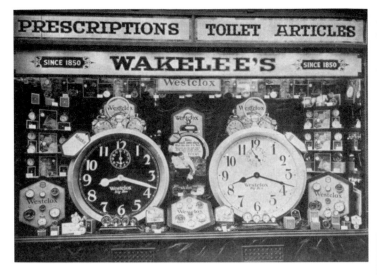

This 1926 Westclox display was put together by John Leed for Wakelee's of San Francisco. The window display, 14 feet long and 30 inches deep, contains 72 clocks and 24 watches in addition to the 2 giant Big Ben models. The models, made of tin and wood, are 6 feet high. The store reported selling 103 clocks during the first few days after installing the window display. (Photo: *Tick Talk*, May 1926)

This window display was prepared by New Orleans hardware dealer Baldwin & Company. (Photo: *Tick Talk*, April 1928)

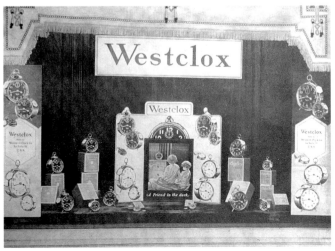

This 1927 window display is from Myer's Emporium in Melbourne, Australia. The store sold 200 clocks within three days after installing the window. The giant Big Ben Luminous at the back of the display is 5 feet high. The hands and numerals in the display were cut out and filled with green celophane and illuminated from the back. (Photo: *Tick Talk*, February 1927)

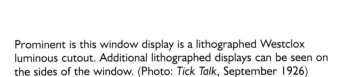

Prominent is this window display is a lithographed Westclox luminous cutout. Additional lithographed displays can be seen on the sides of the window. (Photo: *Tick Talk*, September 1926)

Big Ben Goes Public

While giant replica's of Big Ben had been erected for display at the 1933-34 Chicago World's Fair and at San Francisco's 1939 Golden Gate Exposition, it was not until 1959 that a giant Big Ben went on permanent display.

On August 7, 1959, the world's largest indoor clock was put into service in New York's Grand Central Station. Westclox built it at a cost of over $10,000.

Six years later another giant Big Ben was installed in Duffy Square near Broadway and Times Square.

Big Ben Opens on Broadway

January 1965 marked Big Ben's Broadway debut. An exact replica of Big Ben, 25 feet in diameter, was erected in Duffy Square in the Broadway-Times Square area. The clock, which weighs between 100 and 150 pounds, has an 8-1/2 foot hour hand and 11-1/2 foot minute hand.

The overall sign is 36 feet wide and 46 feet high and took six men over a week to install. The 13 sections of the clock and sign weighing 300 to 500 pounds, respectively, were lifted into place by a 100-foot crane and then bolted together. It took over a day just to mount and set the hands.

The clock was fitted with a "Tyme-Stryke" which sounds the Westminster strike and tolls the hour. The "Tyme-Stryke" consists of bell-tone generators of bronze bell metal that produce exact true-tone bell tones almost inaudible to the ear. The vibrations are then amplified over 100,000 times by specially designed electronic equipment.

The giant Big Ben installed in New York's Grand Central Station graces the cover to the August 1959 *Tick Talk*.

Big Ben's Broadway opening. This replica, 65 times larger than Big Ben, was erected in Duffy Square in the Broadway-Times Square area. The dial is 25 feet in diameter. (Photo: *Tick Talk*, January 1965)

A worker puts the finishing touches on the dial to the giant Big Ben installed in New York's Grand Central Station. (Photo: *Tick Talk*, August 1959)

Although Westclox was founded to pursue innovations in the field of spring wound clocks, it was a late entrant into the field of electric clocks. It was not until twelve years after Henry Warren began marketing synchronous-motored electric clocks through the Warren Telechron Company (initially the Warren Clock Company) that the Western Clock Company produced its first electric clock. Initially, it entered the field of both electric clocks and electric automobile clocks through acquisition rather than invention. Through the next forty years, however, Westclox would become a leader in electric clocks both for the home and the automobile.

Westclox Automation Started in 1885

The Westclox plant was founded in 1885 on a basic principle of automation—the development of a new and better process for casting together the components of clock parts. (*Tick Talk*, January 1957)

First Westclox Electrics Used Sangamo Movement

When Westclox introduced its first two electric clocks in 1931—Big Ben Electrics—they were fitted with Sangamo electric movements. Sangamo, a company formed as a joint venture between the Sangamo Electric Company and the Hamilton Watch Company, was, like the Warren Telechron Company, a pioneer in the development of synchronous electric clocks. Among the inventors developing and perfecting the Sangamo movement was Frederick C. Holtz.

Although Westclox initially produced Sangamo movements in its own factory under license from Sangamo, within a year, the General Time Instruments Corporation had acquired the Sangamo Clock Company. The expectation was that Sangamo Clocks would be produced at the Seth Thomas factory in Thomaston, Connecticut.

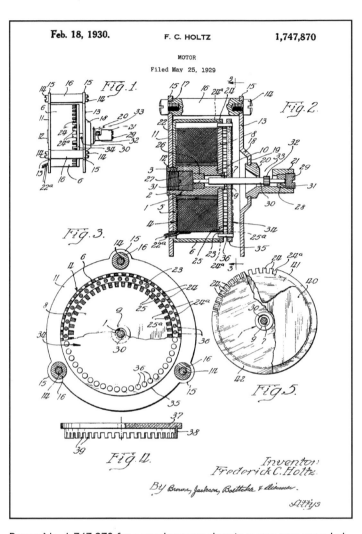

Patent No. 1,747,870 for a synchronous electric motor was awarded to Frederick C. Holtz of Springfield, Illinois, on February 18, 1930. Rights to the patent were assigned to the Sangamo Electric Company.

Westclox also entered the market for electric automobile clocks through acquisition, acquiring the Sterling Clock Company in the late 1920s. Sterling was an established leader in the electric automobile clocks industry, providing clocks for companies such as Chrysler and Graham-Paige. Initially, Sterling continued to operate under its own name even after its equipment was moved from Meriden, Connecticut, to the Westclox factory in Peru-La Salle.

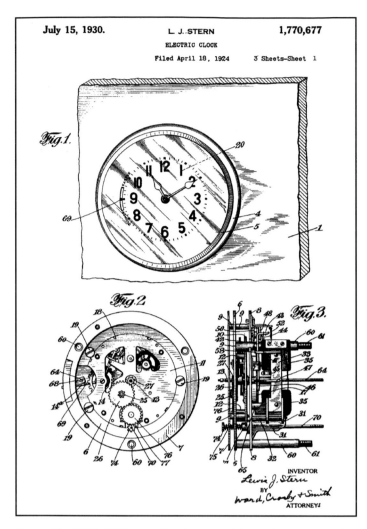

Patent No. 1,770,677 for an electric automobile clock was awarded to Lewis J. Stern of New York, New York, on July 15, 1930. Rights to the patent were assigned to the Sterling Clock Co., Inc.

Martin Hermann Kaefer

Just as George Kern was the innovator behind the developmet of the spring-wound Big Ben, Martin Hermann Kaefer had a significant role in the development of the Big Ben Electric and subsequent electric clocks. Kaefer designed the case for the initial Big Ben Electric and also received the Western Clock Company's first patent for a synchronous electric clock movement.

Kaefer's first application for a patent on an electric clock driving mechanism was approved October 21, 1930 (No. 1,779,214). One of the stated objectives of his invention was to produce a driving mechanism that would be both durable enough to be used in automobile clocks and quiet enough to be used in the home. He was awarded a second mechanical patent for improvements in electric clock-driving mechanisms in April 1931. In 1933, Kaefer received a patent for an improvement in the manufacture of electric plugs, developing a method for producing plugs using a molded insulating material (Bakelite) at significantly lower cost.

Kaefer appears to have received no additional patents until he resurfaced in Thomaston, Connecticut, in 1950. Kaefer may

have moved to Thomaston sometime after the merger of Westclox and Seth Thomas. The Seth Thomas factory was located in Thomaston. Unlike Westclox, which actively pursued patent protection for its inventions and designs, few patents were identified for Seth Thomas during the 1930s and 1940s. Those that were issued were generally design patents awarded to General Time's head of design, Paul Darrot.

The patents issued to Kaefer in 1950 and 1951 were for timing mechanisms used in electric ranges.

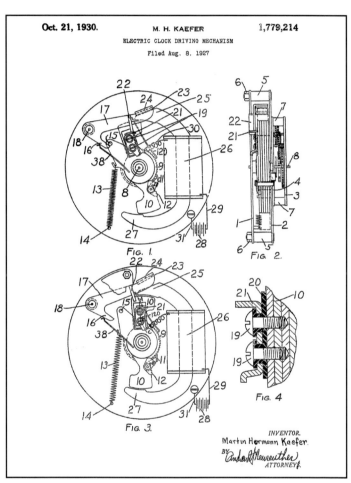

Patent No. 1,779,214 for an electric clock driving mechanism was awarded to Martin Hermann Kaefer of La Salle, Illinois, on October 21, 1930. Rights to the invention were assigned to the Western Clock Company.

Kern the Gambler

In addition to his work for the Western Clock Company, Big Ben inventor George Kern designed two early coin-operated machines. The 1917 patents begin "Be it known that I, George Kern, a subject of the Emperor of Germany, and a resident of the city of Peru, Illinois…"

Kern's coin-operated machines were novel in that they combined vending with games of chance—although all vending machines are in a sense games of chance. Kern's machines accepted a single coin, but would periodically yield two or more cigars, packs of gum, etc. similar to a slot machine.

Kern developed the machines in secrecy and even those who worked with him in the Experimental Department were apparently not aware of his inventions. It is rumored that company president F.W. Matthiessen did not approve of gambling, which could help explain the secrecy.

William H. Greenleaf

Although the Western Clock Company did not produce its first electric clock until 1930, William H. Greenleaf of Chicago, Illinois, filed applications for a series of patents relating to electric clocks in 1926, rights to each patent being assigned to the Western Clock Company. Strangely, none of the patents were approved before 1931. His patent applications covered:

—improvements in accelerator switches (Nos. 1,983,026; 1,950,846; and 1,822,927);
—power-controlling mechanisms for timepieces (No. 1,796,890);
—means for supplementing and maintaining a driving force on the clock mechanism when the main source of power is momentarily interrupted (Nos. 1,874,967 and 1,895,923); and
—means for setting the hands of a timepiece (No. 1,848,562).

Matthiessen the Inventor

Ralph H. Matthiessen, grandson of Westclox founder F.W. Matthiessen, in addition to running a successful motor haulage company in New York and serving as General Time's Board Chairman, found the time to invent a new automobile clock that can be mounted on the dash board without the necessity of having to cut a large hole in the dash board. His invention (No. 1,871,750) was quickly put into production.

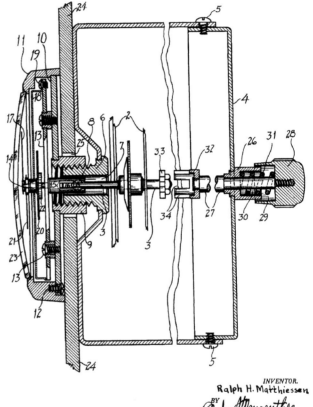

Jan. 19, 1932.   R. H. MATTHIESSEN   1,841,750
AUTOMOBILE CLOCK
Filed July 11, 1928

INVENTOR.
Ralph H. Matthiessen
BY
ATTORNEY.

Ralph H. Matthiessen of Irvington, New York, was awarded Patent No. 1,871,750 for an automobile clock on January 19, 1932. Rights to the patent were awarded to the Western Clock Company.

Andrew Neureuther

Andrew H. Neureuther was the Western Clock Company's most prolific inventor, contributing to the development of spring-wound clocks, electric clocks, and clock-making machinery. In his spare time, he served as an attorney, filing almost all Westclox patent applications between 1907 and mid-1930s.

Neureuther's contributions to electric time keeping included:

—An electric driving mechanism for use with automobile clocks. Under Neureuther's invention, electrical current from the car's battery is used intermittently for a very short time activating an electrically operated mechanism that transforms the power into mechanical power. The power is stored for use by the clock as needed (No. 1,811,278; awarded June 23, 1931).

—Improvements in electric driving and switching mechanisms (Nos. 1,811,278; 1,823,556; 1,869,610; and 1,882,229).

—An electric clock with auxiliary movement that keeps the clock running during current interruptions (No. 1,913,849; awarded June 13, 1933).

—A small synchronous electric motor for use in clocks (No. 1,957,281; awarded May 1, 1934).

—A self-starting synchronous single-phase electric motor (No. 1,962,832).

—A current interruption indicator that resets automatically when the hands are reset (No. 1,977,350; awarded October 16, 1934).

—A small synchronous motor that will remain in step with the electric current despite fluctuations in load on the power lines (No. 2,046,130; awarded June 30, 1936).

—An electric clock with an auxiliary mechanical or balance wheel movement that keeps time during periods of current interruption (No. 2,079,029; awarded May 4, 1937).

Max Schlenker

Although the most recognizable contributions Max Schlenker made to Westclox were his Art Deco case designs, he also made significant contributions to the development of Westclox as a leader in the production of electric clocks. Among his inventions were:

—An electric clock-driving mechanism in which the electric contacts are quickly activated or snapped when the electrical circuit is broken (No. 1,801,985; awarded April 21, 1931).

—An improved electric switch (No. 1,912,163; awarded May 30, 1933).

—An automobile clock for mounting in the glove box that is lit at night by means of a small light operated off the

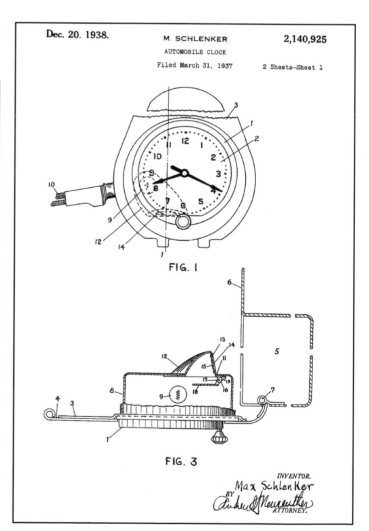

Andrew H. Neureuther of Peru, Illinois, was awarded Patent No. 1,962,832 for a self-starting synchronous motor on June 12, 1934.

Patent No. 2,140,925 for an automobile clock was awarded December 20, 1938, to Max Schlenker. Rights to the patent were assigned to General Time.

car's battery. The invention also covers a switch that illuminates the interior of the glove box whenever it is opened (No. 2,140,925; awarded December 20, 1938).

—Improvements in automobile clocks whereby the power is supplied intermittently by electro-magnetic means (No. 2,279,015; awarded April 7, 1942).

—An improved casing for small synchronous motors and associated gearing (No. 2,465,042; awarded March 22, 1949).

—A clock case that allows the user to change the color of the case by simply replacing a color ring without the use of tools. The same patent covers a cord storage capacity that enables users to reduce the length of the cord based on the distance between the clock placement and the electrical outlet (No. 2,638,735; awarded May 19, 1953).

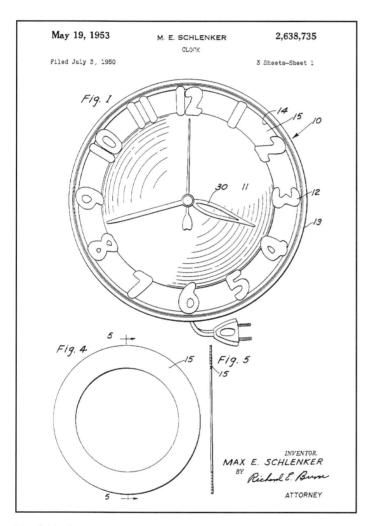

Max Schlenker was awarded Patent No. 2,638,735 for a clock case with interchangeable color rings on May 19, 1953. Rights were assigned to General Time.

Westclox brought out eleven new electric and spring clock designs in 1954 as well as a unique radio switch clock that changes stations while you sleep. RCA Victor used the switch in its latest clock radio.

William A. Hilliard

William A. Hilliard joined Westclox on August 1, 1962, as Chief Engineer of Consumer Products. In this capacity, he was responsible for development and design of clocks and watches. He reported to Max Schlenker, Manager of Engineering. His area of responsibility was expanded in July 1966 when he was named Chief Engineer of Consumer and Military Products for the La Salle-Peru plant, reporting directly to the Plant Manager.

Before coming to Westclox, Hilliard was with the Aerosonic Corporation of Clearwater, Florida. He graduated from the College of Horology in Philadelphia, Pennsylvania, and was a teacher on their staff for a number of years. He also served as Director of Research for Longine-Wittnauer before coming to Westclox.

W.A. Hilliard, Chief Engineer of Consumer Products. In this capacity, Hilliard was responsible for the design and development of clocks and watches. (Photo: *Tick Talk*, August 1962)

Ralph H. Preiser

In July 1966, Ralph H. Preiser was named Westclox's Chief Engineer of New Products, with responsibility for the conception and development of new products. Although the July 1966 *Tick Talk* indicates that Preiser joined Westclox in July 1961, his patents and presence in Peru predate that period by at least five years. His first patent assigned to General Time was for an automatic crescendo alarm that starts sounding softly and quietly but automatically and gradually increases in volume (No. 2,856,751, awarded October 21, 1958).

Most of Presier's inventions, however, related to the introduction of Westclox weather instruments in the late 1960s. Such patents covered:

—a change indicator for a barometer (No. 3,374,765; awarded March 26, 1968);
—a hygrometer (Nos. 3,410,140 and 3,460,388);

–an instrument for measuring the temperature-humidity index (No. 3,521,488); and

–a comfort humidity indicator (No. 3,709,039; awarded January 9, 1973).

In 1976, Preiser, along with Frank Stellwagen and Anthony Rigazio, invented a new low power synchronous motor and line cord (No. 3,988,639).

Ralph Preiser, Chief Engineer of New Products. (Photo: *Tick Talk*, July 1967)

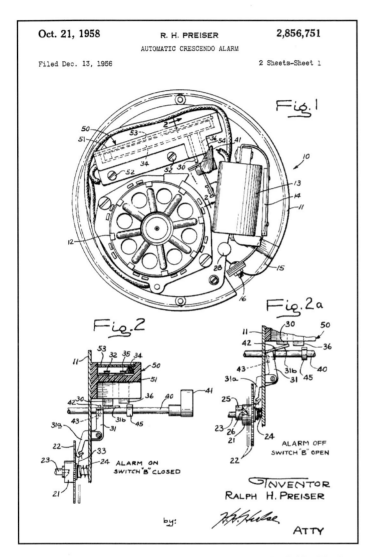

Ralph Preiser of Peru, Illinois, was awarded Patent No. 2,856,751 for an alarm with automatically controlled alarm intensity. Rights were assigned to General Time.

An Automatic Perpetual Clock

One of the more unusual patents awarded to the Western Clock Company was for an automatic perpetual calendar intended to be electrically driven. The calendar had rotating wheels to indicate the days of the week, months of the year, and days of the month and was claimed to automatically show the correct date throughout the years irrespective of the number of days in the month. It also adjusted automatically for leap year. Arthur P. Neyhart invented the automatic perpetual clock in 1933 but Westclox does not appear to have employed the invention in a production model.

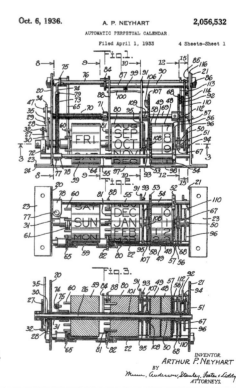

Arthur P. Neyhart of Los Angeles was awarded Patent No. 2,056,532 for an automatic perpetual calendar on October 6, 1936. Although rights to the invention were assigned to the Western Clock Company, Westclox does not appear to have put the invention into production.

Other Peru-La Salle Innovations

Many other staff from the Peru-La Salle factory also contributed to improvements and innovations in electric time keeping. These include Jesse J. Kennedy, Robert Olinger, Elmer H. Beiser, Roger G. Kramer, Arthur B. Campbell, Emil F. Henry, Ernest L. Berninger, Dale L. Richards, Elmer A. Traeger, August L. Spetzler, Walter F. Kolodziej, Philippe G. Kueffer, Clarence J. Goodwin, Robert L. Reimann, and Hubertus G. Frey. Among the innovations coming out of the Peru-La Salle factory were:

–an indicator for self-starting synchronous clocks to show whether current has been reduced or interrupted (No. 1,956,028; awarded to Emil F. Henry on April 24, 1934)

–an improved synchronous electric motor (No. 2,234,420; awarded to Elmer A. Traeger on March 11, 1941)

–an improved time-controlled switch in which the control knob always indicates whether there is current flowing through the device and through which heavy drain electrical appliances can be safely operated (No. 2,587,026; awarded to Elmer H. Beiser on February 26, 1952);

–an improved casing for an electric clock movement having a cord storage compartment (No. 2,644,853; awarded to Ernest L. Berninger and Dale L. Richards on July 7, 1953);

–push-button operation of the clock-timer features of a clock radio (No. 2,977,433; awarded to Elmer H. Beiser and Roger H. Eme on March 28, 1961);

–an improved means for providing controlled illumination to a clock face which allows user-controlled intensity (No. 2,875,320; awarded to Arthur B. Campbell on February 24, 1959);

–an automatic regulator adjusting mechanism for automobile clocks that self corrects the clock speed when minor adjustments are made to the position of the clock hands (No. 3,141,291; awarded to August L. Spetzler on July 21, 1964) and improvements to that mechanism (No. 3,287,896; awarded to Walter F. Kolodziej on November 29, 1966)

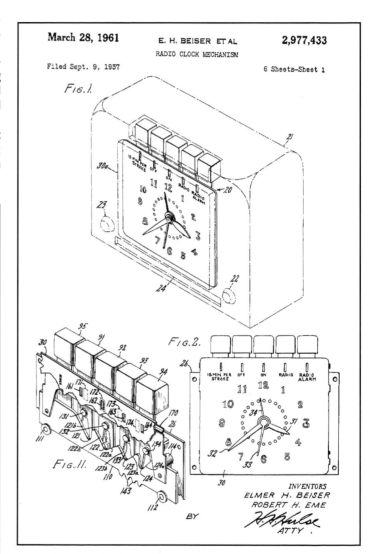

Beiser and Robert Eme of Chicago were awarded Patent No. 2,977,433 for a push button clock radio mechanism on March 28, 1961. Rights were assigned to General Time.

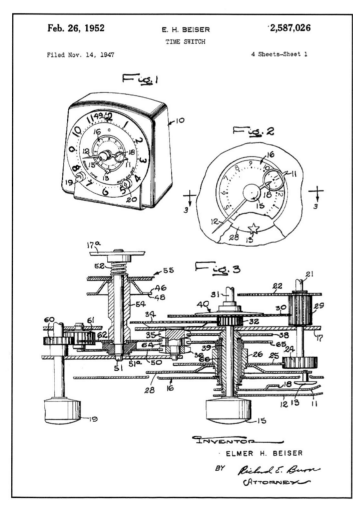

Elmer H. Beiser of Peru, Illinois, was awarded Patent No. 2,587,026 for a compact time switch on February 26, 1952. Rights were assigned to General Time.

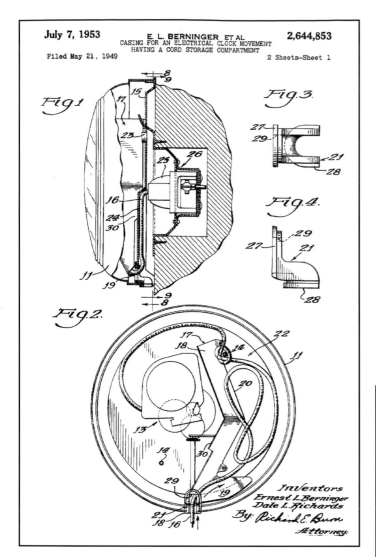

July 7, 1953   E. L. BERNINGER ET AL   2,644,853
CASING FOR AN ELECTRICAL CLOCK MOVEMENT
HAVING A CORD STORAGE COMPARTMENT
Filed May 21, 1949   2 Sheets—Sheet 1

Patent No. 2,644,853 for a clock casing with cord storage was awarded to Ernest L. Berninger of Peru, Illinois, and Dale L. Richards of La Salle, Illinois, on July 7, 1953. Rights were assigned to General Time.

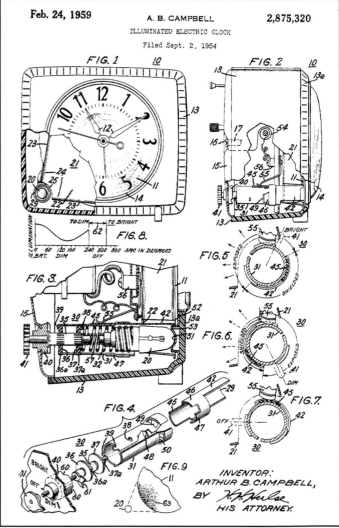

Feb. 24, 1959   A. B. CAMPBELL   2,875,320
ILLUMINATED ELECTRIC CLOCK
Filed Sept. 2, 1954

Arthur B. Campbell of Peru, Illinois, was awarded Patent No. 2,875,320 for an illuminated electric clock on February 24, 1959. Rights were assigned to General Time.

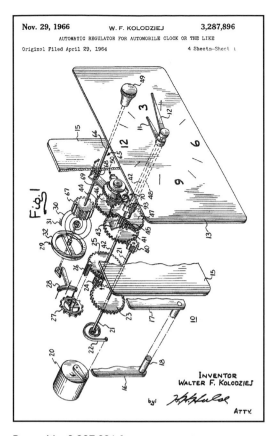

Nov. 29, 1966   W. F. KOLODZIEJ   3,287,896

AUTOMATIC REGULATOR FOR AUTOMOBILE CLOCK OR THE LIKE

Original Filed April 29, 1964   4 Sheets-Sheet 1

INVENTOR
WALTER F. KOLODZIEJ
by:
ATTY.

Acrotyne Movement Introduced

In September 1965, Westclox announced the development of a revolutionary new clock movement through a joint venture between Jeco Company, Ltd. of Tokyo, and General Time. The "Acrotyne" movement was the first electronic tuning fork movement with a magnetic transmission specifically designed for clocks.

The new movement differed from existing tuning fork movements in that those movements rely on a mechanical ratchet type coupling whereas the General Time movement used magnetic coupling between a high precision tuning fork of special temperature compensated alloy and the drive (or escapement drive train), resulting in less wear, less need for lubrication, quieter operation, and reduced sensitivity to temperature changes.

The new movement, which operated for a year on a single 1.5 volt battery, had a claimed accuracy of plus or minus two seconds per day.

The first clock to incorporate the new movement was a Seth Thomas "Mark I."

Patent No. 3,287,896 for an automatic regulator for an automobile clock was awarded to Walter F. Kolodziej of La Salle, Illinois, on November 29, 1966. Rights were assigned to General Time.

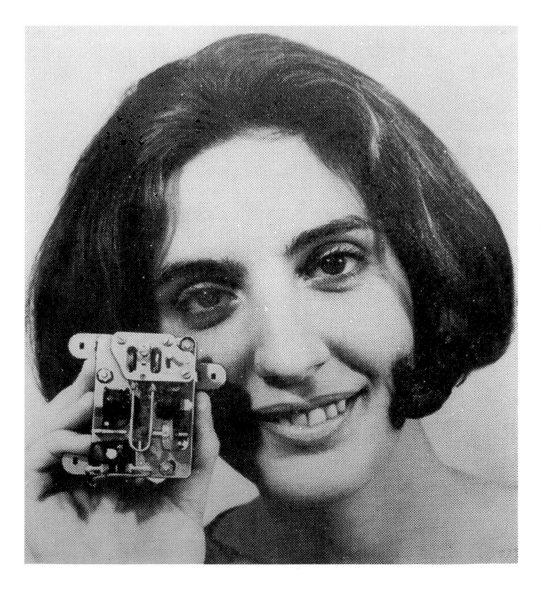

General Time, in association with the Jeco Company, Ltd. of Japan, announced a new battery operated "Acrotyne" movement in September 1965. (Photo: *Tick Talk*, September 1965)

Athens, Georgia, Assumes Leadership in Electric Clocks

By the late 1950s, much of the research in electric time keeping had moved south to the Athens, Georgia, plant. David Morrison and Ralph Robinson were responsible for many of the innovations introduced in the late 1950s and 1960s. Their innovations, often developed together or with other staff members, include:

–an improved pull-set mechanism that provides accurate adjustments without the precise alignment problems associated with prior mechanisms (No. 2,914,907; awarded to Morrison, December 1, 1959);

–a drowse alarm mechanism allowing users to select the amount of extra time they want to snooze (No. 3,039,260; awarded to Morrison and Robinson, June 19, 1962)

–a clock controlled switch to operate household appliances (No. 3,068,331; awarded to Morrison and George P. Postell, December 11, 1962);

–a front-set mechanism for a switch control timer (No. 3,264,818; awarded to Morrision and Robinson, August 9, 1966);

–a percussion type alarm mechanism for use in battery-operated clocks (No. 3,407,402; awarded to Morrision and Robinson, October 22, 1968);

–a 24-hour time switch having the general appearance and setting properties of a typical alarm clock switch (No. 3,485,968; awarded to Morrison and Robinson, December 23, 1969);

–a full feature alarm timer including a settable alarm, a function control switch with on, switch off, alarm, and auto-alarm positions, a "sleep" mechanism providing delayed operation of the switch, and a "drowse" mechanism. (No. 3,109,280; awarded to Robinson and Thomas F. Ring);

–an improved drowse alarm mechanism requiring fewer parts (No. 3,127,733; awarded to Robinson, April 7, 1964);

–a touch type mechanism for shutting off an alarm (No. 3,371,478; awarded to Robinson, March 5, 1968);

–a switch operating alarm timer in which a single cam times both the "drowse" and "sleep" features (No. 3,387,452; awarded to Thomas Ring, Raymond Keane, and Ralph Robinson, June 11, 1968);

–a test system for determining whether a battery-operated alarm clock has sufficient power remaining to sound the alarm (No. 3,405,518; awarded to Robinson and Alan E. Patrick, October 15, 1968);

–a modified alarm clock set to give both an audible and visual alarm at pre-selected intervals prompting the user to take medication from a compartment built into the top of the case. (No. 3,474,617; awarded to Robinson and Morrison, October 29, 1969);

–a 24-hour alarm mechanism that converts a standard alarm into one that sounds automatically every 24 hours. It operates by way of a latch that holds the alarm disabled during one 12-hour cycle. (No. 3,517,499; awarded to Raymond A. Keane and Ralph Robinson, June 30, 1970);

–a digital clock-timer utilizing endless loops of tape, each carrying numbers for hours, minutes, or seconds. (No. 3,597,918; awarded to Robinson, August 10, 1971);

–a digitally indicating alarm clock (No. 3,924,399; awarded to Robinson, December 9, 1975)

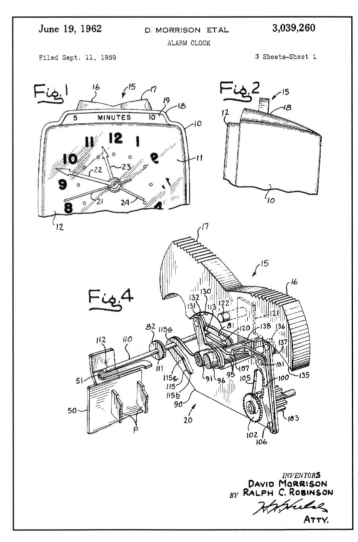

Patent No. 3,039,260 for an alarm clock with a delay feature was awarded to David Morrision and Ralph Robinson of Athens, Georgia, on June 19, 1962. Rights were assigned to General Time.

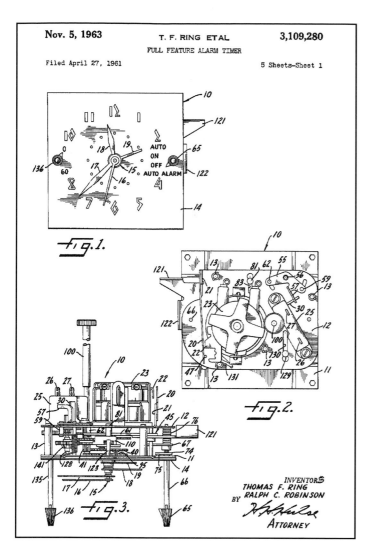

Nov. 5, 1963   T. F. RING ETAL   3,109,280
                    FULL FEATURE ALARM TIMER

Filed April 27, 1961   5 Sheets—Sheet 1

Thomas F. Ring and Ralph C. Robinson of Athens, Georgia, were awarded Patent No. 3,109,280 for a full-feature alarm timer on November 5, 1963. Rights were assigned to General Time.

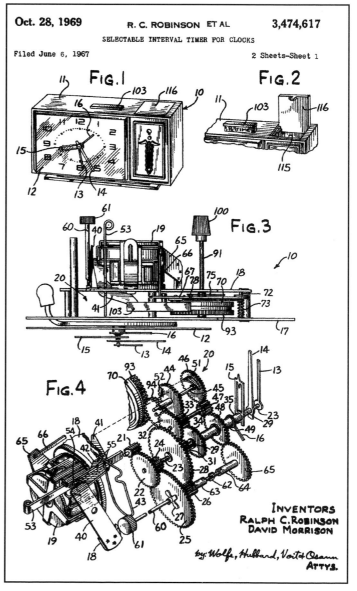

Oct. 28, 1969   R. C. ROBINSON ET AL   3,474,617
                    SELECTABLE INTERVAL TIMER FOR CLOCKS

Filed June 6, 1967   2 Sheets—Sheet 1

Ralph Robinson and David Morrison were awarded Patent No. 3,474,617 for a selectable interval timer on October 28, 1969. The timer formed the basis for the "Medi-Chron." Rights were assigned to General Time.

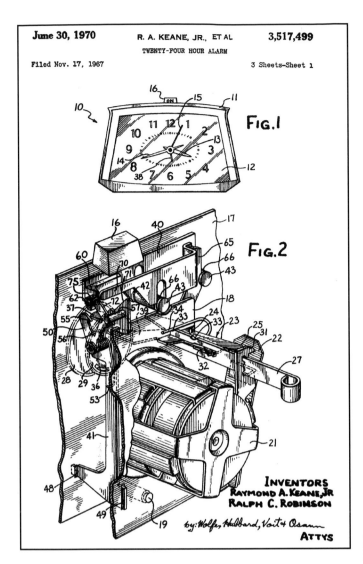

June 30, 1970   R. A. KEANE, JR., ET AL   3,517,499

TWENTY-FOUR HOUR ALARM

Filed Nov. 17, 1967   3 Sheets-Sheet 1

FIG.1

FIG.2

INVENTORS
RAYMOND A. KEANE, JR
RALPH C. ROBINSON

by: Wolfe, Hubbard, Voit & Osann
ATTYS

Patent No. 3,517,499 for a 24-hour alarm clock was awarded to Raymond A. Keane and Ralph C. Robinson of Athens, Georgia, on June 30, 1970. Rights were assigned to General Time.

United States Patent   [11] 3,597,918

[72]	Inventor	**Ralph C. Robinson**
		Mooresville, N.C.
[21]	Appl. No.	863,886
[22]	Filed	Oct. 6, 1969
[45]	Patented	Aug. 10, 1971
[73]	Assignee	**General Time Corporation**
		Stamford, Conn.

Primary Examiner—Richard B. Wilkinson
Assistant Examiner—Stanley A. Wal
Attorney—Pennie, Edmonds, Morton, Taylor & Adams

ABSTRACT: A digitally indicating clock-timer having endless loops of tape, each carrying a cycle of numerals for direct time indication, with the tapes being driven by drums of small diameter which are coupled together by geneva-type mechanisms so constructed that each tape is advanced one unit only upon completion of passage of a complete cycle of numerals on the tape of next lower order. In the preferred embodiment, such "cycle stepping" is achieved by employing two geneva stages in series with one another. The tape is disposed in a folded, reentrant arrangement for maximum compactness with the driving drums in alignment in central position. A transparent guide member enables illumination of the tape by transmitted light. A synchronous motor serves to drive the minute tape via a timing train and geneva mechanism for stepped advancement of the "minutes" drum. An hour wheel coupled to the minutes drum, and cooperating with an alarm set wheel under the control of a function lever, serves to operate a switch for turning on the associated radio and, a short time thereafter, for sounding an alarm. A settable "sleep" lever cooperating with the timing train permits the user to fall asleep with the radio on with subsequent automatic turnoff. The "sleep" lever, by disabling of the alarm, also serves upon actuation of the associated "drowse" button, to give the user the option of a few minutes of additional sleep after the alarm goes off.

The tape display and driving arrangement and a particular form of positive locking geneva mechanism have features of general utility not limited to clocks or timers.

[54] **DIGITALLY INDICATING CLOCK-TIMER**
    14 Claims, 33 Drawing Figs.

[52]	U.S. Cl.	58/125
[51]	Int. Cl.	G04b 19/02
[50]	Field of Search	58/125, 126, 2, 6 A, 7, 19, 50, 125 C

[56]   **References Cited**
UNITED STATES PATENTS

1,667,210	4/1928	Leon	58/50
1,998,763	4/1935	Janson	58/125
2,040,421	5/1936	Almquist	58/125
2,072,457	3/1937	Larrabee	58/125 X
2,645,896	7/1953	Uhlig et al.	58/125

FOREIGN PATENTS

| 834,890 | 12/1938 | France | 58/125 |
| 339,871 | 9/1959 | Switzerland | 58/125 |

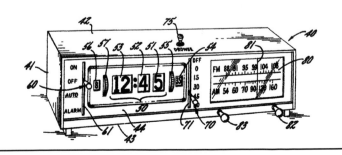

Ralph Robinson was awarded Patent No. 3,597,918 on August 10, 1971, for this digital clock timer. Rights were assigned to General Time.

Other Innovations

Among the other innovations in electric timekeeping patented by General Time were:

—a battery-operated impulse electric clock for use in automobiles designed to be highly accurate despite wide variations in battery voltage (No. 2,632,292; awarded to Adolph Amend, March 24, 1953);

—a skip mechanism for a switch activated timer that can be set to automatically skip a certain day or days of the week (No. 2,940,317; awarded to Carl J. Goodhouse, June 14, 1960);

—improvements in lighted numerical display clocks in which electric lamps are successively illuminated in different patterns (No. 3,015,094; awarded to Andrew Craig Reynolds, December 26, 1961);

—a solid state clock having no moving parts which is thin enough to be applied to a flat wall (No. 3,258,906; awarded to Sanford J. Demby, July 5, 1966);

—a touch-controlled alarm clock in which a gentle tap on the case will both illuminate the clock and operate the alarm (No. 3,352,101; awarded to Eugene M. Michel and Gerald R. Toovey, November 14, 1967);

—a touch type drowse feature (No. 3,367,103; awarded to Lee C. Bowden, February 6, 1968).

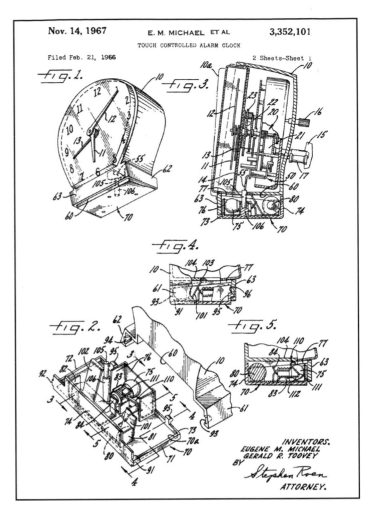

Eugene M. Michael of Spring Valley and Gerald R. Toovey of Du Pue, Illinois, were awarded Patent No. 3,352,101 for the "Magic Touch" alarm on November 14, 1967. Rights were assigned to General Time.

Westclox General Manager M.C. Budlong (right) shows D.J. Hawthorne, President of General Time, how the new automatic regulator for automobile clocks, introduced for the 1957 model year, works. (Photo: *Tick Talk*, August 1956)

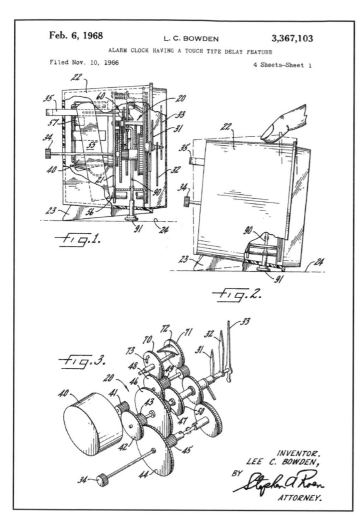

Feb. 6, 1968   L. C. BOWDEN   3,367,103

ALARM CLOCK HAVING A TOUCH TYPE DELAY FEATURE

Filed Nov. 10, 1966   4 Sheets—Sheet 1

Lee C. Bowden of Bowling Green, Kentucky, was awarded Patent No. 3,367,103 for a touch type delay feature on February 6, 1968. Rights were assigned to General Time.

Westclox Introduces Clock Unit for Transistor Radios

In 1958, Westclox introduced a timing unit specially designed for use in the small battery-operated transistor radios sweeping the country at the time. The invention, believed to be the first in the country, made possible the manufacture of completely portable, battery-operated clock radios.

The clock was designed to operate off a 1-1/2 volt flashlight battery lasting six months to a year. The clock unit had a three-position switch to turn the radio on or off, or to start the radio automatically at a preset alarm time. A variation was also introduced with a sleep switch to turn the radio off automatically after an interval of up to sixty minutes.

Another new feature of this clock was its ability to self correct its speed. If the clock was running fast or slow, the user could automatically correct its speed by merely resetting the hands to the proper time.

At the time of its introduction, Westclox already had orders from several radio manufacturers.

Travelaire–A New Kind of Clock Radio Introduced

In October 1960, Westclox announced the introduction of a transistor radio with a built-in key wound clock. According to Westclox, this combination was important because it meant no drain on the radio battery.

The six-transistor radio was small enough to tuck in a pocket or purse and was offered in "his" and "hers" finishes. "His" had an oxford gray finish with ivory trim while "hers" was turquoise with ivory trim. Leather carrying cases were also available, "his" in gray cowhide; "hers" in light tan. Earphones were included in the package.

Quartzmatic Clock Movement

In a May 3, 1971, press release, Talley Industries announced the introduction of a revolutionary new quartz crystal clock— the "Quartzmatic™" described as the "most accurate and reliable consumer clock in the world." In announcing the new movement, Talley indicated that it expected some clocks to achieve an average accuracy within one second per month.

The new movement had three modules—an electronic module, a motor module, and a gear train module. The gear train module was specially designed by General Time. A standard synchronous electric clock requires about 10,000 times more power that the new motor, which operates on 300 microwatts of power. The press release goes on to note that the electronic module is mounted on a printed circuit board designed for use in industrial clock and timer applications as well as in consumer clocks.

Initial prices for the new "Quartzmatic" clocks were expected to be in the $50 to $500 range.

Development of the new Quartzmatic movement was initiated at the Westclox Division's La Salle plant in 1968. Development involved a coordinated effort between General Time engineers and their counterparts from the semiconductor and quartz crystal industries.

Design Awards

La Salle Series—Two of George Graff's La Salle Series clocks, Models 402 and 403, were chosen for display in the Third International Industrial Exhibition sponsored by the American Federation of Arts. Items included in the 1930 display were chosen by a selective procedure and general invitations to exhibit were not issued. In addition to the United States, works were included from Czechoslovakia, Denmark, England, France, Germany, The Netherlands, Sweden, and Switzerland.

The two clocks were entered in the Exhibition of Decorative Metalwork Division which included objects of silver, pewter, copper, brass, aluminum, lead, bronze, steel, and iron, or any combination of these.

The traveling Exhibition was shown at the Museum of Fine Arts (Boston), Metropolitan Museum of Art (New York), Art Institute of Chicago, and the Cleveland Museum of Art.

Hand Bag Watch—At the prestigious Industrial Arts Exposition held in New York's Rockefeller Center in 1935, Westclox's Hand Bag Watch, designed by DeVaulchier and Blow, won the coveted Kaufmann Award, the exposition's top prize. The prize, donated by Pittsburgh department store magnate, Edgar J. Kaufman, was awarded to "that product which exhibits in the greatest degree the merits of beauty, utility, and availability." The Hand Bag Watch was judged by a group of sixteen Bryn Mawr graduates to be the top design of the hundreds of articles submitted for judging.

Tick Talk noted that a scroll and knob bookend took second place (Author's note: probably Fred Farr's design for Revere). Other items considered in the final selection were a Telechron clock and a General Electric range.

Kaufman is best remembered for commissioning Frank Lloyd Wright to design his mountain retreat in western Pennsylvania—Falling Waters.

Travalarm—At a 1953 competition sponsored by the Canadian Industrial Design Committee, the "Travalarm" was honored for its outstanding design. The more than 350 products entered in the competition ranged from small items like clocks, bicycle horns, and toasters to household furniture.

Noted industrial designer Ben Nash is shown holding a Handbag Watch as Mrs. Gerald Swope, Chairman of the judges, displays the Kaufman Award, the grand prize of the Industrial Design competition held at Rockefeller Center. (Photo: *Tick Talk*, June 1935)

George W. Blow

Although George W. Blow was awarded only two design patents, his designs were among the most distinctive of the Art Deco era. A partner in the design firm DeVaulchier and Blow (formerly Industrial Design Inc., it was Blow who was credited with the design of the Handbag Watch that won the Kaufmann Award in 1934. No design patent was awarded for the Handbag Watch, but Blow was awarded a patent for his design of the "Table Clock," a small but stunning masterpiece of design. He also received a patent for his design of the "Clip Easel Watch." In addition to winning the Kaufmann Award, the Handbag Watch was included in the landmark 1934 Museum of Modern Art exhibit "Machine Art." One of only three clocks included in the exhibit, it shared the stage with a Gilbert Rohde design for the Herman Miller Clock Company and a Magnetic clock by the Jaegar Watch Company.

Little is known about George W. Blow or his partner Simon DeVaulchier, who counts among his designs several clocks for the Warren Telechron company. Blow served on the Board of Directors of both the Western Clock Company and General Time. He was elected to the Western Clock Company Board in 1923, filling the vacancy caused by the death of his father, George P. Blow, one of the three original members of the Board.

Blow's firm—by then DeVaulchier, Blow, and Wilmet—designed the General Time exhibition at the 1939 Golden Gate Exposition in San Francisco.

Blow appears to be from an artistic family as his brother Richard was listed in *Who's Who in American Art*, 1940 Edition.

This Westclox electric alarm, made in Scotland, was selected by the British Council of Industrial Design as one of the best designs of 1962. I found no evidence that the design was marketed in the United States. (Photo: 1962 General Time annual report)

Ellworth R. Danz

Ellworth R. Danz joined Westclox in 1940 and, except for service in the Pacific Theater during World War II, spent almost his entire career in styling. He was made Styling Engineer in March 1955. In April 1964 he was named Chief Stylist for the La Salle-Peru and Athens plants.

Ellworth Danz continued to style clocks for Westclox after the Peru plant closed in August 1980, working from the basement of his home. He was awarded over twenty patents for his clock designs and doubtless created many other designs that were not patented.

Danz created most of his designs at a time of change in the clock industry when cheaper materials and construction methods were beginning to make clocks disposable. His styling abilities are perhaps best displayed in the "707," a clock that captures the spirit of the 1950s and is the equal of the best designs of the 1950s.

Danz also took over the styling of Big Ben and Baby Ben from Henry Dreyfuss during the 1950s.

At the time of this writing, Danz currently lives in Wisconsin.

W.J. Hardill, general sales manager for Western Clock Company Limited, General Time's Canadian plant, receives a design award from Trade Commissioner C.D. Howe. In the center is Canadian Prime Minister St. Laurent. (Photo: *Tick Talk*, May 1953)

Paul G. Darrot

Paul G. Darrot was the Director of Design for General Time from the 1930s into the 1950s. He contributed designs to both Westclox and Seth Thomas. His designs for both firms are among the best modern designs of the period.

Little is known about Darrot's life. He is listed in the 1930 Federal Census as having been born in Paris in 1930. Similarly, the Connecticut Death Index for 1949-96 shows that he died February 14, 1958, at age 58. At the time of death he lived in Southbury, Connecticut.

Darrot was an accomplished amateur photographer and gave a presentation on a photographic printing process to the Westclox camera club in April 1947.

Ellworth R. Danz, Chief Stylist. (Photo: *Tick Talk*, July 1966)

General Time's Director of Design, Paul G. Darrot, gives a talk to the Westclox Camera Club in March 1947. (Photo: *Tick Talk*, April 1947)

United States Patent Office

Des. 189,200
Patented Nov. 8, 1960

189,200

CLOCK

Ellworth R. Danz, La Salle, Ill., assignor to General Time Corporation, New York, N.Y., a corporation of Delaware

Filed Oct. 27, 1959, Ser. No. 58,084

Term of patent 14 years

(Cl. D42—7)

FIG.-1

One of Ellworth Danz' most innovative designs was the "707." (Des. 189,200, awarded November 8, 1960)

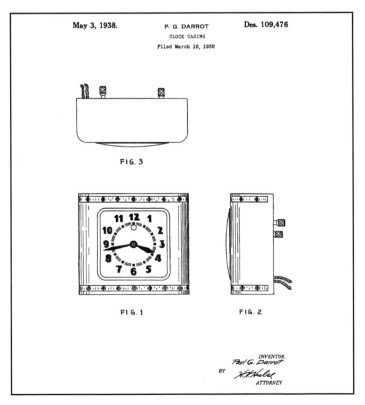

May 3, 1938.   P. G. DARROT   Des. 109,476

CLOCK CASING

Filed March 16, 1938

FIG. 3

FIG. 1   FIG. 2

INVENTOR.
Paul G. Darrot
BY
ATTORNEY

Among Paul Darrot's designs was the "Bachelor" (No. 873). (Des. 109,476, awarded May 3, 1938)

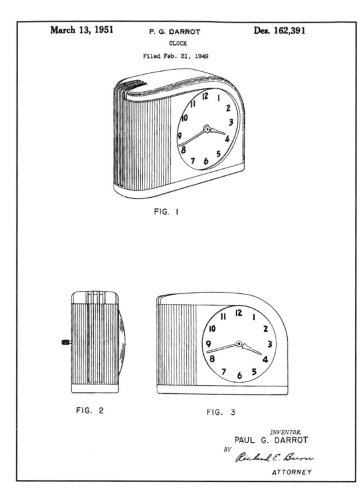

March 13, 1951   P. G. DARROT   Des. 162,391

CLOCK

Filed Feb. 21, 1949

FIG. I

FIG. 2   FIG. 3

INVENTOR.
PAUL G. DARROT
BY
Richard E. Burn
ATTORNEY

Perhaps Darrot's best known design for Westclox was the original "Moonbeam" (No. 904). (Des. 162,391, awarded March 13, 1951)

Henry Dreyfuss

Henry Dreyfuss (1904-1972) was one of the giants of American industrial design and lent his talents to the design and redesign of Big Ben and the rest of the family from 1932 to 1947. Like several other designers, he began his career as a stage designer. After graduating from the Ethical Culture School in New York, Dreyfuss worked with Norman Bel Geddes on set designs for a number of Broadway shows.

Dreyfuss next found brief employment as a design consultant for Macy's, but soon left to open his own Madison Avenue design firm, followed several years later by a West Coast office in Pasadena, California.

A founding member of the Society of Industrial Design and the first President of the Industrial Designers Society of America, Dreyfuss became known for his ability to add beauty to everyday objects. In addition to his designs for Westclox, Dreyfuss designed General Electric's first flattop refrigerator, a thermos jug for the American Thermos Bottle Company, Bell telephones, Hoover vacuum cleaners, and washing machines for Sears.

On a larger scale, his design work ranged from John Deere tractors to New York Central locomotives. He also designed the ocean liners *Constitution* and *Independence*.

Although it has been suggested that Dreyfuss redesigned Big Ben to make the clock look thinner, it is not clear which came first, the thinner case or the thinner movement. The Dreyfuss

cased Big Bens do not seem to have as much appeal to collectors as the first series cases designed by George Kern.

In terms of modern design, Dreyfuss' late 1940s redesign of the Ben Electric is perhaps his best design for Westclox, but even it is hardly a match for Martin Hermann Kaefer's original Big Ben Electric of 1931.

Although Dreyfuss received only three patents for his designs at Westclox, it is generally considered that he designed the entire Ben Family from 1932 through 1949. Russell Flincham's book *Henry Dreyfuss: The Man in the Brown Suit* shows the Western Clock Company as a Dreyfuss client from 1930-1936 and a General Time client from 1933 to 1945. It appears, however, that Dreyfuss continued to design for Westclox and General Time after 1945 as his application for a patent for a redesigned Ben Electric was filed in January 1947.

In addition, Westclox expert Bill Stoddard donated two Westclox style models to the American Clock and Watch Museum, Bristol, Connecticut. The first model, made of plastic and metal, is of the Style 6 Baby Ben introduced in 1949. The base is marked:

Henry Dreyfuss
501 Madison Avenue
New York City

It is thus clear that although the 1949 updates of Big Ben and Baby Ben were not patented, Henry Dreyfuss should be credited with the designs.

The second model Stoddard donated to the American Clock and Watch Museum was a big Ben style model constructed out of wood and marked on the bottom "MOD 48H." The back of the model has the key and knob arrangement of the single key wind Big Ben movement introduced in 1956. The model is black with nickel trim with a white dial. The model was not put in

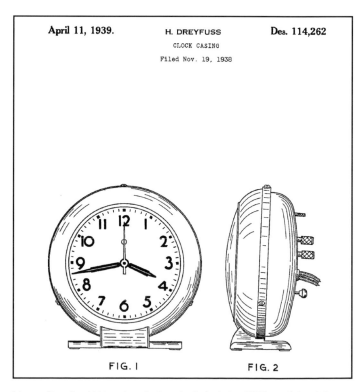

April 11, 1939.   H. DREYFUSS   Des. 114,262

CLOCK CASING

Filed Nov. 19, 1938

FIG. I   FIG. 2

Henry Dreyfuss' Westclox designs included the 1939 models of the Big Ben, Baby Ben, and Big Ben Electric. Although the electric cord shows the patent drawing to be of the Big Ben Electric, the spring-wound models shared the same case design. (Des. 114,262, awarded April 11, 1939)

production but appears to be a prototype for the Style 7 Big Ben introduced in 1956. Stoddard notes that while the first model is clearly labeled as coming from Dreyfuss' offices, the second model is not labeled as to source.

In addition to Big Ben and Ben Electric, Dreyfuss was responsible for the 1932 redesign of Pocket Ben, although this design was not patented. Dreyfuss took credit for the design in a 1933 article on modern design.

After ending his work for Westclox, Dreyfuss designed clock cases for the E. Ingraham Company during the mid-1950s.

Dreyfuss was not reluctant to share his views on industrial design and lectured extensively. He also wrote two books on industrial design—*Designing for People* (1955) and *The Measure of Man* (1960). Dreyfuss closed his design firm in 1968, but continued to design on a consulting basis until his death in 1972.

Aug. 30, 1949.   H. DREYFUSS   Des. 154.995

CLOCK

Filed Jan. 8, 1947

FIG. 1

FIG. 2   FIG. 3

INVENTOR.
HENRY DREYFUSS
BY
Richard E. Burns
ATTORNEY

Perhaps Dreyfuss' most innovative design for Westclox was the 1947 Big Ben Electric (No. 963). (Des. 154,995, awarded August 30, 1949)

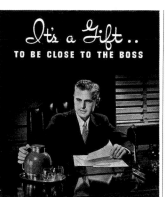

This advertisement that ran in *Time* November 6, 1939, clearly illustrates the sales power associated with the term "styled by Henry Dreyfuss."

Robert A. Janz

Although Robert A. Janz has no designs to his credit, he nonetheless played an important role in the development of new products through his role in the Model Shop. Janz started his Westclox career in 1919 in the Machinist Training School. After completing the course in 1923, he began work in the Experimental Department, which became a part of the Engineering Department in 1934. Janz also completed a course in watch and clock making at the Elgin Watchmakers' College.

With the September 1954 retirement of August Schierholtz, Robert A. Janz was made foreman of the Model Shop in the Engineering Department. He resigned the position because of poor health in 1959, but continued to serve as a senior model maker until his retirement in October 1967 after more than forty-eight years with Westclox.

Robert A. Janz. (Photo: *Tick Talk*, August 1954)

H. August Schierholtz

Henry August Schierholtz joined the Western Clock Company March 13, 1913, after completing a course in watch and clock making at the Canadian Horological Institute in Toronto. He initially worked in the Experimental Department devoted to developing new products and improving the old. He worked under George Kern, inventor/designer of the original Big Ben.

Schierholtz was awarded only one design patent, but his 1927 design represented the first major restyling of Big Ben since its introduction in 1910.

Following a stint in the Army during World War I, Schierholtz returned to Westclox, resuming his experimental work. He became the head of the model shop in the Engineering Department, a position he held until his retirement, September 3, 1954, after more than forty years service. During his final years with Westclox he also served as an instructor in the Westclox Watch and Clock Makers' School.

Following retirement, Schierholtz returned to his native Canada.

Max E. Schlenker

Max Schlenker was born in Wurttenberg, Germany in 1905 and attended a technical high school. He worked in the experimental department of a clock factory in Schwenigen, Germany before immigrating to the United States.

He joined the Manufacturing Experimental Department at the Western Clock Company in August 1924 and was appointed Chief Designer in 1929. He became Chief Engineer in 1940 and was given the title Manager of Engineering in 1958.

Schlenker was awarded twenty-eight design patents from the 1930s to early 1950s. Although most of the designs entered production, no record of production models was found for several of his 1930s designs.

In addition to his design work, Schlenker made a number of contributions to the development of electric time keeping and electric automobile clocks.

In March 1952, Schlenker was made Consulting Engineer of General Time Corporation. The new title and duties were in addition to his duties in La Salle.

Schlenker moved into a new capacity with General Time in April 1963, becoming Director of Overseas Procurement. In this new role, Schlenker was responsible for all Westclox overseas procurement as well as acting in a staff capacity for other General Time divisions making overseas purchases. While Director of Overseas Procurement was a new title, it appears that Schlenker had been working on overseas procurement issues for some time. The April 1963 *Tick Talk* noted that over that the past ten years, Schlenker had made forty trips to Europe to meet with foreign manufacturers, explore and investigate new ideas, and assist in technical improvements in any products purchased abroad. He continued to serve as Manager of Engineering at the La Salle plant.

In July 1966, Schlenker was placed on special assignment to the General Manager. In this capacity he continued to handle overseas procurement and acted as a consultant for Westclox and General Time on international operations. He retired four years later, on April 30, 1970, after almost forty-six years with Westclox and General Time.

Max Schlenker assumed the role of Consulting Engineer of General Time Corporation in addition to his position of Westclox Chief Engineer in March 1952. (Photo: *Tick Talk*, March 1952)

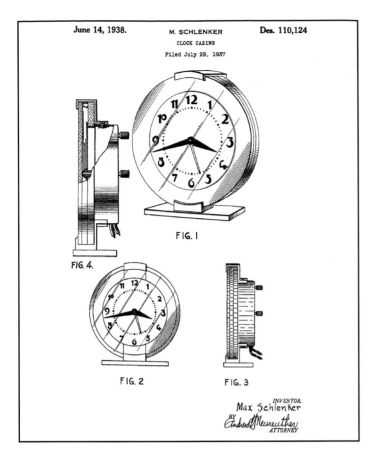

June 14, 1938. M. SCHLENKER Des. 110,124
CLOCK CASING
Filed July 29, 1937

FIG. 1

FIG. 4.

FIG. 2

FIG. 3

INVENTOR.
Max Schlenker
BY
Andrew Meierreuther
ATTORNEY

Among Max Schenker's most distinctive designs was the "Andover" (No. 865), reintroduced after World War II as the "Oracle." (Des. 110,124, awarded June 14, 1938)

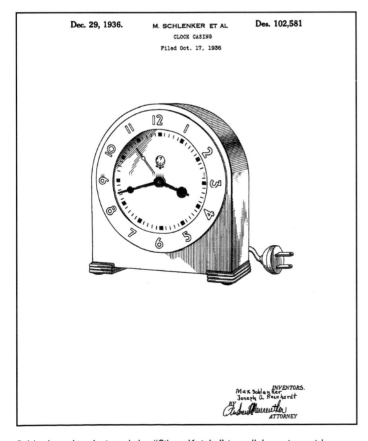

Dec. 29, 1936. M. SCHLENKER ET AL Des. 102,581
CLOCK CASING
Filed Oct. 17, 1936

INVENTORS.
Max Schlenker,
Joseph A. Reinhardt
BY
Andrew Meierreuther
ATTORNEY

Schlenker also designed the "Silent Knight" in collaboration with Joseph A. Reinhardt. (Des. 102,581, awarded December 29, 1936)

Other Designers

Mel Appel of Livingston, New Jersey, and **Martin Schnur** of West Orange, New Jersey, were awarded five design patents for novelty children's clocks including the Hickory Dickory Dock, See-Saw, Grenadiers, and Fairy Tale. Appel also designed the cases for the two Man-Time watches.

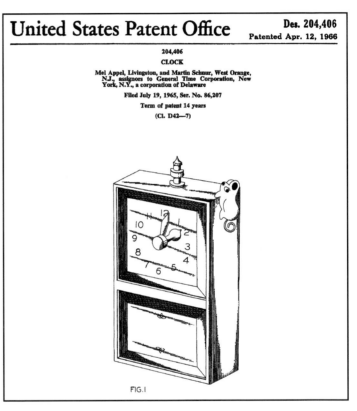

United States Patent Office Des. 204,406
Patented Apr. 12, 1966

204,406
CLOCK
Mel Appel, Livingston, and Martin Schnur, West Orange, N.J., assignors to General Time Corporation, New York, N.Y., a corporation of Delaware
Filed July 19, 1965, Ser. No. 86,207
Term of patent 14 years
(Cl. D42—7)

FIG.1

Mel Appel and Martin Schnur designed the Hickory-Dickory-Dock and other children's novelty clocks of the late 1960s. (Des. 204,406, awarded April 12, 1966)

Leo Ivan Bruce Jr. of Framingham Center, Massachusetts, apparently the son of Telechron designer Leo Ivan Bruce, designed the distinctive "Tambourine" wall clock. He received two other design patents that were assigned to General Time.

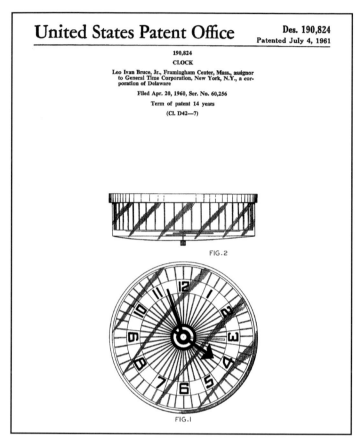

Leo Ivan Bruce Jr.'s clock designs included the "Tambourine". (Des. 190,824, awarded July 4, 1961)

Giacinto C. D'Ercoli of Park Forest, Illinois, teamed with **Roman J. Szalek** of La Salle, Illinois, on the design of the "Woodfair." D'Ercoli was awarded a total of four design patents including the 1968 version of the "Logan;" Szalek was awarded fourteen, including the "Medi-Chron" and "Seville."

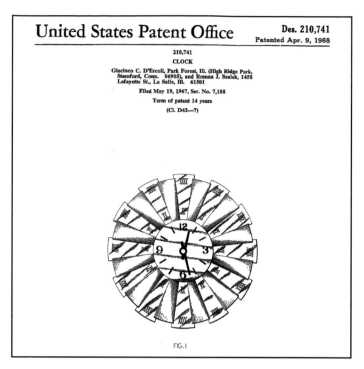

Giacinco D'Ercoli's designs included the "Woodfair" (No. 46103). (Des. 210,741, awarded April 9, 1968)

Harold D. Fetty of Birmingham, Michigan, designed the 1958 "Kenyon" but appears to have done no other design work for Westclox.

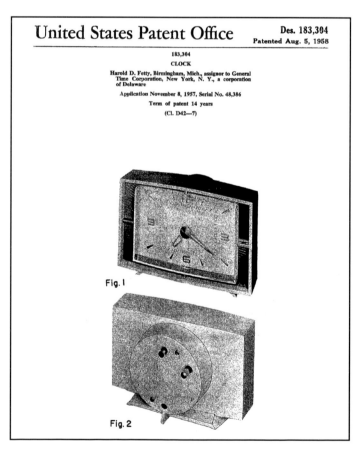

Harold D. Fetty's only design was the 1958 "Kenyon" (No. 1291). (Des. 183 304, awarded August 5, 1958)

Martin Hermann Kaefer of Peru, Illinois, designed the case for the original Big Ben Electric Model 820. Although no design patent was awarded, he likely designed the case for the companion Model 840. Kaefer was primarily an engineer and contributed a number of innovations in electric time keeping discussed in Chapter 4.

Kaefer had relocated to Thomaston, Connecticut, by the late 1940s where he apparently continued work for General Time in the field of range timers.

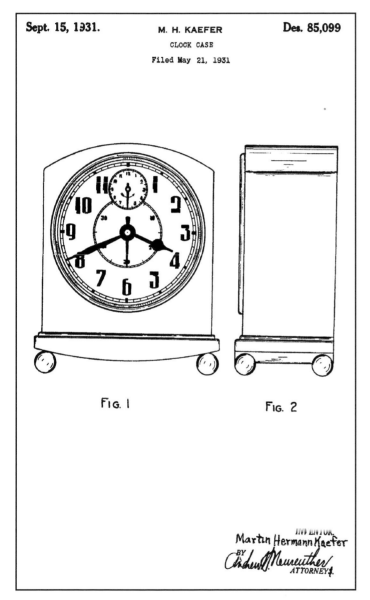

Martin Hermann Kaefer designed the first Big Ben Electric (No. 820). (Des. 85099, awarded September 15, 1931)

Keith D. Kitts of Livonia, Michigan, designed the distinctive Mid-Century Modern "Dynamic," apparently his only design work for General Time.

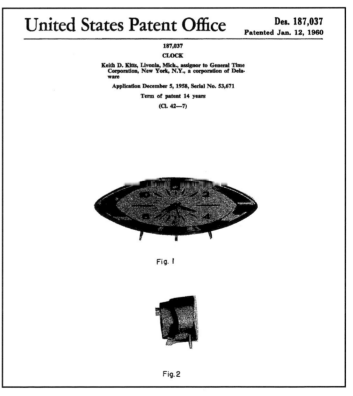

Keith Kitts' only Westclox design became the 1958 "Dynamic" (No. 1400) one of the most distinctive designs of the 1950s. (Des. 187,037, awarded January 12, 1960)

David W. Miley of Peru, Illinois, designed the "Bell-Vue." His eight other Westclox designs included the "Lookout Switch Timer," "Renfield Magic Touch," and several collaborative efforts with Ellworth Danz.

United States Patent Office

Des. 210,676
Patented Apr. 2, 1968

210,676

CLOCK

David W. Miley, Peru, Ill., assignor to General Time Corporation, Stamford, Conn., a corporation of Delaware

Filed Feb. 20, 1967, Ser. No. 5,881

Term of patent 14 years

(Cl. D42—7)

FIG.1

David Miley designed the Bell-Vue (No. 20189). (Des. 210,676, April 2, 1968)

Jean Otis Reineke of Glenview, Illinois, designed the distinctive Mid-Century Modern "Contessa" as well as the equally impressive "Shadow Box," two of the better designs of the 1960s. Sadly, those were his only designs for Westclox.

United States Patent Office

Des. 204,778
Patented May 17, 1966

204,778

CLOCK

Jean Otis Reinecke, Glenview, Ill., assignor to General Time Corporation, New York, N.Y., a corporation of Delaware

Filed Aug. 10, 1965, Ser. No. 86,518

Term of patent 14 years

(Cl. D42—7)

One of the most innovative Westclox designs of the 1960s was Jean Otis Reineke's "Contessa" (No. 20163) one of the few 1960s designs likely to become highly collectible. (Des. 204,778, awarded May 17, 1966)

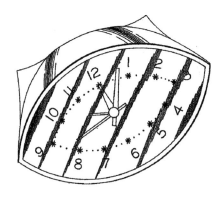

FIG.1

Joseph A. Reinhardt, a member of the Westclox Engineering Department, occasionally tried his hand at case design, creating the case for the Art Deco-styled "Ben Franklin." He also collaborated with Max Schlenker on design of the "Silent Knight."

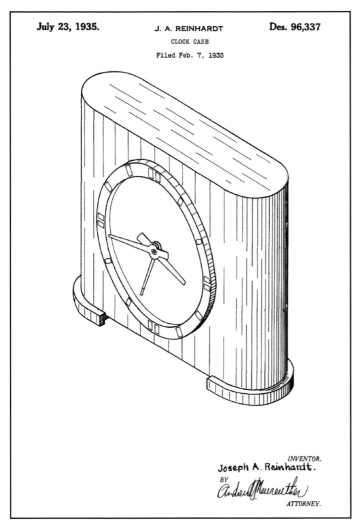

July 23, 1935.

J. A. REINHARDT

CLOCK CASE

Filed Feb. 7, 1935

Des. 96,337

INVENTOR.

Joseph A. Reinhardt.

BY

ATTORNEY.

Joseph A. Reinhardt was awarded the design patent for the distinctive "Ben Franklin" (No. 850). (Des. 96,337, awarded July 23, 1935)

Lawrence J. Wilson of Grosse Pointe, Michigan, designed the popular 1950s "Snowflake" wall clock as well as the "Town Crier" from the same era but appears to have contributed no other designs to Westclox.

Additional designers who worked only on spring wound clocks are discussed in *Westclox: "Wind-up"*.

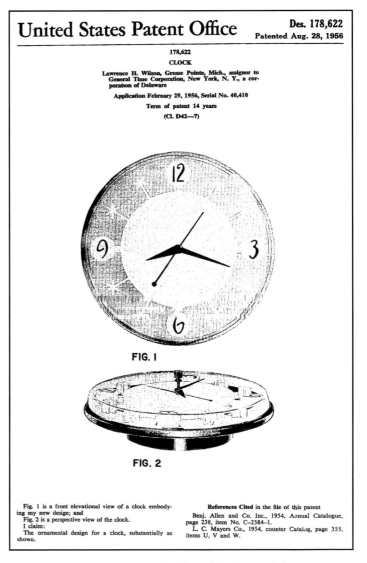

United States Patent Office

Des. 178,622
Patented Aug. 28, 1956

178,622

CLOCK

Lawrence H. Wilson, Grosse Pointe, Mich., assignor to General Time Corporation, New York, N. Y., a corporation of Delaware

Application February 29, 1956, Serial No. 40,410

Term of patent 14 years

(Cl. D42—7)

FIG. 1

FIG. 2

Fig. 1 is a front elevational view of a clock embodying my new design; and
Fig. 2 is a perspective view of the clock.
I claim:
The ornamental design for a clock, substantially as shown.

References Cited in the file of this patent
Benj. Allen and Co. Inc., 1954, Annual Catalogue, page 238, item No. C–2384–1.
L. C. Mayers Co., 1954, counter Catalog, page 355, items U, V and W.

Lawrence H. Wilson designed the "Snowflake," one of the more popular 1950s designs. (Des. 178,622, awarded August 28, 1956)

Big Ben Electric

Rear view of the Model 820 "Big Ben Electric." Note the detachable cord fitted with both screw-in and push-in connectors so that it could be plugged into a wall outlet or screwed into a light socket. (Photo: *Tick Talk*, August 20, 1931)

August 1931 saw the introduction of the "Big Ben Electric" (No. 820, $8.75), 5-3/16" x 4-1/2" x 2-1/2". It has a jet black composition case trimmed in chromium. The dial is metal with easy to read numerals. It was also available with a luminous dial at a slightly higher price. Self-starting electric movement and alarm with rear shut-off. Designed by Martin Hermann Kaefer (Des.85,099, awarded September 15, 1931). **($75-85)**

Also introduced in August 1931 was a second version of the "Big Ben Electric" (No. 840, $12.50). It has a solid mahogany case with an inlaid strip of light wood. Silvered metal dial with etched numerals. Felt cushions on the base protect fine furniture from marring. Self-starting electric movement and alarm. The alarm has a clear, mellow tone and rear shut-off. (Photo: *Tick Talk*, August 20, 1931) **($65-75)**

Sangamo Synchronous Movements

The motor used in Westclox's first electric alarms—Big Ben Models 820 and 840—is a self-starting Sangamo synchronous movement. It is a slow speed motor running at 240 revolutions a minute. It will run synchronously from 85 to 150 volts.

The key marked "A" on the back of the clock is to wind the alarm spring for demonstration purpose, before the clock has been run sufficiently to wind electrically.

The clock is equipped with a detachable cord and a high grade composition plug—complete so that it will fit either a screw in or push in socket.

Although the movement is a Sangamo, it was assembled in Westclox's Four Inch Assembling Department.

Big Ben Electric Movement

The 1931 Big Ben Electric Movement. Although it is a Sangamo movement, it was assembled in Westclox's Four Inch Assembly Department. (Photo: *Tick Talk*, August 20, 1931)

Introduced in January 1939, the "Big Ben Chime Alarm Electric" ($4.95 w/plain dial, $5.95 w/luminous dial) has a self-starting electric movement with current interruption indicator. The pleasant sounding gong alarm starts with a series of gentle chime calls followed by an extra loud alarm—"First He Whispers, Then He Shouts." Designed by Henry Dreyfuss (Des. 114,262, awarded April 11, 1939). Choice of plain dial with black (No. 880) or ivory (No. 882) finish or luminous dial with black (No. 885) or ivory (No. 886) finish. (Photo: *Tick Talk*, January 20, 1939) **($55-65)**

Henry Dreyfuss' new design for the Big Ben Electric was featured in the Westclox ad appearing in the April 11, 1939, *Saturday Evening Post*. The ad mentions the new streamlined styling but never mentions Dreyfuss.

Big Ben for the *hard-to-get-up* farm hands

A new model "Big Ben Electric" Alarm (No. 963, $8.95), 5-3/4" x 5", was introduced in the December 1947 *Tick Talk*. It features a brown molded plastic case with gold color trim. It has a gong alarm with adjustable volume. The alarm is set via a sweep indicator on a two-tone convex metal dial. Polished gold color numerals outlined in brown to match the pierced hands. The wide base is cushioned underneath to protect polished surfaces. The current interruption indicator is reset by simply tilting the clock backward while the current is on. Quiet, self-starting low-speed motor with rubber mounts. On the left is the luminous version (No. 967, $9.95) added within a year. Designed by Henry Dreyfuss (Des. 154,995, awarded August 30, 1949). **($75-85)**

A new "Big Ben Electric" ($3.95 w/plain dial, $4.95 w/ luminous dial), similar in appearance to the "Big Ben Chime Alarm," was introduced in the September 1941 *Tick Talk*. A loud and soft alarm replaced the chime alarm. Self-starting electric movement. Offered only in ivory with gold-colored trim. Designed by Henry Dreyfuss (Des. 114,262, awarded April 11, 1939). (Photo: *Tick Talk*, Sept. 1941) **($45-55)**

Front and rear, the new Big Ben Electric displays smooth lines.

A new "Big Ben Electric," 4-7/8" h, was introduced in the May 1956 *Tick Talk*. The new model, with the same styling as the new spring model, was offered with plain ($6.95) or luminous ($7.95) dial. Choice of white with gold color trim (No. 1206, plain; No. 1216, luminous) or bronze with gold color trim (No. 1207, plain; No. 1217, luminous). Cone-shaped shatter-proof crystal. Single knob sets time and alarm. Cushioned base and insistent alarm. (Photo: 1957 catalog) **($35-45)**

In 1958, the "Big Ben Electric" acquired a new dial with "easy-to-read" vertical numbers. (Photo: 1958 catalog) **($35-45)**

Introduced in the March 1960 *Tick Talk*, this variation of "Big Ben Electric" (No. 1208-L, $8.98) has a "Golden" case with spun dial. By 1962, the plain dial had been dropped as an option on "Big Ben Electric" and new model numbers assigned to the three luminous versions—white (No. 20008), bronze (No. 20006), and golden (No. 20010). Dropped after the 1963-64 catalog. The golden version was known as the "Big Ben Deluxe Electric" during its last two years of production. (Photo: 1962 catalog) **($40-50)**

When the "Big Ben Electric" was restyled in January 1965, it was also renamed "Ben Electric" (No. 20156, $8.98), 4-1/4" h. "Ben Electric" received the same oval shape as "Baby Ben" and "Big Ben." All metal case finished in white with solid brass trim. Choice of plain (No. 20157) or luminous (No. 20156) dial. Cushioned base. Shatterproof crystal. Sweep second hand and alarm indicator. Dropped from the 1966-67 catalog. Designed by Ellworth Danz. (Des. 201,895, awarded August 10, 1965) (Photo: 1965 catalog) **($20-25)**

Introduced in the March 1966 *Tick Talk*, the "Big Ben Electric Dialite" (No. 20184, $8.98), 4-1/4" h, has the same case design as the remainder of the Ben family, but features an illuminated dial and sweep second hand. All metal case finished in white with brass trim. Cushioned base. Self-starting electric movement. Remained in the catalog until at least 1970. Based on original design by Ellworth Danz. (Photo: 1967-68 catalog) **($20-25)**

Baby Ben Electric

Introduced in August 1940, the "Baby Ben Electric" (No. 900, $3.95 w/plain dial; No. 905, $4.95 w/luminous dial) was initially offered only in an ivory case with gold-colored trim. Although slightly taller, at 4-inches, than the spring wound model, "Baby Ben Electric" was believed to be the smallest electric clock on the market at the time. Dropped at the beginning of World War II and not reintroduced following the war. (Photo: *Tick Talk*, August 1940) **($35-45)**

Introduced in the 1970 catalog, the "Big Ben Electric Fashion Brite" ($10.95), 4-1/4" h, has a case, dial, and trim that are color coordinated. Lighted dial. Buzzer alarm. Alarm set indicator light. Cushioned base. Choice of Avocado (No. 20304) or Shaded Wedgwood Blue (No. 20306) finish. Shown on the left is the "Big Ben Electric Dialite" (No. 20184), the same clock without the designer color. Original design by Ellworth Danz. (Photo: 1970-71 catalog) **($20-25)**

By 1957 a new "Baby Ben Electric" ($6.95, plain dial; $7.95, luminous dial), 3-3/4" h, had been introduced with metal case and gold color trim. Cushioned base and shatterproof cone-shaped crystal. Insistent alarm. Choice of Beige (No. 1240, plain; No. 1250, luminous); Pink (No. 1241, plain; No. 1251, luminous); or Jade Green (No. 1242, plain; No.1253, luminous) finish. By 1962, new model numbers were assigned and only the pink (No. 20018) and beige (No. 20016) models with luminous dials remained. Dropped from the 1964-65 catalog when the new oval-cased models were introduced. (Photo: 1957 catalog) **($25-30)**

Alarm Clocks

Introduced in the August 1932 *Tick Talk*, the "America Electric" has a thin metal case finished in black and nickel. The dial has a touch of red to augment the usual black. Convex crystal. Steady, buzzer-type alarm. Rear alarm indicator and shut off. Not offered with luminous dial. Slow speed movement mounted in rubber. Designed by Max Schlenker (Des. 87,597; awarded August 16, 1932). (Photo: *Tick Talk*, August 1932) **($55-65)**

The Westclox fire fighters pose for a picture with the new fire truck. The truck replaced the man-drawn hose cart in use until 1929. (Photo: *Tick Talk*, July 20, 1929)

Ballad Of A Wife

"He always sent flowers
Before we were wed,
To get any now,
I'd have to drop dead."

Reprinted from *Tick Talk*, August 20, 1927

Introduced in the August 1933 *Tick Talk*, "Ben Bolt" ($2.95) is a small electric alarm with case finished in combination of black and nickel. Pleasant toned internal bell. Modernistic dial and hands. Convex nonbreakable crystal. Rear alarm indicator and shut off. Offered in choice of plain (No. 828) or luminous (No. 835) dial. By 1937, an ivory-cased version was added (No. 829). Designed by Max Schlenker (Des. 90,091, awarded June 6, 1933) **($105-120)**

The "Hustler Electric," introduced in August 1933, was part of the nondescript series of clocks produced by Westclox but not bearing the Westclox name. It was available in choice or blue or green case. Manual starting electric movement with forward motion only. A revolving disc on the dial shows that the clock is running as there is no second hand. The case is the same as the "Hustler" spring clock introduced in May 1933. (Photo: *Tick Talk*, August 1933) **($40-50)**

Introduced in October 1935, the "Country Club" (No. 815, $2.50) has a black lacquered metal case with nickel trim. A small leg at the back of the clock keeps it upright. A low speed motor is used with simplified manual starting. The motor is mounted in rubber to ensure silent operation. The dial has a two-tone effect with a darker numeral band sporting stylized Roman numerals. The alarm indicator is visible through a small window near the top of the dial. **($35-45)**

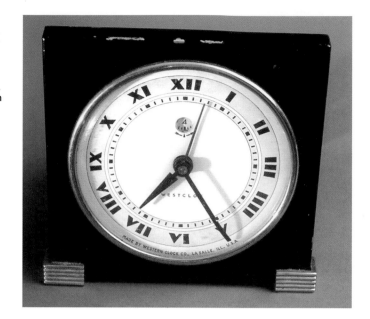

In August 1937, a new version of the "Country Club" (Model 815, $3.45) was introduced with an ivory finish and luminous dial. Note the novel window style alarm indicator. Manual starting electric movement. Also listed from 1937-1941 is a maroon finish with plain dial (No. 814). (Photo: *Tick Talk*, August 13, 1937) **($35-45)**

Westclockers were paid by check for the first time in March 1922. Previously, they were paid in cash.

and of th
This n
for $6.95
The n
Bantam
pieces, ar
Westclox
$1.25.
Bingo
tractive
brownish
nickel tri

Introduced in April 1936, the "Greenwich" (No. 846, $6.95) is an electric alarm with walnut colored wood case with gold-colored trim. die-cast feet with felt cushioning to prevent scratching. Etched metal dial with window type alarm indicator. Convex glass. Self-starting slow-speed synchronous movement. (Photo: *Tick Talk*, April 1936) **($40-50)**

Fittingly introduced in December 1936 was the "Silent Knight" (No. 826, $4.95), 5-1/4" x 4-7/8" x 2", a self-starting electric alarm. It has a die-cast case with gun metal finish. A wide, polished gold-colored bezel doubles as a numeral band with inlaid Arabic numerals. Red sweep second hand, window type alarm indicator, and convex glass. Mellow sounding gong alarm. Self-starting Sangamo motor. An ivory version (No. 827) with gold trim was added in 1937. Designed by Max Schlenker and Joseph A. Reinhardt (Des. 102,581, awarded December 29, 1936). (Photo: *Tick Talk*, December 1936) **($65-75)**

This ad from the December 4, 1937, *Saturday Evening Post* displays the 1937 Westclox product line.

Although the case of this "Silent Knight" is in excellent condition, the clock is missing its second hand and does not work, significantly reducing its value. **($25-30)**

The Christmas box for 1936. (Photo: *Tick Talk*, December 1936)

Introduced in September 1938, the "Bachelor" (No. 873, $3.95), 4-3/4" x 5-1/8" x 2", was initially offered in a dark blue molded plastic case trimmed in gold-colored flutings. The "Bachelor" was the first Westclox to use a new self-starting movement and motor incorporating a current interruption indicator. The Westclox interruptor signal was designed to ignore momentary interruptions of less than two seconds. Designed by Paul G. Darrot (Des. 109,476, awarded May 3, 1938). **($75-85)**

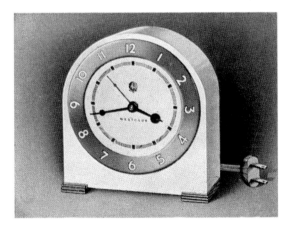

An ivory version of the "Silent Knight" (Model 827, $5.45) was introduced in August 1937. Self-starting electric movement. die-cast case with gold-colored trim. (Photo: *Tick Talk*, August 13, 1937) **($85-95)**

Two new finishes were added to the "Bachelor" line in July 1939. In addition to the original blue case, an ivory case with luminous dial (No. 877, $4.95) and black case with plain dial (No. 875, $3.95) were offered (Photo: *Tick Talk*, July 1939) **($75-85)**

In August 1940, another variation was added to the Bachelor lineup. The ivory model was made available with a plain dial (No. 879) and the fluted metal trim at the top and bottom was replaced with a flat band. **($75-85)**

Introduced in January 1939, the "Pittsfield" (No. 871, $5.95), 5-3/4" x 5-5/8" x 2", has an ivory finish case with gold color trim. Debossed brown numerals on an outside band of ivory Plaskon®. Gold color dial. Self-starting electric movement with current interruption indicator. Alarm movement. Designed by Max Schlenker (Des. 107,102, awarded November 23, 1937). **($55-65)**

"Dignity of manners always conveys a sense of reserve force."

(*Tick Talk*, August 20, 1926)

Introduced in the September 15, 1938, *Tick Talk*, the "Orb" ($2.95) has a two-piece molded plastic case with the front and back tapered to a gold-colored band encircling the case. Manual starting electric movement and buzzer alarm. The movement is the same as the one used in the "Country Club." Designed by Paul G. Darrot (Des. 109,210, awarded April 12, 1938). The base in the production model differs from that in the patent drawing. (Photo: *Tick Talk*, September 15, 1938) **($60-70)**

The "Logan," 4-3/4" sq., was the first new model introduced after the war. Introduced in October 1945, the "Logan" was initially offered in an ivory lacquered case with gold-colored trim in both plain (No. 862, $5.95) and luminous (No. 866, $6.95) dials. It has a self-starting electric movement with current interruption indicator. The signal is reset by tilting the clock backwards while the current is on. Two-tone dial. Bell alarm setting and shut-off are located on the back. The movement is mounted in rubber for quietness. Dropped by 1955. (Photo: *Tick Talk*, October 1945) **($40-50)**

"Which is the wrong side of a bed?" asks this April 19, 1941, ad from the *Saturday Evening Post*. Turns out people get up on the wrong side of the bed when they toss and turn all night because they don't have confidence in their alarm clock.

Luminous Dials

Luminous hands and dials were painted by hand. *Tick Talk* noted in its June 1927 issue that mechanical processes such as embossing or printing would destroy the illuminating properties of the compound. As a result, a needle-like stylus was used to apply the material by hand to the numerals. On the hour and minute hands, a fine brush was used to apply the paste-like compound.

Efficient applicators completed from fifty to sixty dials per day, depending on the model. *Tick Talk* noted that only about a quarter of the "girls" who attempted to paint dials ever became proficient. Several months of training was provided, starting with work on Big Ben, because of the large numerals, and progressing to Baby Ben and Glo Ben.

Because of the expense of the Radium compound, each operator was given a carefully measured portion of the compound in the morning.

Introduced in the August 1948 *Tick Talk*, the "Moonbeam" (No. 904, $9.95), 5-1/2" x 6-1/2", rapidly became a favorite. It uses a novel flashing light to awaken sleepers. A light concealed in the case flashes at regular intervals for approximately seven minutes. If this silent alarm does not work, a regular alarm follows. *Tick Talk* notes that the room need not be dark for the flashing light to awaken the sleeper. Self starting electric movement. White plastic case with gold-color base. Two-toned dial with brown numerals. A luminous version (No. 907, $12.95) was added by 1955. Dropped from the 1958 catalog. Designed by Paul G. Darrot (Des. 162,391, awarded March 13, 1951). The recent reintroduction of the "Big Ben Moonbeam" by Salton is likely to deflate values for the originals in the short term. **($75-85)**

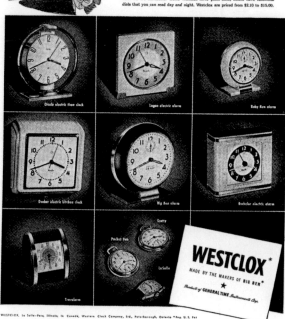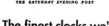

Saturday Evening Post ad, September 27, 1947. (Photo: *Tick Talk*, September 1947)

This weird contraption is an early effort to create an alarm clock capable of waking the deaf. A telephone buzzer was connected to a Big Ben so that Big Ben's alarm would set off the buzzer. The buzzer was placed under the deaf person's pillow. The buzzer set off enough vibration to wake the sleeper. (*Tick Talk*, March 1921)

The "Moonbeam" was featured in Westclox's February 1951 *Saturday Evening Post* ad. (Photo: *Tick Talk*, February 1951)

The Moonbeam was again featured in the *Saturday Evening Post* ad for October 1952. (Photo: *Tick Talk*, October 1952)

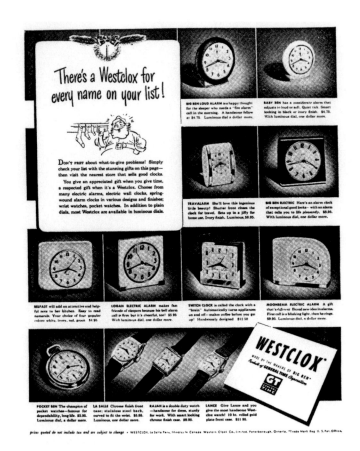

"There's a Westclox for every name on your list" is the theme of the December 1949 Westclox ad in the *Saturday Evening Post*. (Photo: *Tick Talk*, December 1949)

The 1948 "Barry" (No. 960, $4.95), 4-3/4" x 4-1/2", is a self-starting electric alarm in molded black plastic case with horizontal fluting. Bright finish bezel surrounds decorative two-tone dial with legible numerals. Brown pierced hands and alarm indicator on the dial. Bell alarm. Interruption signal on dial is reset by simply tilting the clock backwards. **($45-55)**

Introduced in July 1949, the "Bantam" ($3.95), 3-1/2" h, has an ivory finish molded plastic case. The numerals and hands are brown; the sweep second hand, gold. Front alarm indicator with rear shut off. Self-starting electric movement. (Photo: *Tick Talk*, July 1949) **($40-50)**

The 200,000,000th timepiece produced by Westclox rolled off the assembly line February 16, 1948. Shown holding up the historic clock are Paul Kerp, left, the foreman of the Big Ben Assembling Department, and Herman Willmeroth, assistant in the Big Ben Finishing Department. (Photo: *Tick Talk*, February 1948)

"Wanted: A good looking boy with a 'ritzy' car. See Frances Foley."

Reprinted from *Tick Talk*, December 1929

Westclox Week ad appearing in the *Saturday Evening Post*, September 24, 1949. (Photo: *Tick Talk*, September 1949)

The new Bantam alarm clock was promoted in the October 22, 1949, *Saturday Evening Post*. The ad was also carried in Collier's and Sunday newspapers in sixty-six cities. (Photo: *Tick Talk*, October 1949)

In 1929, 447 Westclockers completed the year without being absent or tardy. Henry Cohard completed his ninth consecutive perfect year.

The cover of the June 1947 *Tick Talk* shows a movement winding operation in the Wrist Watch Department.

Table Clocks

Introduced in February 1935, the "Ben Franklin" (No. 850), 5-1/4" x 7-1/4" x 2-1/8", is a self-starting, time-only, electric clock. It has a highly polished jet black composition case. The bezel, hands, and base are gold-colored metal. White inlaid index numeral markings replace numbers. The movement is the same one used in the Big Ben Electric except that the alarm mechanism is omitted. The motor is a Sangamo motor purchased from the Sangamo Electric Company of Springfield, Illinois. Designed by Joseph A. Reinhardt (Des. 96,337, awarded July 23, 1935). **($85-95)**

> "Some people who can't see the other side of a question remind us of the fish called the flounder; it has both its eyes on one side of its head."
>
> (*Tick Talk*, September 5, 1930)

Introduced in April 1938, the "Andover" (No. 865, $4.95) has a manual-starting (S2) electric movement. The nickel case encloses two pieces of glass; the front is clear, the back is blue. A two-tone metal dial is sandwiched between the two pieces of glass. The same basic design was reintroduced as the "Oracle," a self-starting electric table clock after the war. Designed by Max Schlenker (Des. 110,124, awarded June 14, 1938). (Photo: *Tick Talk*, April 25, 1938) **($115-125)**

Introduced in September 1941, the "Troy" ($3.50), 4-1/2" x 5" x 2", was offered in a choice of ivory or maroon molded plastic case, both with gold-colored trim. Self-starting electric movement with current interruption indicator. It has the same case design as the spring-wound "Shelby." The "Troy" was not reintroduced after World War II. Designed by Max Schlenker (Des. 117,912, awarded December 5, 1939). (Photo: *Tick Talk*, September 1941) **($35-45)**

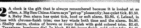

"What kind of gift is best remembered?" is the question posed by the Westclox ad appearing in the May 17, 1941, *Saturday Evening Post*. The answer, of course, is a clock because it is looked at so often.

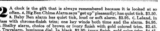

The *Saturday Evening Post* ad from November 1, 1941, emphasized the importance of Westclox's careful construction and testing. What is the most common thief of sleep? The ad notes that sleep experts agree that the fear of not waking up on time—being late for work—is the main culprit.

Introduced in the October 1946 *Tick Talk*, the "Oracle," 6-1/4" h, ($15.00), has a case of glass and gold-colored metal. The die-cast base is cushioned underneath to prevent marring surfaces. Etched silvered dial with polished numerals. Self-starting electric movement (M 3B type). Although announced in October 1946, production was delayed because of a shortage of material. The January 1947 *Tick Talk* announced the availability of the new model. The "Oracle" was dropped from the 1948 Electric Clocks Catalog despite what appears to be brisk sales. Postwar version of the 1938 "Andover." Based on Max Schlenker's prewar design for the "Andover" (Des. 110,124, awarded June 14, 1938). (*Tick Talk*, October 1946, January 1947) **($75-85)**

A "restyled" Oracle? While the clock on the left has a bright new dial with stick numerals, it is not a factory update. The tell-tale signs that this is a home project are the paint drips on the dial and the irregular spacing of the hour markers. Such clocks have little appeal to collectors.

Tick Talk frequently featured the children and grandchildren of Westclox employees. Pictured are Jeanne and John Zywica, grandchildren of Bill Overroeder. (Photo: *Tick Talk*, December 1947)

The new "Oracle" moves down the production line. (Photo: *Tick Talk*, April 1947)

Grandchildren of BILL OVERROEDER, Auto Screw

Jeanne Zywica
Age 7

John Zywica

Introduced in the August 1948 *Tick Talk*, the "Ardmore" (No. 943, $8.95) has a lustrous brown plastic case. The numeral band is bordered by twin gold-colored bezels. The numbers are cut into the narrow rims of plastic between the two bezels. The numerals are the same brown color as the case. The hands are gold colored. Self-starting electric movement. Current interruption indicator can be reset by simply tilting the clock while the power is on. Designed in 1941 by Max Schlenker (Des. 127,817, awarded June 17, 1941) but not produced until after the war. (Photo: 1948 catalog) **($50-60)**

Wall Clocks

Introduced in March 1936, this new "Electric Wall Clock" ($2.95), 5-3/4" diameter, was available in red (No. 853) or ivory (No. 841) finish, both with chrome trim. Four inch metal dial with easy to read numerals and red sweep second hand. Simplified manual starting electric movement. The red version was dropped in January 1938 and a chrome finish added as an option. Designed by Max Schlenker (Des. 100,478, awarded July 21, 1936). (Photo: *Tick Talk*, April 1936) **($55-65)**

Introduced in April 1938, the "Manor" is a self-starting (Type M) electric wall clock with die-cast case finished in a combination of black and ivory. Designed by Max Schlenker (Des. 107,458, awarded December 14, 1937). (Photo: *Tick Talk*, April 25, 1938) **($55-65)**

Westclox introduced its first "Electric Wall Clock" shortly after Christmas 1931. The case, available in choice of green (No. 803) or ivory (No. 800), is made of Plaskon, a product of the Mellon Institute Laboratories. It is believed that this was the first use of Plaskon in a clock case. The manual-starting electric movement was completely manufactured at the Westclox plant, with the exception of the small coil. The tiny coil is one and one-half inches long and three-quarters of an inch wide and contains 8,000 turns of wire about the thickness of a human hair. A new dial was announced in the July 1935 *Tick Talk*. At the same time, a chrome plated bezel replaced the original painted bezel. Designed by Max Schlenker (Des. 85,665, awarded December 1, 1931). (Photo: *Tick Talk*, January 1932) **($45-55)**

In April 1938, a chrome finish with black trim was added to the options for the "Round Wall Clock," formerly known simply as the "Electric Wall Clock." Notice the different dial used for the chrome version compared to the ivory version in the rear. *Tick Talk* reported that the red finish was discontinued but it was still listed in an April 18, 1941 price list. The finishes available in April 1941 were ivory (No. 807), red (No. 809), green (No. 810), and white (No. 811). (Photo: *Tick Talk*, April 25, 1938) **($65-75)**

DECEMBER, 1939   VOL. 24   NUMBER 12

Cover to the December 1939 *Tick Talk*.

In March 1939, the "Manor" ($3.95) became available in a choice of four finishes—ivory and red, ivory and green, ivory and black, and all ivory. Self-starting (S4) electric movement and M1A motor. (Photo: *Tick Talk*, March 1939) **($55-65)**

Introduced in March 1939, the "Belfast" ($2.95) has a square metal case available in choice of Ivory (No. 833-L), Chinese Red (No. 833-R), or Jade Green (No. 833-G) enamel finish. The unusual dial features debossed black numerals on a bright metal ring with black hands set against an ivory tinted background. Brass sweep second hand. Manual-starting S2 movement. Designed by Max Schlenker (Des. 113,120, awarded January 31, 1939). (Photo: *Tick Talk*, March 28, 1939) **($45-55)**

The original "Belfast" was not among the models reintroduced after the war, but a new "Belfast" ($4.95), 7-3/4" x 6-1/2", appeared in the 1948 catalog. Metal case with a single "raised rib" running horizontally in the center. Hands can be reset by turning the knob at the bottom in either direction. Self-starting electric movement with current interruption indicator. Baked lacquer finish in choice of Ivory (No. 981), Red (No. 982), Green (No. 983), or White (No. 984). (Photo: 1948 catalog) **($35-45)**

Introduced in April 1941, the "Dunbar" ($3.95), 7" h, was offered in choice of ivory (No. 920), red (No. 921), green (No. 922), or white (No. 923) finish. The dial on this self-starting electric clock is tilted slightly forward for easier reading. It is also the first Westclox wall clock with a square dial. The back of the case is recessed to allow the cord to be completely hidden when the clock is mounted directly over an electrical outlet. The "Dunbar" uses the same M2 movement used in the "Manor." The "Dunbar" was one of the first Westclox reintroduced after the war and was included in the 1948 catalog. (Photo: *Tick Talk*, April 1941) **($60 70)**

Tickle Talk

Among *Tick Talk*'s regular features was "Tickle Talk," a page of jokes.

In 1938, 181 million separate and distinct advertisements were released through the *Saturday Evening Post*, metropolitan newspapers, and farm publications.

The Dunbar, with its slanted front, was a very popular model and is still fairly easy to find.

By October 1945, Westclox was again producing clocks as shown by this ad appearing in the October 27, 1947 *Saturday Evening Post*.

As the economic downturn in the early 1930s continued, Westclox management tried to economize whenever possible, including the posting of signs over paper towel dispensers advising that "One Towel Will Dry the Hands." *Tick Talk* noted that a few Westclockers with "less sense than the proverbial first grade dunce" had occasionally scribbled "half witticisms" on the cards criticizing the effort.

Tick Talk noted that writing on company property was wrong at any time but that "at a time like this when you have to stretch the eagle on a dollar until it looks like a stork, it is a heinous offense."

What should be done to the culprits? The article is titled "We Suggest Boiling in Oil."

Introduced in the December 1947 *Tick Talk*, the "Monitor Commercial Wall Clock" has a 12-1/2" convex dial with white finish, black numerals, and black hands. The streamlined case has a brown metallic finish. Intended for use in businesses, schools, and offices. Self-starting electric movement and red sweep second hand. Current interruption indicator. Choice of Brown Metallic (No. 999, $12.50) or Chrome (No. 1000, $14.50) finish. Dropped from the 1958 catalog and replaced by a new model. (Photo: 1948 catalog) **($25-35)**

Plaskon, a new material made by the Mellon Institute Laboratory, was used in the Electric Wall Clock introduced in the January 1932 *Tick Talk*, marking the first use of Plaskon in a clock case.

The Westclox payroll in 1949 was $9,500,000.

Another milestone was reached February 16, 1948, as the 200,000,000th Westclox rolled off the assembly line in La Salle, the largest total production in timepiece history. Clock number 200,000,000 was inscribed and placed on display in the factory.

Tick Talk pointed out that if all 200 million timepieces were shipped at once, it would require a train with 5,000 standard size boxcars stretching 40 miles. Placed end to end the 200 million timepieces would stretch half way around the world at the equator. If the 200 million timepieces were stretched end-to-end, they could make two trips from New York to San Francisco, San Francisco to New Orleans, and New Orleans back to New York.

If a clock and watch maker started a factory in 117 A. D. and produced one timepiece every minute for the same number of hours that Westclockers worked in 1948, that clock and watch maker would be reaching the 200 million milestone in 1948.

Pictured on the cover of the October 1948 *Tick Talk* is movement inspector Otto W. Danz of the Big Ben Assembly Department. (Photo: *Tick Talk*, October 1948)

Alarm Clocks

Introduced in July 1950, the "Greenwich," 4" h, has a mahogany finished wood case and a pleasant toned bell alarm. It is trimmed in gold color metal. Self-starting electric movement. (Photo: *Tick Talk*, July 1950) **($50-60)**

View of a Westclox assembly line as the "Greenwich" comes down the line. (Photo: *Tick Talk*, September 1950)

Seven new models were added to the Westclox line in 1955.

(*Tick Talk*, March 1956)

"Who is 'Chuck' Zaleski spending his noon hours with now? That's the sixty-four dollar question, isn't it Chuck?"

Reprinted from *Tick Talk*, March 1950

"Allen was sporting his new Easter bonnet. It's quite the latest fashion"

Reprinted from *Tick Talk*, April 1950

Introduced at the sales convention in May 1952, the "Sphinx," 4-1/2" h, a self-starting electric alarm, has a mahogany-finished wood case in a modern style. The case is accented with gold color feet and bezel. (Photo: *Tick Talk*, July 1952) **($45-55)**

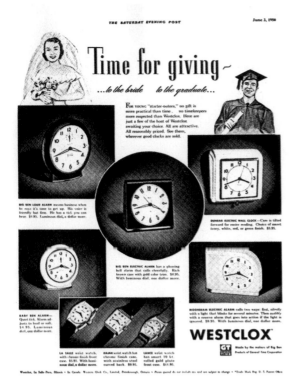

Saturday Evening Post ad, June 3, 1950. The bride is joined by the graduate. (Photo: Tick Talk, June 1950)

The original "Moonbeam" continued to be promoted in Westclox's March 8, 1952, Saturday Evening Post ad.

Westclox of Scotland produced its millionth timepiece in December 1950. Here, a stewardess for the British Overseas Airways Corporation presents the millionth clock to Arnold J. Wilson, President of General Time, as John H. Schmidt, Secretary-Treasurer looks on. The plant in Scotland allowed Westclox to sell its products in foreign markets where trade conditions prevented clocks produced at the US plant from being competitive. (Photo: Tick Talk, December 1950)

A new blond finish was introduced for the "Sphinx" ($7.95) in May 1953. Tick Talk notes that "It is believed Sphinx in the blond finish will prove particularly popular with householders who have equipped their homes with the increasingly popular blond finish furniture." (Photo: Tick Talk, May 1953) **($45-55)**

Is it true cats have more fun? Chessie inspects the blond Sphinx.

Introduced in the October 1953 *Tick Talk*, the "Glo-Larm" ($8.95), 4-1/4" h, was offered in choice of beige (No. 1025), ivory (No. 1026), or aqua green (No. 1027) plastic case. It features a face illuminated by a hidden light that glows through the dial. The catalog notes that "After dark his whole face glows." The light can be turned to bright, dim, or off. Self-starting electric movement. Dropped by 1957. (Photo: *Tick Talk*, Oct. 1953) **($50-60)**

Letters, We Get Letters

Westclox,

I was just thinking that I cannot keep this to myself. So here I am writing and telling you.

For Christmas we bought our daughter a Westclox Moonbeam Blinking Light Alarm Clock. Our daughter is 19 years old and happens to be stone deaf. The story begins:

We tried a Big Ben Alarm Clock to ring under her sleeping pillow and she said she didn't even get the vibration of the ring. We really were trying everything, but nothing would awaken her.

One Sunday she was reading the paper and saw an advertisement about the Moonbeam Blinking Light Alarm and said, 'Mother, why don't you ask Mr. Checil (he is our jewelry man) if he could order a Blinking Light Alarm clock. Maybe it would help me.'

We did not tell our daughter about the clock, but Mr. Checil ordered it and at Christmas time we set the Blinking Light Alarm in her bedroom for the time that I was going to awaken her for Sunday church hour. Christmas morning she ran to our bedroom and said, 'Oh, Mother, did it wake me up! I thought I was dreaming that all the stars in heaven were down in my bedroom and the surprise when I saw the blinking light clock!' (God bless the inventor)

I just wanted you to know how happy we are that something was invented for the deaf people and that she is very happy with her blinking light alarm.

If people visit us, the first thing she shows them is her precious blinking light alarm.

Thank you.

I remain,

Mrs. Edward F. Kalal

Cleveland, Ohio

Reprinted from *Tick Talk*, August 1950.

"Woods by Westclox" was the theme of the May 1953 *Saturday Evening Post* ad featuring the Sphinx and Greenwich. (Photo: *Tick Talk*, May 1953)

Columbia Time Products is a promotional line of time-pieces made by Westclox but not bearing the Westclox name. They are used in the premium field or for large buyer's private brands. (*Tick Talk*, August 1957)

In 1957, the Athens plant was producing 6,500 electric clocks and 2,000 radio timers each day. It employed 430. (*Tick Talk*, September 1957)

THE GOOSE THAT LAYS THE GOLDEN EGGS

Some things never change. This political cartoon appeared in the December 4, 1936, *Tick Talk*, but could just as easily have appeared in today's *Washington Post*.

Glo-Larm

So new... and so comforting to live with

$8⁹⁵ Plus tax

By day nobody knows...that after dark his whole face glows and glows and glows

It's really a joy to have this new electric alarm clock around. For two unusual—and delightful—reasons. You can read it effortlessly in the dark. And its soft, gentle glow is always such a comforting presence in your room. You see, the *entire* face of Glo-Larm is illuminated. A hidden light glows *through* the dial, clearly outlining hands and numerals, so that you may read the time at a glance. Oh yes, you can turn the glow to Bright, Dim—or Off. Only 4 inches high, the distinctive new Glo-Larm by Westclox is available in beige, aqua green or ivory. It has a pleasant bell alarm. And the price is only $8.95. Why not make up your mind to live with this delightful new clock ... starting right now?

THE NEW **GLO-LARM** BY
WESTCLOX*
Electric Clocks
made by the makers of **BIG BEN**
Products of **GT** *Corporation*

WESTCLOX, La Salle-Peru, Illinois • In Canada: Western Clock Co., Ltd., Peterborough, Ontario • *Price quoted for U.S.A. only, does not include tax and is subject to change* • *Trade Mark Reg. U. S. Patent Office.

The "Glo-Larm" was featured in the February 1954 *Saturday Evening Post* ad. (Photo: *Tick Talk*, February 1954)

Introduced in the April 1954 *Tick Talk*, the "Country Club Electric Alarm" ($9.45, plain dial; $10.45, luminous dial) has a molded plastic case in choice of ivory (No. 1045, plain & No. 1055, luminous) or green (No. 1046, plain; No. 1056, luminous). Simple, clean cut lines. Self-starting electric movement. Dropped from the 1957 catalog. (Photo: *Tick Talk*, April 1954) **($30-40)**

Introduced in the April 1954 *Tick Talk*, the "Byron Electric Alarm" ($10.95), 5-1/4" h, has a metal case finished in red (No. 926), green (No. 927), or silver (No. 925). The base tilts slightly, making the plain dial, with gold color Roman numerals, easier to read. Pleasant bell alarm. Non-breakable domed plastic crystal. Cushioned base. Self-starting electric movement. Based on a 1948 design by Max Schlenker (Des. 149,091, March 23, 1948). **($45-55)**

The January 1958 *Tick Talk* announced that the Fawn was now being offered with luminous dial. It also announced the availability of Monitor in a smaller 8" size and the availability of Baby Ben in pink (luminous dial only)

Introduced in the January 1965 *Tick Talk*, the "Kendall Dialite" (No. 20160, $7.98), has the same case design as the "Kendall" but adds a softly lighted dial with side decoration and alarm set indicator light, White case. Self-starting electric movement. Dropped from the 1968-69 catalog. (Photo: 1965 catalog) **($15-20)**

Introduced in the April 1954 *Tick Talk*, the "Kendall Electric Alarm" ($7.95) has a wood case in choice of blond (No. 1041) or mahogany (No. 1040) finish. Also offered with luminous dial ($8.95) in blond (No. 1051) or mahogany (No. 1000). Sweep alarm hand. Gold color trim. Dropped by 1957. (Photo: *Tick Talk*, April 1954) **($50-60)**

Sleepmeter

Introduced in October 1954, the "Sleepmeter," 4-3/16" h, has an ivory plastic case and nonbreakable crystal. Self-starting electric movement with bell alarm. Choice of plain ($5.45) or luminous ($6.45) dial. (Photo: *Tick Talk*, October 1954) **($15-20)**

Introduced in the January 1965 *Tick Talk*, the "Kendall" ($5.98), 3-1/2" h, was described as a "sparkling new design achievement in Modern-Transitional spirit." Large, easy to read numerals and sweep second hand. Buzzer alarm. Self-starting electric movement. Choice of white with plain dial (No. 20159) or Sandalwood with plain dial (No. 20161). Dropped from the 1967-68 catalog. (Photo: 1965 catalog) **($15-20)**

Introduced in the October 1954 *Tick Talk*, the "Pittsfield," 4-1/2" h, has a wood case in choice of plain ($7.98) or luminous ($8.95) dial in mahogany (No. 1100, plain; No. 1110, luminous) or blond (No. 1101, plain; No. 1111, luminous) finish. Gold color trim. Pleasant bell alarm and easy to set alarm indicator. Self-starting electric movement. Dropped from the 1958 catalog. (Photo: 1957 catalog) **($40-50)**

Introduced in the February 1955 *Tick Talk*, the "Piper" electric alarm clock, 3-1/2" h, has a streamlined metal case and choice of plain ($3.98) or luminous ($4.98) dial. Offered in Ivory (No. 947, plain; No. 957, luminous) and Saddle Brown (No. 948, plain; No. 958, luminous) finish supported on brass finish "legs." A single knob operates both the alarm and time hands. Dropped from the 1959-60 catalog. (Photo: 1957 catalog) **($35-40)**

The "Pittsfield" with mahogany case and luminous dial. **($40-50)**

Introduced in the June 1955 *Tick Talk*, the "Town Crier," 4-1/2" h, has a beige plastic case with "hobnail" pattern front. It has a non-breakable crystal and a sweep second hand. Choice of plain (No. 1107, $4.95) or luminous (No. 1117, $5.95) dial. Self-starting electric movement. Dropped from the 1957 catalog. Designed by Lawrence H. Wilson (Des. 177,865, awarded May 29, 1956). (Photo: *Tick Talk*, June-July 1955) **($15-20)**

Introduced in the June 1955 *Tick Talk*, "Dash," 4-1/2" h, is described as "a clock for the young at heart, with dramatic new lines." Black plastic case with recessed front of gold color metal. Unbreakable crystal and sweep second hand. Self-starting electric movement. Steady call alarm. Choice of plain (No. 1088, $5.95) or luminous (No. 1098, $6.95) dial. Dropped from the 1958 catalog. Designed by Ellworth Danz (Des. 177,666, awarded May 15, 1956). (Photo: 1957 catalog) **($15-20)**

Introduced in the June 1955 *Tick Talk*, "Fortune" (No. 1102, $6.95) has a gray-tone plastic case with gold-colored trim and modern dimensional stick dial. Self-starting electric movement. Luminous dial. Insistent alarm. Two additional finishes—black (No. 1122) and egg-shell (No. 1123)—both with luminous dial, were added to the 1958 catalog. All three finishes were combined under one model number—1102-L—in the 1959-60 catalog. Dropped by 1962. (Photo: 1957 catalog) **($55-65)**

Introduced in the May 1960 *Tick Talk*, the "Dash," 3-1/4" h, was offered in a new high impact plastic case with a 5-year guarantee against breakage. Sweep second hand and alarm indicator. Self-starting electric movement. Offered in choice of plain dial (No. 807, $4.98) in pink or white or luminous dial (No. 807-L, $5.98) in antique white. By 1962, new model numbers had been assigned to each finish— Antique White Plain Dial (No. 20073); Pink Plain Dial (No. 20075); Antique White Luminous Dial (No. 20074). Dropped from the 1962-63 catalog. (Photo: 1962 catalog) **($15-20)**

Introduced in the January 1956 *Tick Talk*, the "Sheraton" ($8.95), 4-1/2" h, has a wood case finished in choice of Fruitwood (No. 1085, plain dial) or Mahogany (No. 1096, luminous). It has traditional styling with scrolled dial and spherical brass legs. Bell alarm. Self-starting electric movement. Produced at the Athens, Georgia, plant. In 1958, the "Fruitwood" finish was renamed "Light Mahogany." Both light and dark mahogany versions used the same 1085 model number in 1959. By 1962, a new finish— Maple (No. 21019, plain dial)—had been added and new numbers assigned to the light mahogany (No. 21021, plain) and dark mahogany (No. 21022, luminous) finishes. The light mahogany finish was dropped from the 1968-69 catalog but the two remaining finishes remained in the catalog until at least 1970. (Photo: 1957 catalog) **($25-35)**

Introduced in the November 1956 *Tick Talk*, the "Ellsworth" ($8.95), 3-7/8" high, was the first clock introduced with a high impact Cycolac case. Cycolac was a new plastic that "can't crack, chip or peel." The "Ellsworth" has a satin-finished metal dial, shatter-proof Plexiglas crystal, and a sweep alarm indicator on the dial. It was offered in two colors—decorator gray with a red and brass dial (No. 1042) and gleaming black with a pearl-white and brass dial (No. 1043). Dropped from the 1959-60 catalog. It was produced at the Athens plant. (Photo: 1957 catalog) **($20-25)**

Tick Talk welcomes the 1958 New Year. (Photo: *Tick Talk*, December 1957)

The 1957 "Tide," 3-1/4" h, has an embossed flamingo design on its side panels. Shatterproof crystal. Self-starting electric movement with sweep second and alarm hands. Insistent alarm. Choice of Ivory with plain dial (No. 1244, $3.98), Pink with luminous dial (No. 1255, $4.98), or Yellow with luminous dial (No. 1256, $4.98). (Photo: 1957 catalog) **($15-20)**

The "Tide" was restyled for 1958, receiving a new dial, hands, and side panel design. Luminous versions combined under No. 1244-L in the 1959-60 catalog. By 1962, only the ivory version remained in the catalog and a new number had again been assigned—No. 20087. (Photo: 1958 catalog) **($15-20)**

A luminous version of the "Tide" (No. 20088) was reintroduced in the 1963-64 catalog, this time on the ivory case. (Photo: 1963-64 catalog) **($15-20)**

Introduced in the March 1966 *Tick Talk*, the "Tide Drowse" (No. 20193, $4.98), 3-1/2" h, has an Antique White plastic case and plain dial. Drowse alarm. Full numeral dial. Dropped from the 1969-70 catalog. (Photo: 1966-67 catalog) **($15-20)**

3¼" high

The "Tide" received another freshening in the 1964-65 catalog with new side panels. Remained in the catalog essentially unchanged for the remainder of the 1960s. (Photo: 1965 catalog) **($15-20)**

Introduced in the 1958 catalog, the "Dynamic" ($12.95), 10-3/4" x 4-1/4", is described as "the last word in original modern decorator styling…" Medium impact plastic case in choice of Maple Sugar (No. 1400) or Bittersweet (No. 1401). Gold recessed bezel, hands, and raised numerals. Self-starting electric movement with buzzer alarm and single knob time/alarm set. Sweep second and alarm hands. Models combined under No. 1400 in 1959-60 catalog. Dropped by 1962. Designed by Keith D. Kitts (Des. 187,037, awarded January 12, 1960). (Photo: 1959-60 catalog) **($55-65)**

The cracked crystal on this example of the Dynamic lowers its value. Repair/ replacement of unusually shaped crystals is very difficult and likely to exceed the value of the clock. **($25-30)**

Introduced in the 1958 catalog, the "Andover" ($7.98), 4" h, has that "sculptured look." Embossed metal dial with luminous hour marks and hands. Self-starting electric movement with buzzer alarm and sweep second and alarm hands. Choice of Driftwood (No. 1410) or Black (No. 1411) finish plastic case. Model numbers consolidated as No. 1410-L in the 1959-60 catalog. Dropped by 1962. (Photo: 1958 catalog) **($20-25)**

Introduced in the 1958 catalog, the "Brucewood," 4-1/8" x 5-1/2" x 3-1/4", has a solid mahogany case that "suits today's homes to a T." Gold color trim. Self-starting electric movement with buzzer alarm. Sweep second and alarm hands. Shatterproof crystal. Choice of plain (No. 1347, $8.98) or luminous (No. 1357, $9.98) dial. Luminous version became No. 1347-L in the 1959-60 catalog. New model numbers assigned in 1962 catalog—No. 21027 (plain); No. 21028 (luminous). Dropped from the 1962-63 catalog. (Photo: 1958 catalog) **($35-45)**

Introduced in the 1958 catalog, the "Lace," 4" x 3-3/4" h, was described as "new and charming for girls of any age!" Plastic case with filigree insert. Self-starting electric movement with sweep second and alarm hands. Choice of Antique White with plain dial (No. 1320, $5.98); Pink with luminous dial (No. 1325, $6.98); or Dusty Blue with luminous dial (No. 1326, $6.98). Catalog numbers combined in 1959-60 as No. 1320 (plain dial) and 1320-L (luminous dial). New catalog numbers appear in the 1962 catalog—No. 20055 (Antique white, plain); No. 20056 (Pink, luminous); No. 20058 (Dusty Blue, luminous). Dropped from the 1962-63 catalog. Designed by Ellworth Danz (Des. 183,243, awarded July 22, 1958). (Photo: 1958 catalog) **($15-20)**

Introduced in the April 1959 *Tick Talk*, the "Drowse" ($5.98), 3-3/4" h, is a self-starting electric alarm featuring the exclusive "Sleep Selector" that permits the user to choose five or ten minutes of extra sleep. The plastic case was available in "cloud gray" (No. 800, $5.98) with a plain dial and "doeskin" (No. 800-L, $6.98) with a luminous dial. This 1959-60 catalog photo also shows the free counter display provided to dealers purchasing an assortment of "Drowse" alarms. Two new colors—pine frost green and pastel pink were added in March 1960. Manufactured in Athens, Georgia. (Photo: 1959-60 catalog) **($10-15)**

3¼" high

Introduced in the May 1959 *Tick Talk*, "Colt" (Nos. 804 & 804-L, $4.98), 3-1/4" h, has an "ultra modern" plastic case in "smart" sand beige color. Self-starting electric movement. Sweep second hand. Also available with luminous dial for one dollar extra. The sand beige case was gone by 1962 and two new finishes were offered—Antique White with plain dial (No. 20081) and Pink with luminous dial (No. 20082). (Photo: 1965 catalog) **($10-15)**

3¾" high

In June 1961, the case of the "Drowse," 3-3/4" h, was redesigned and new colors and models numbers added. Color choices in 1962 were: Antique white with luminous dial (No. 20102, $6.98); Buckskin Beige with plain dial (No. 20101, $5.98); and Seaspray Green with luminous dial (No. 20104, $6.98). Seaspray Green was dropped from the 1963-64 catalog and "Buckskin Beige" became "Sandalwood." Dropped from the 1970 catalog. (Photo: 1964-65 catalog) **($10-15)**

Introduced in the May 1959 *Tick Talk*, "Award" (No. 803-L, $14.95), 4-1/8" h, has a mahogany case of classic design. Silvered dial, raised gold-color numerals, luminous hands and hour marks, gold color bezel and feet, sweep second hand. Self-starting electric alarm movement. New solid walnut case added in 1962 catalog (No. 21012) and new number assigned to mahogany case (No. 21014). Dropped after the 1962-63 catalog and replaced by the "Award II." Designed by Ellworth Danz (Des. 187,746, awarded April 26, 1960). (Photo: 1962 catalog) **($40-50)**

Introduced in the May 1959 *Tick Talk*, the "707" ($19.95), 4-5/8" h, has a solid mahogany case in a "different contemporary design." Rich spun brass finish dial, luminous hands, solid brass bezel and trim, and shatterproof crystal. Self-starting electric alarm movement. Dropped by 1962. Designed by Ellworth Danz (Des. 189,200, awarded November 8, 1960). **($110-125)**

Introduced in the May 1963 *Tick Talk*, the "Award II" ($14.95), 4-1/2" h, has traditional styling with fancy luminous dial and hand-rubbed wood grain finish. Cushioned base. Available in choice of walnut (No. 21040) or mahogany (No. 21042) finish. Self-starting electric movement with sweep alarm and second hands. Dropped from the 1965-66 catalog. (Photo: 1963-64 catalog) **($35-45)**

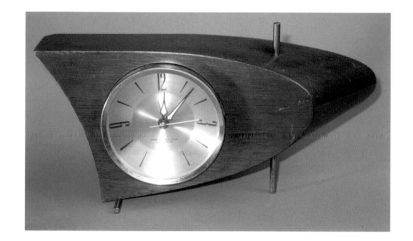

The "707" may have been the most stylish Westclox of the 1950s.

Introduced in May 1960, the "Oracle" (No. 805, $27.50) was described as "the ultimate in fashion design." Etched silver panels on a solid brass case and applied brass numerals on a silvered dial. Sweep second indicator and alarm indicator. Self-starting electric movement. Not found in the 1962 catalog. (Photo: *Tick Talk*, May 1960) **($30-40)**

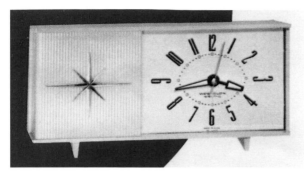

Introduced in the January 1961 *Tick Talk*, the completely redesigned "Moonbeam Silent Alarm" ($11.95), 7-5/8" x 3-3/4", was available in choice of Antique White (No. 20024) or Buckskin Beige (No. 20026) plastic case. Like the original "Moonbeam," this new model uses a flashing light to awaken the sleeper. If the sleeper does not respond to the flashing light, a regular alarm follows. Self-starting electric movement. Designed by Ellworth Danz (Des. 191,756, awarded November 14, 1961). (Photo: 1962 catalog) **($20-25)**

The "Moonbeam" received another new dial in the 1963-64 catalog as well as new case colors. Buckskin Beige was dropped in favor of Brown (No. 20028) and Yellow (No. 20030). By 1967-68, only the Antique White case remained. It remained in production, essentially unchanged for the remainder of the 1960s. (Photo: 1964-65 catalog) **($20-25)**

The "Moonbeam" sports a new dial design in the 1962-63 catalog. (Photo: 1962-63 catalog)

Introduced in the April 1962 *Tick Talk*, the "Moonbeam Nite-Lite" (No. 20022, $12.95) has the same case as the "Moonbeam" but adds a switch that turns on a steady night light. Antique white plastic case and luminous dial. Self-starting electric alarm movement. (Photo: 1962-63 catalog) **($20-25)**

The 1963-64 catalog added the option of a brown case (No. 20020) to the "Moonbeam Nite-Lite" and introduced a new dial. Remained essentially unchanged for the remainder of the 1960s. (Photo: 1966-67 catalog)

Introduced in the June-July 1961 *Tick Talk*, the "Dialite Drowsewood" (No. 21038, $12.95) has solid walnut side panels and a dial that is lighted from behind to glow at night. Self-starting electric movement. Also offered in 1962-63 with luminous features rather than the lighted dial (No. 21036, $10.95). Dropped from the 1966-67 catalog. (Photo: 1963-64 catalog) **($30-35)**

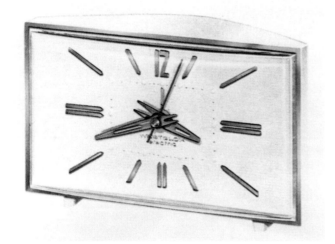

Introduced in the June-July 1961 *Tick Talk*, the "Aspen" ($7.98) has a plastic case, raised gold color numerals, shatterproof crystal, sweep second hand, and luminous dial. Self-starting electric movement. Offered in Antique White (No. 20090), Beige (No. 20092), Seaspray Green (No. 20094), and Black (No. 20096). The Antique White case was added to the 1962-63 catalog; the Black case to the 1963-64 catalog. Dropped from the 1966-67 catalog. (Photo: 1963-64 catalog) **($20-25)**

The "Dialite Drowsewood" was featured on the cover of the August 1961 *Tick Talk*.

Introduced in the June-July 1961 *Tick Talk*, the "Dialite Dunbar" (No. 20076, $6.98), 3-1/2" h, has a lighted dial that glows at night for full visibility. Antique white plastic case. Self-starting electric movement. Sweep second hand. Shatterproof crystal. Alarm set indicator. Dropped from the 1966-67 catalog. (Photo: 1964-65 catalog) **($10-15)**

Introduced in the June 1962 *Tick Talk*, the "Dunbar" (No. 20118, $6.98), 3-1/2" h, has a wood grain finish case with parquet luminous dial. Shatterproof crystal, sweep second hand. Renamed the "Dunmar" in the 1969-70 catalog and then dropped from the 1970 catalog. (Photo: 1968-69 catalog) **($15-20)**

Introduced in the April 1962 *Tick Talk*, the "Woodbriar" electric alarm has a walnut finish case and was offered with both plain (No. 21029, $8.98) and luminous (No. 21030, $9.98) dial. Remained in the catalog throughout the remainder of the 1960s. (Photo: 1968-69 catalog) **($25-30)**

"He has to learn the facts of life some time! All I did was show him the size of the National Debt, and tell him what his share was." . . .

(The size of the National Debt, by the way, was $256,777,727,579.56— as of October 31, 1949—and the per capita share of each man, woman and child is $1,712.)

Although not a regular feature of *Tick Talk*, political cartoons occasionally appeared. Although this cartoon is from the January 1950 *Tick Talk*, change the numbers and it could easily be from 2002. (Photo: *Tick Talk*, January 1950)

The 1962-1970 "Drowse Dialite" (No. 20106, $7.98), 3-3/4" h, has an antique white plastic case with lighted dial. The drowse alarm lets the user select between five and ten minutes extra sleep. Dropped from the 1970 catalog. (Photo: 1966-67 catalog). **($10-15)**

Introduced in the June 1962 *Tick Talk*, the "Dunbar Drowse" (No. 20128, $7.98), 3-1/2" h, adds the famous Westclox drowse feature to the wood finish "Dunbar." The drowse feature "allows leisurely rested arisings." Luminous dial. Renamed the "Dunmar Drowse in the 1969-70 catalog and then dropped from the 1970 catalog. (Photo: 1968-69 catalog) **($10-15)**

Introduced in the 1968-69 catalog, the "Drowse II," 3-3/4" h, added jumbo-sized selector buttons to the top of the case so users could select 5 or 10 minutes extra sleep. Raised numeral dial. Antique white plastic case with choice of plain (No. 20227, $5.98), luminous (No. 20224, $6.98), or Dialite (No. 20228, $7.98). (Photo: 1968-69 catalog) **($10-15)**

Introduced in the June-July 1962 *Tick Talk*, the "Dunbar Drowse" was also available with Sand Beige (No. 20120, $6.98), Jonquil Yellow (No. 20122, $6.98), or Green (No. 20124) case, all with a luminous dial. The beige case was available only in the 1962-63 model years. Dropped from the 1965-66 catalog. (Photo: 1963-64 catalog) **($10-15)**

Introduced in the June-July 1962 *Tick Talk*, the basic "Dunbar" was available with Antique White (No. 20113, $4.98) or Sandalwood (No. 20115, $4.98) plastic case, both with plain dial. Within the year, a luminous version was added to the Antique White case (No. 20114, $5.98). Renamed "Dunmar" in the 1969-70 catalog and then dropped from the 1970 catalog. (Photo: 1968-69 catalog) **($10-15)**

◯ ⬤ 3¾" x 7⅝"

Introduced in the June 1964 *Tick Talk*, "Tangier" ($9.98), 3-3/4" x 7-5/8", is an electric alarm clock available in choice of antique white (No. 20084) or brown (No. 20086) case. The grille is a rich gold tone on both versions. Luminous dial. Dropped from the 1967-68 catalog. (Photo: 1966-67 catalog) **($15-20)**

Introduced in the June-July 1962 *Tick Talk*, the "Dunbar Drowse Dialite" ($7.98), 3-1/2" h, combined two of Westclox's popular features—the Drowse alarm and the Dialite lighted dial—in one clock. Offered in Sand Beige (No. 20132, $7.98), Robin's Egg Blue (No. 20134, $7.98), and Green (No. 20136). The Green case replaced the Sand Beige case in the 1963-64 model year. Dropped from the 1966-67 catalog. (Photo: 1963-64 catalog) **($10-15)**

Introduced in the March 1965 *Tick Talk*, the "Branford," 3-5/8" h, has a sweep second hand and easy-to-read dial. Offered in Wedgwood Blue with plain dial (No. 20097, $5.98), Wedgwood Green with plain dial (No. 20099, $5.98) and Wedgwood Blue with luminous dial (No. 20098, $6.98). Dropped from the 1967-68 catalog. (Photo: 1965 catalog) **($15-20)**

Introduced in the June 1965 *Tick Talk*, the "Branford Dialite" (No. 20170, $7.98) has "traditional good taste." The case is finished in antique white with a decorative border around the crystal. Lighted dial with sweep second hand. Buzzer alarm. Self-starting electric movement. Dropped from the 1968-69 catalog. (Photo: 1965 catalog) **($15-20)**

The "Contessa" looks shapely from any angle. (Photo: *Tick Talk*, March 1965) **($35-45)**

Introduced in the March 1965 *Tick Talk*, the "Contessa" ($6.98), 3-5/8" h, has a tilted oval face "loaded with feminine appeal." It features a sculptured modern case with circular brushed aluminum finish dial. Sweep second hand. Also offered with luminous dial for $1.00 extra. Choice of Antique White with plain dial (No. 20163), Burnt Orange with plain dial (No. 20165), Champagne Gold with plain dial (No. 20167), Pastel Blue with plain dial (No. 20169) or Antique White with luminous dial (No. 20162). Electric alarm movement. Dropped from the 1967-68 catalog. Designed by Jean Otis Reineke (Des. 204,778, awarded May 17, 1966). (Photo: 1965 catalog) **($35-45)**

Introduced in the June 1965 *Tick Talk* as part of the "Crown Series," the "Woodcrest," 4-1/4" h, has a walnut finish wood case with contemporary styling. Gold color foil dial and gilded trim. Buzzer alarm. Choice of plain (No. 21043, $8.98) or luminous (No. 21044, $9.98) dial. Remained in the catalog for the remainder of the 1960s. (Photo: 1965 catalog) **($35-45)**

Introduced in the January 1966 *Tick Talk*, the "Magic Touch Drowse Dialite" ($7.98), 3-9/16" h, combines the Magic Touch feature with a drowse alarm and lighted dial. The drowse alarm can be repeated three times during one alarm period. Choice of Antique White (No. 20178), Antique Gold (No. 20180), or Fern Green (No. 20182) plastic case. Dropped from the 1970 catalog. (Photo: 1968-69 catalog) **($15-20)**

Introduced in the January 1966 *Tick Talk*, the "Magic Touch Drowse" ($5.98), 3-1/4" h, has an electric alarm that wakes you, lets you drowse seven minutes, and then wakes you again. Magic touch feature allows user to shut off the alarm by touching the top of the case. Choice of Antique White (No. 20175) or Clove Brown (No. 20177) case, both with plain dial. Dropped from the 1969-70 catalog. (Photo: 1968-69 catalog) **($10-15)**

Introduced in the January 1966 *Tick Talk*, the "Magic Touch Dialite" ($5.98), 3-1/4" h, has a softly lighted dial for full night view. A simple tap on the top of the case silences the alarm. Choice of White (No. 20186) or Antique Gold (No. 20188) plastic case. In the 1969-70 catalog, a new wood grain finish (No. 20258) was added. Available through at least 1970. (Photo: 1968-69 catalog) **($10-15)**

7" x 3⅞"

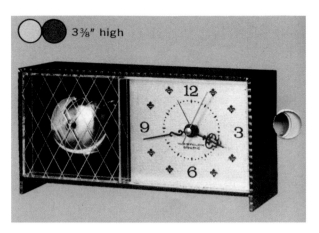

3⅜" high

Introduced in the March 1966 *Tick Talk*, the "Twin-Face Alarm" ($12.95), 7" x 3-7/8", was an electric alarm that featured two separate alarms and faces "ideal for twin-bed couples who get up at different times." Separate "his" and "hers" alarm tones. Choice of Antique White (No. 20195), Clove Brown (No. 20197), or Pastel Blue (No. 20199) plastic case, all with plain dial. The plain dial versions were dropped from the 1967-68 catalog and replaced by luminous dials—Antique White (No. 20194), Clove Brown (No. 20196), and Pastel Blue (No. 20198). Designed by Ellworth Danz and Roman Szalek (Des. 210,677; awarded April 2, 1968). (Photo: 1967-68 catalog) **($25-35)**

Introduced in March 1966, the "Bell-Vue" ($10.95), 3-3/8" h, was an electric alarm featuring a bell and striker visible through a molded lattice on the front of the case. A soft bell-tone alarm rings for approximately ten minutes followed by a distinct buzzer sound. Brushed gold color metal dial with black numerals. Choice of brushed brass (No. 20189) or wood grain (No. 20191) finish. Dropped from the 1968-69 catalog. Designed by David W. Miley (Des. 210,676, awarded April 2, 1968). (Photo: 1966-67 catalog) **($25-35)**

The "Twin-Face" was changed again in the 1968-69 catalog, becoming the "Twin-Face Nite-Lite" ($14.95) as a night light was added to the center panel with a push button switch. Choice of Antique White (No. 20230), Clove Brown (No. 20232), or Pastel Blue (No. 20234), all with luminous dial. Only the Antique White case remained in the 1969-70 catalog. (Photo: 1968-69 catalog) **($25-35)**

"Time on her hands" is the caption Westclox applies to this cover photo of Elizabeth Lenzi, Four Inch Finishing Department, posing with some of Westclox's electric clocks. (Photo: *Tick Talk*, March 1952)

Introduced in the 1966-67 catalog, the "Magic Touch" electric alarm ($4.98), 3-1/4" h, has traditional styling coupled with a plain dial and decorative alarm set markers. Choice of Antique White (No. 20171) or Sandalwood (No. 20173) plastic case. The Sandalwood case was dropped from the 1968-69 catalog; the Antique White case from the 1970 catalog. The 1966-67 catalog also shows the availability of the Antique White "Magic Touch" in a "blister pack" with it's own catalog number (No. 20671). Dropped from the 1969-70 catalog. (Photo: 1968-69 catalog) **($10-15)**

Introduced in the 1967-68 catalog, the "Bold," ($3.98, plain dial; $4.98, luminous dial), 3" h, was a low-priced alarm with plastic case and crystal. Choice of Antique White (No. 20213, plain; No. 20214, luminous) or Sandalwood (No. 20215, plain; No. 20216, luminous). Replaced by the "Bold II" in 1970. Self-starting electric movement. (Photo: 1968-69 catalog) **($10-15)**

Introduced in the 1967-68 catalog, the "Renfield Magic Touch"($6.98, plain; $7.98, luminous), 3-7/8" h, has an "easy-vue" design with wood finish trim. Brushed gold color embossed dial. Drowse alarm wakes you, lets you drowse ten minutes, then wakes you again. Choice of Antique White (No. 20217, plain; 20218, luminous) or Sandalwood (No. 20219, plain; No. 20220, luminous). Sandalwood available only in 1967-68. Dropped from the 1969-70 catalog. Designed by David W. Miley (Des. 212,032, awarded August 20, 1968). (Photo: 1968-69 catalog) **($10-15)**

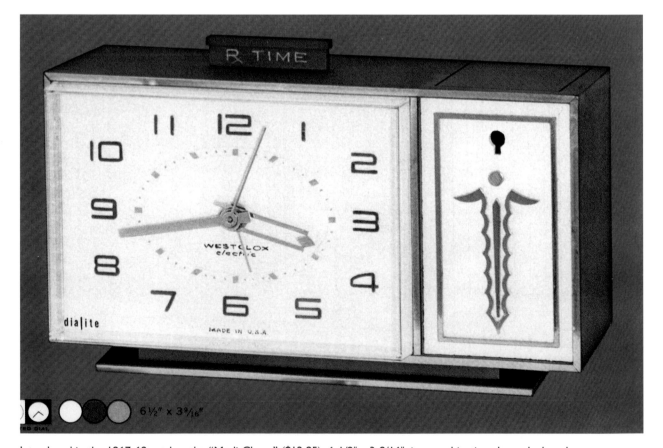

Introduced in the 1967-68 catalog, the "Medi-Chron" ($12.95), 6-1/2" x 3-9/16", is a combination alarm clock and medication reminder. The prescription time bar pops up and the medication alarm sounds at 4-6-12 or 24-hour settings. There is a key lock to the medication compartment. Separate clock alarm. Lighted dial. Choice of Antique White (No. 20208), Woodtone (No. 20210), or Antique Gold (No. 20212) plastic case. Dropped from the 1969-70 catalog. Designed by Roman J. Szalek (Des. 213,455, awarded March 4, 1969). (Photo: 1967-68 catalog) **($25-35)**

Introduced in the 1968-69 catalog, the "Electric Beltone Dialite" ($9.98), 6" h, has an oval-shaped lighted dial and features a gentle bell tone alarm. Antique bronze top ornament. Choice of White (No. 20246) or Woodtone (No. 20248) case. (Photo: 1968-69 catalog) **($25-35)**

Introduced in the 1968-69 catalog, the "Berwyn Magic Touch" ($8.98), 4" h, has a lighted dial and a drowse alarm that wakes you, allows you to sleep another ten minutes, and then wakes you again. Alarm is silenced by simply touching the top. Choice of Antique White Dialite (No. 20242) or Woodtone Dialite (No. 20244) finish. Self-starting electric movement. (Photo: 1969-70 catalog) **($15-20)**

Making its first appearance in the 1968-69 catalog, the "Alarm-O-Matic," 3-3/4" h, has an exclusive automatic alarm that resets itself to resound the buzzer at the same time every day. Offered with plain dial ($7.98) in Antique White (No. 20235) and Antique Gold (No. 20237) or Dialite dial ($9.98) in Antique White (No. 20236) and Woodtone (No. 20238). Self-starting electric movement. (Photo: 1969-70 catalog) **($15-20)**

The cover of the August 1952 *Tick Talk* shows Mary L. Fitzke of the Four Inch Finishing Department inspecting Bantam electric alarms. (Photo: *Tick Talk*, August 1952)

Introduced in the 1969-70 catalog, the "Kenyon Dialite" ($8.98), 7-1/4" sq., has a lighted dial with filigree border around the dial. White case with colored dial insert in choice of Avocado (No. 25356), Woodtone (No. 25358), or Flame (No. 25360). (Photo: 1969-70 catalog) **($20-25)**

Introduced in the 1969-70 catalog, the "Minikin," 3" h, was offered in choice of Antique White with plain (No. 20255, $3.98) or luminous (No. 20256, $4.98) dial or Woodtone with plain dial (No. 20257, $3.98). (Photo: 1969-70 catalog) **($5-10)**

Introduced in the 1969-70 catalog, the "Lampliter" ($9.98), 3-1/2" h, converts a table lamp into an alarm signal. Simply plug your lamp into the back of the clock and it will flash on and off at the appointed hour to wake you. An audible alarm follows. Lighted dial. Choice of Antique White (No. 20268) or Woodtone (No. 20270) case. Renamed the "Lampalarm" in the 1970 catalog. (Photo: 1969-70 catalog) **($10-15)**

Introduced in the 1969-70 catalog, the "Minikin Drowse" ($4.98), 3" h, adds a drowse button to the top of the case. Allows seven minutes extra sleep before the alarm sounds again. Choice of Antique White (No. 20259), Woodtone (No. 20261), or Blue (No. 20263) plastic case, all with plain dial. (Photo: 1969-70 catalog) **($5-10)**

Introduced in the 1969-70 catalog, the "Minikin Dialite" ($4.98), 3" h, adds a lighted dial and decorative side panels to the basic "Minikin." Choice of Antique White (No. 20262), Woodtone (No. 20264), or Blue (No. 20266) case. (Photo: 1969-70 catalog) **($5-10)**

Santa departs on his rounds from Westclox's North Pole plant. (Photo: *Tick Talk*, December 1955)

Introduced in 1970, the "Bold II" ($3.98), 2-15/16" h, has a plastic case and crystal. Self-starting electric movement. Plain dial with bold numerals. Choice of White (No. 20291) or Sandalwood (No. 20293). (Photo: 1970 catalog) **($5-10)**

Table clocks

Introduced in the February 1958 *Tick Talk*, the "Kenyon" (No. 1291, $9.98), 6" x 4", features a "masculine look" and has a sturdy, non-breakable "sage tan" plastic case with gold-color hands, silvered dial, and raised gold-color numerals. Luminous dial and hands. Described as a "Western style" occasional clock. Dropped from the 1959-60 catalog. Designed by Harold D. Fetty (Des. 183,304, awarded August 5, 1958). (Photo: 1958 catalog) **($15-20)**

Westclox added three major farm magazines—*Country Gentlemen*, *Successful Farming*, and *Capper's Farming*—to its national advertising campaign in the fall of 1934. Combined circulation of the three magazines was over 3.7 million.

Tick Talk plugs the "Kenyon" as the ideal gift. Apparently not many consumers agreed as it was dropped after only one year. (Photo: *Tick Talk*, February 1958)

Introduced in the June 1965 *Tick Talk*, the "Hickory-Dickory-Dock" (No. 82019, $8.98), 12-5/8" h, is another of the "Wee Winkie" series of nursery clocks. It features a gray mouse perched on a peacock blue case. The nursery rhyme appears on the case. Electric movement. Dropped from the 1968-69 catalog. Designed by Mel Appel and Martin Schnur (Des. 204,406, awarded April 12, 1966). (Photo: 1966-67 catalog) **($85-95)**

Introduced in the 1967-68 catalog, this second version of the "Direct Reading" (No. 20225, $16.95), 7-1/4" x 3-3/4", has a rectangular case with wood grain finished face and gilded trim. Smooth brown plastic case. Rotating dials show hours, minutes, and five second intervals. Hours are spelled out "for fast, easy reading." Plain dial protected by clear lens. (Photo: 1968-69 catalog) **($15-20)**

Introduced in the 1967-68 catalog, the "Direct Reading" ($14.95), 6-3/4" x 3-5/8", has a rectangular case with gracefully rounded corners. Leather-grained texture and brushed aluminum face. Bold numerals on rotating cylinders. Clear lens protects the cylinders. Choice of Black/Silver color with plain dial (No. 20221) or Brown/Gold with plain dial (No. 20223). (Photo: 1968-69 catalog) **($15-20)**

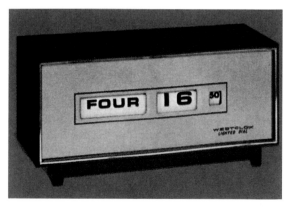

Introduced in the 1967-68 catalog was the "Direct Reading Dialite" (No. 20222, $19.95), 7-1/4" x 3-3/4". Same case design as No. 20225, but has a wood grain case with brushed gold color face. Lighted dial. (Photo: 1968-69 catalog) **($15-20)**

Wall clocks

Introduced in the January 1950 *Tick Talk*, the "Orb" ($3.95) has a metal case with baked enamel finish in choice of ivory, red, white, or yellow. Self-starting electric movement. Five inch dial with black numerals and hands. Convex glass and red second hand. Dropped by 1955. (Photo: *Tick Talk*, January 1950) **($55-65)**

Letters, We Get Letters

Dear Sirs:

Would you like a bouquet today? Let me tell you about our Westclox white kitchen clock which is seventeen years old this month. About ten years ago after washing the wall we returned our clock to its hook in its original position (so we thought), walked away and the clock fell crashing to the floor. The plastic was cracked in several places. We decided, however, to plug it in for a while. To our surprise the Westclox still worked perfectly. We applied a wide strip of white adhesive tape. About two weeks later I was painting the bell fixture which is about one foot diagonally up from the clock. Yes, it happened again. The clock fell. The plastic case really cracked and broke this time. My husband said, 'Goodbye clock.' We laughed, picked it up and really taped it this time. By the way, the glass did not break either time. We put the clock back on the wall again. It has kept perfect time all these years despite the two mishaps. Occasionally we change its bandages. Aren't you proud of your product?

Yours truly,
Mrs. P.C.

(Authors Note: If the writers from *Home and Garden* television's *Decorating Cents* program read the above letter, you may see this unique decorating scheme promoted on a future episode.)

Reprinted from *Tick Talk*, June 1964

The March 1950 *Saturday Evening Post* ad featured the new "Orb" kitchen clock. The ad also appeared in *Colliers*, *Life*, *Better Homes and Gardens*, *American Magazine*, *Sunset*, *American Home* and the Sunday rotogravure sections of sixty-nine big city newspapers. (Photo: *Tick Talk*, March 1950)

Workers assemble the Westclox Melody. (Photo: *Tick Talk*, August 1950)

Introduced in the July 1950 *Tick Talk*, the "Melody" is a self-starting electric wall clock. It has a white plastic case with a colored metal ring under the numerals. The ring can be changed to harmonize with any décor. Although each clock comes with one ring, the two sides are painted different colors. In addition, "the housewife, if she chooses, may cover the ring with wallpaper, material to match her curtains, or paint it herself." The back of the case has a place to conceal the excess cord. Dropped by 1955. Designed by Max Schlenker (Des. 160,434, awarded October 10, 1950). (Photo: *Tick Talk*, July 1950) **($35-45)**

The "Melody" electric wall clock was featured in the *Saturday Evening Post* ad on October 21, 1950. (Photo: *Tick Talk*, October 1950)

Introduced in the April 1954 *Tick Talk*, the "Manor Electric Wall Clock" ($3.98, colors; $4.98, chrome) was "designed for volume leadership in the low priced field." It was available in choice of red, green, white, yellow, or chrome finish. Self-starting electric movement. Not found in 1955-56 catalog. (Photo: *Tick Talk*, April 1954) **($45-55)**

The *Saturday Evening Post* ad for May 1951 pushed Westclox as the perfect wedding gift. (Photo: *Tick Talk*, May 1951)

Introduced in the May 1960 *Tick Talk*, the "Manor" (No. 912, $6.98), 6-1/4" x 7-1/2", has a tilt-down, glare free dial. It mounts flush against the wall and has a self-starting electric movement with front hand set and sweep second hand. The 3-dimensional dial has full easy-to-read numerals. Initially offered in white, turquoise, and yellow plastic cases. By 1962, new model numbers were assigned—White (No. 25017), Turquoise (No. 25019), and Yellow (No. 25021). The turquoise and yellow cases were dropped from the 1963-64 catalog and were replaced by a new Wood Finish (No. 25023) case. Dropped from the 1969-70 catalog. (Photo: 1968-69 catalog) **($35-45)**

"…Westclox electric clocks which first you buy as equipment for your home and soon accept as intimate members of your family" reads the copy in this August 1953 *Saturday Evening Post* ad. (Photo: *Tick Talk*, August 1953)

The "Prim" ($3.98), 6-1/2" dia., was a corded electric wall clock introduced in the 1966-67 catalog. It was offered in White (No. 25201), Sandalwood (No. 25203), and Yellow (No. 25205). Also available in blister pack in White (No. 25701) and Sandalwood (No. 25703). Dropped from the 1969-70 catalog. (Photo: 1968-69 catalog) **($15-20)**

Introduced in the October 1954 *Tick Talk*, "Prim" ($4.98, chrome; $3.98, colors), 5-3/4" dia., was described as ideal for kitchen, bedroom, den, recreation room, laundry, workshop, or office or anywhere else a small electric wall clock was needed. White enameled metal case with dial in choice of red (No. 1140), yellow (No. 1143), white (No. 1142), or green (No. 1141). Also offered in chrome (No. 1144) finish. Self-starting electric movement and nonbreakable crystal. Chrome finish dropped from 1957 catalog; colors from the 1958 catalog. (Photo: 1957 catalog) **($20-25)**

Introduced in the February 1955 *Tick Talk*, the "Zest" ($6.95) is a uniquely styled wall clock with white plastic case and choice of red (No. 1180), charcoal (No. 1181), or yellow (No. 1183) dial. Self-starting electric movement with convenient cord storage in the back of the clock. Non-breakable dial. Dropped by 1957. Designed by Ellworth Danz (Des. 177,797, awarded May 29, 1956). (Photo: *Tick Talk*, February 1955) **($10-15)**

Introduced in the February 1955 *Tick Talk*, "Spice" ($4.95) has a 5-1/2" dial and two-toned polished aluminum case initially available in red (No. 1160), white (No. 1162), or yellow (No. 1163). "Spice" was also available in a copper (No. 1164), chrome (No. 1165) or brass (No. 1166) finish for one dollar more. Model numbers were consolidated under Nos. 1160 (red, white, yellow) and 1164 (copper, chrome, brass) in the 1959-60 catalog. Individual model numbers were again in use by 1962—white (No. 25033), yellow (No. 25035), red (No. 25031), chrome (No. 25027), and copper (No. 25029). The brass version had been dropped by 1962. Self-starting electric movement. (Photo: 1957 catalog) **($25-30)**

The "Spice" ($6.98) was again updated in June 1966 with the addition of an embossed filigree pattern on the dial coordinating with the case design. Bold easy-to-read numerals and sweep second hand. Flush mount. Shatterproof dial. Choice of Antique Copper (No. 25207) or Antique Silver (No. 25209) finish. Dropped from the 1968-69 catalog. (Photo: 1967-68 catalog) **($25-30)**

The "Spice," 6" dia., was updated in the 1963-64 catalog with new dial and hands. Finish options were reduced to chrome (No. 25027), copper (No. 25029), and white (No. 25033). Metal case. Self-starting electric movement with sweep second hand. The white finish was dropped from the 1967-68 catalog. (Photo: 1963-64 catalog) **($25-30)**

Introduced in the January 1956 *Tick Talk*, the aptly named "Snowflake" ($5.95), 7" dia., has a three-dimensional dial that pops out against the colorful background of the concave plastic case. Non-breakable crystal. Self-starting electric movement with front hand-set knob. Available in red (No. 1200), mint green (No. 1201), pink (No. 1202), and charcoal (No. 1203). Dropped from the 1959-60 catalog. Produced in Westclox's Athens, Georgia, plant. Designed by Lawrence H. Wilson (Des. 178,622, awarded August 28, 1956). (Photo: 1957 catalog) **($30-35)**

This ad appeared in the *Saturday Evening Post* in August 1956. It features the "Snowflake" (left) and "Sheraton" (right). (Photo: *Tick Talk*, August 1956)

Introduced in the 1958 catalog, "Orbit" (No. 1440, $12.95), 12" dia., is described as an entirely new approach in a decorative wall clock. It has a "cartwheel" design with black dial face, white "spokes" and solid brass rings. Self-starting electric movement with sweep second hand. Also available with white dial and black spokes (No. 1441). Dropped by 1962. Designed by Ellworth Danz (Des. 186,532, awarded November 3, 1959). (Photo: 1958 catalog) **($30-40)**

The 1957 "Frill" (Nos. 1147, $8.95), 12" dia., has a gleaming brass finish case with "graceful petal design." Self-starting electric movement with sweep second hand. In 1958, a wrought iron version (No. 1148) was added. In 1959, a copper version was added under the same model number as the brass version. New, individual model numbers assigned around 1962—brass (No. 26045), copper (No. 26047), and wrought iron (No. 26049). The dial was restyled on the brass case for the 1963-64 catalog with Roman numerals replacing the Arabic numerals. Arabic numerals remained on the copper and wrought iron version. Dropped from the 1966-67 catalog. (Photo: 1957 catalog) **($40-50)**

Introduced in the 1958 catalog, the "Wallmate" ($4.50), 6" sq., has a colorful patterned plastic design. Unique roller-type hand set on side of case. Storage space for excess cord in the back of the case. Choice of red (No. 1370), white (No. 1371), or turquoise (No. 1372) case. All finishes used the 1370 model number in the 1959-60 catalog. New model numbers issued by 1962—red (No. 25061); white (No. 25063); and turquoise (No. 25065). The red and turquoise cases were replaced by Sandalwood (No. 25067) and Pink (No. 25069) in the 1962-63 catalog. Dropped from the 1966-67 catalog. (Photo: 1958 catalog) **($15-20)**

The egg-shell white plastic case and colorful dials of the "Glendale" were dropped in the 1959-60 catalog in favor of a choice of white case with gold color side panels, yellow case with copper side panels, or turquoise case with copper side panels. All three finishes were given the same model number—1305. The dial was also redesigned. Dropped by 1962. (Photo: 1959-60 catalog) **($15-20)**

Introduced in the August 1957 *Tick Talk*, the "Glendale" ($6.98), 5-3/4" x 7-3/4", has an egg-shell white plastic case with gold-color patterned side panels. It was available with choice of red (No. 1305), charcoal (No. 1306), or turquoise (No. 1307) dial. Self-starting electric movement. Designed to be used as either a shelf or wall clock. Excess cord can be concealed in the back of the case. Made in Athens, Georgia, plant. (Photo: 1957 catalog) **($15-20)**

Introduced in the August 1957 *Tick Talk*, the "Frolic" ($4.98), 6-3/4" sq., has a "picture frame" plastic case that can be mounted on the wall or used on a counter. Metallic dial with embossed numerals. Choice of red (No. 1285), white (No. 1286), or yellow (No.1287) case. Self-starting electric movement. The red, white, and yellow cases were dropped from the 1959-60 catalog and replaced by chrome and copper finishes, both offered under model number 1285. Dropped by 1962. Made in the Athens, Georgia, plant. (Photo: 1957 catalog) **($15-20)**

The clock doc checks out an "Orb" wall clock on the cover of the May 1952 *Tick Talk*.

New case designs and sizes were created for the "Monitor" in 1958. An 8" size with a new thin movement and modern-styled case was added in choice of Desert Tan (No. 1380, $11.95), Chrome (No. 1381, $13.95) or Brass (No. 1382, $13.95). The new model's features include an all-steel flush mounting case that hugs the wall; a clear, full-figure dial with bold black hands and bright red sweep second hand; an easy-to-read convex dial and crystal; bottom hand-set knob; and self-starting electric movement with current interruption indicator. A 12" "Monitor" was available in choice of Desert Tan (No. 1386, $13.95) or Chrome (No. 1387, $15.95). Finally, a 10" "Monitor" was introduced with a square metal case. Available only in Desert Tan (No. 1384, $13.84). New model numbers were assigned in 1962—No. 25101 (12" dia., Desert Tan); No. 25103 (12" dia., Chrome); No. 25111 (8" dia., Desert Tan); No. 25113 (8" dia., Chrome); No. 25115 (8" dia., Brass); No. 25121 (10" sq., Desert Tan). The square and brass "Monitors" were dropped from the 1964-65 catalog. A new "Monitor" with 7-1/2" dial was added to the 1968-69 catalog in choice of Desert Tan (No. 25363) or Chrome (No. 25365) finish. (Photo: 1963-64 catalog) **($20-25)**

Added to the catalog in 1958, the "Choo Choo" (No. 1420, $5.98), 6-7/8" dia., is a children's electric wall clock. A "Toyland" train attached to the sweep second hand moves through the tunnel and around the countryside scene on the dial. White enameled case. Center hand set. Gone by 1962. **($65-75)**

The gift box that accompanied the "Choo Choo." Because it is decorative, the box has a stong value on its own. (Photo: 1958 catalog) **($45-55)**

A "24-Hour Monitor" was added to the line in the 1969-70 catalog. It has a 12" dial with full 24-hour clock for military, airline, and other specialized applications [Such as ebay®]. Self-starting movement. Sweep second hand. Choice of Desert Tan (No. 25389, $14.95) or Chrome (No. 25391, $16.95) finish. (Photo: 1969-70 catalog) **($35-45)**

Alhambra

Introduced in April 1959, the "Alhambra" (No. 900, $14.95), 12-1/2" square, is a wall clock with "high style delicate lace work as a feature of its design." Silvered dial with embossed numerals. Long life movement with only one moving part. Front hand set knob. Manufactured in Athens, Georgia. Dropped by 1962. (Photo: *Tick Talk*, April 1959) **($25-35)**

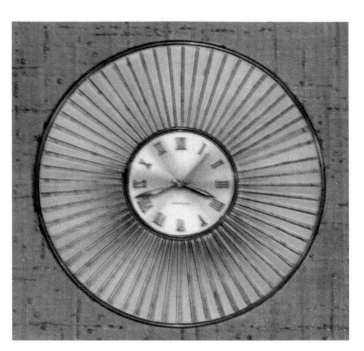

Introduced in the May 1959 *Tick Talk*, "Parliament" (No. 901, $29.95), 16" dia., has a solid brass case with a circularly-brushed silver-plated finish. Spun silver-plated dial with applied solid brass numerals. Self-starting electric movement. Dropped from the 1962 catalog. Based on a design by Ellworth Danz. (Photo: 1959-60 catalog) **($45-55)**

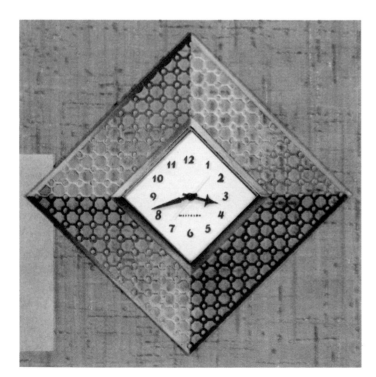

The 1959-60 "Alhambra" (No. 910) was also offered in a diamond design case, 17-1/4" w, with gold color finish and intricate lacework pattern. Sweep second hand. Dropped by 1962. (Photo: 1959-60 catalog) **($35-45)**

Introduced in the May 1959 *Tick Talk*, the "Walltone" (No. 902, $4.98), 5" h, has a plastic case with glare proof dial . Front hand set and sweep second hand. Available in choice of white (No. 25051), yellow (No. 25053), or pinefrost green (No. 25055). Pinefrost Green was dropped in the 1963-64 catalog in favor of Red (No. 25057). This two-way electric clock can be mounted on the wall or set on a counter. Dropped from the 1969-70 catalog. (Photo: 1968-69 catalog) **($15-20)**

Tick Talk's December 1951 cover.

Introduced in the April 1960 Tick Talk, the "Sonnet" (No. 906, $5.98) is a kitchen wall clock with a plastic case initially offered in choice of yellow, pink, or white. Self-starting electric movement. The April 1962 Tick Talk listed the "Sonnet" among the new models, but no discernable differences were evident from the photographs. Separate catalog numbers were assigned by 1962—White (No. 25041), Yellow (No. 25043), Pink (No. 25045), and Wood finish (No. 25047). The pink case was dropped from the 1963-64 catalog, the yellow case from the 1966-67 catalog, and the remaining finishes from the 1969-70 catalog. (Photo: 1968-69 catalog) **($20-25)**

Introduced in the April 1960 Tick Talk, the "Scroll," 22" h, with self-starting electric movement and sweep second hand (Nos. 908 & 26023, $16.95). Also offered in the 1962-63 catalog with wood finish (No. 26027, $16.95). Dropped from the 1963-64 catalog (Photo: 1962 catalog) **($20-25)**

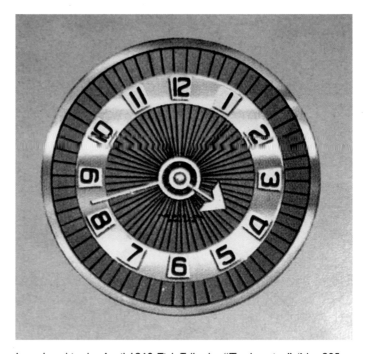

Introduced in the April 1960 Tick Talk, the "Tambourine" (No. 905, $7.98), 8" dia. is a kitchen wall clock in choice of white, yellow, or nutmeg finish. Self-starting electric movement. Renumbered in the 1962 catalog—White (No. 25007); Yellow (No. 25009); Nutmeg (No. 25011). The yellow case was dropped from the 1963-64 catalog and replaced by Charcoal (No. 25013). Dropped from the 1967-68 catalog. Designed by Leo Ivan Bruce, Jr. (Des. 190,824, awarded July 4, 1961). (Photo: 1962-63 catalog) **($55-65)**

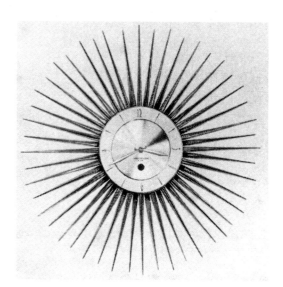

Introduced in April 1960, the "Athens" with 8-day keywound movement (No. 400, $27.50) or self-starting electric movement with sweep second hand (No. 911, $24.95). Both versions were dropped from the 1962 catalog. (Photo: *Tick Talk*, April 1960) **($25-30)**

The March 10, 1951, Westclox ad in the *Saturday Evening Post*. (Photo: *Tick Talk*, March 1951)

Introduced in April 1960, the "Camden" with 8-day keywound movement (No. 401, $22.50) or self-starting electric movement with sweep second hand (No. 909, $19.95). Dropped from the 1962 catalog. (Photo: *Tick Talk*, April 1960) **($20-35)**

Introduced in the June 1961 *Tick Talk*, the "Variety," 9" sq., is a self-starting electric wall clock that fits flush to the wall. Offered in black (No. 26051, $9.98) and brown (No. 26053, $9.98). In the 1962-63 catalog, three free decorator panels were provided to allow the user to match any décor. No mention of the three decorator panels was found in subsequent catalogs and the corded "Variety" was dropped from the 1965-66 catalog. (Photo: 1962-63 catalog) **($35-40)**

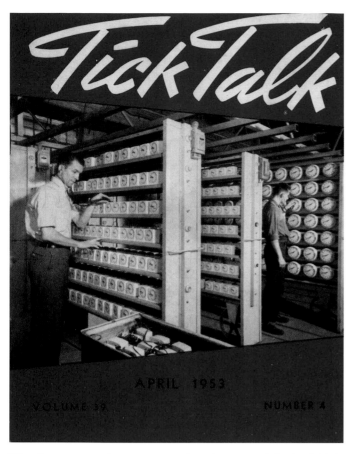

Westclox testing racks were pictured on the cover of the April 1953 *Tick Talk*.

Introduced in the August 1962 *Tick Talk*, the "Variety Mosaic," 9" square, was available in choice of self-starting electric movement (No. 26055, $12.95) or the new transistorized battery-operated movement (No. 46019, $17.95). The case features a mosaic pattern of hand-set ceramic tiles. Gold color embossed hour markers on a rich black dial. Black case with brilliant gold color trim. Front hand set and shatterproof crystal. The corded version was dropped from the 1965-66 catalog; the no-cord version from the 1968-69 catalog. (Photo: 1962-63 catalog) **($25-30)**

Introduced in the 1963-64 catalog, the "Stanton" corded electric wall clock, 9" dia., was offered in Tile White with brown décor (No. 25141, $6.95), Golden Maple (No. 25143, $6.95), and Pink (No. 25145, $6.95). The pink version was dropped as an option in the 1964-65 catalog and the remaining models were dropped from the 1965-66 catalog. (Photo: 1964-65 catalog) **($35-45)**

Included only in the 1964-65 catalog, the Model No. 25191 "Stanton" ($6.95), 9" dia., has black numerals on an Arctic White metal case. Self-starting electric movement. (Photo: 1964-65 catalog) **($35-45)**

Introduced in the May 1963 *Tick Talk*, the corded electric "Shadow Box" (No. 26057, $14.95), 12" x 10-3/4", has a rich spun metal dial in a black matte finish case with silver color trim. Dropped from the 1965-66 catalog. Designed by Jean Otis Reineke (Des. 197,433, awarded February 4, 1964). (Photo: 1963-64 catalog). **($45-55)**

Introduced in the January 1964 *Tick Talk*, the "Lighted Dial" electric wall clock ($7.98), 7-1/8" dia., was offered in white (No. 25300), brown (No. 25302), and yellow (No. 25304). Mounts flush to the wall and has a lighted dial (Dialite®) that is easy to read night or day. Sweep second hand and distinctive hour hand. Dropped from the 1967-68 catalog. (Photo: 1965-66 catalog) **($25-35)**

Introduced in the May 1963 *Tick Talk*, the "Nile" ($5.98), 5-1/2" x 6-1/2", can be used either as a flush wall clock or shelf clock. Front hand set knob. Choice of White (No. 25161), Sandalwood (No. 25163), or Red (No. 25165) case. Listed in the 1966-67 catalog with blister pack packaging—White (No. 25661); Sandalwood (No. 25663). Dropped from the 1968-69 catalog. (Photo: 1963-64 catalog) **($15-20)**

Introduced in the January 1964 *Tick Talk*, the "Legion" electric wall clock ($7.98), 8-3/4" dia., has a spun aluminum center dial with wrap around crystal. Choice of White (No. 25171) or Sandalwood (No. 21173) finish. Easy-to-read numerals with sweep second hand. Front hand set. Dropped from the 1967-68 catalog. (Photo: 1965-66 catalog) **($45-55)**

The December 1955 *Saturday Evening Post* ad featured the new electric models introduced in 1955. (Photo: *Tick Talk*, December 1955)

Introduced in the June 1964 *Tick Talk* but not available until September, the "Accent" ($6.98), 8" diameter, is a corded electric wall clock with large, easy-to-read numerals. The plastic case was offered in choice of white (No. 25189), sandalwood (No. 25195), or turquoise (No. 25197). Front hand-set knob. Sweep second hand. A "no-cord" version of the "Accent" was added to the 1965-66 catalog in choice of white (No. 46065) or sandalwood (No. 46067) case. The "no-cord" version of the "Accent" was dropped from the 1968-69 catalog. (Photo: 1964-65 catalog) **($20-25)**

Introduced in the June 1964 *Tick Talk*, "Pert" ($4.98), 8" h, is a corded electric wall clock with easy to read full numeral dial, sweep second hand, and front hand set knob. The plastic case was available in choice of white (No. 25183), yellow (No. 25185), or sandalwood (No. 25187). (Photo: 1964-65 catalog) **($25-30)**

While the "no-cord" Accent continued unchanged in 1967, the corded "Accent" ($7.98), 8" dia., was all new, sporting a new dial with bold numerals and choice of copper (No. 25321) or chrome (No. 25323) finish case. Sweep second hand. Dropped from the 1970 catalog. (Photo: 1968-69 catalog) **($25-30)**

Introduced in the March 1965 *Tick Talk*, 8-5/8" h, the "Woodbridge Electric" (No. 25199, $8.98) has a rich hand-rubbed woodtone finish. Hexagonal design with white metal dial finish. The "No-Cord Woodbridge" (No. 46063, $12.95) has the same Colonial styling but has a self-starting electric movement with sweep second hand. The corded version was dropped from the 1967-68 catalog, but the no cord version continued in production through 1970. (Photo: 1968-69 catalog) **($25-30)**

The fellow "in a pensive mood" is Otto Unzicker of the Tool Department (Photo: *Tick Talk*, September 1940)

Introduced in the June 1965 *Tick Talk*, "Circus Parade" (No. 82015, $5.98), 9" dia., was one of a series of "Wee Winkie" nursery clocks. It features "jaunty" circus animals parading around the dial. (Photo: 1968-69 catalog) **($65-75)**

Introduced in the June 1965 *Tick Talk*, the "Lace Dialite" ($8.98), 7-1/4" h, is a wall clock with lighted dial. Filigree border design. Sweep second hand. Self-starting electric movement. Choice of White (No. 25306) or Brown (No. 25308) case. Dropped from the 1969-70 catalog. (Photo: 1965 catalog) **($15-20)**

Introduced in the June 1966 *Tick Talk*, the "Starette Dialite" ($6.98), 7" h, is a self-starting electric wall clock with lighted dial and white "lusterkote" dial finish. The round clock is surrounded by an octagonal frame with "sculpted" design. Sweep second hand. Flush mount. Front hand set. Choice of white (No. 25310), turquoise (No. 25312), or woodtone (No. 25314) finish. Still in production in 1970. Designed by Roman J. Szalek (Des. 210,039, awarded January 30, 1968). (Photo: 1968-69 catalog) **($15-20)**

Introduced in the 1967-68 catalog, the "Capella" ($5.98), 5-3/8" h, has a rectangular design with distinctive border. Full numeral dial and sweep second hand. Choice of White/Ocher (No. 25331), Sandalwood/Brown (No. 25333), or Turquoise/Dark Turquoise (No. 25335) plastic case. Dropped from the 1969-70 catalog. (Photo: 1968-69 catalog) **($20-25)**

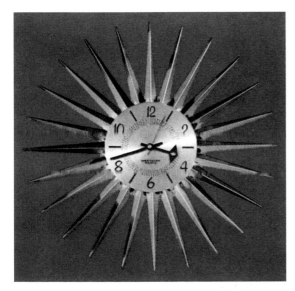

Introduced in the 1967-68 catalog, the "Bonnie" (No. 25349, $9.98), 13" dia., has polished brass finish spokes and circular brushed gold-color dial. Sweep second hand. Open front. Self-starting electric movement. Also available with fully transistorized battery movement (No. 46127, $14.95). Both versions were dropped from the 1969-70 catalog. (Photo: 1968-69 catalog) **($25-30)**

Introduced in the 1968-69 catalog, the "Logan" ($5.98), 6" h, has raised numerals on a "floating" dial. Sweep second hand. Choice of White (No. 25343), Ocher (No. 25345), or Avocado (No. 25347) plastic case. Still in production in 1970. Designed by Giacinto C. D'Ercoli (Des. 215,955, awarded November 11, 1969). (Photo: 1968-69 catalog) **($20-25)**

Introduced in the 1967-68 catalog, the "Countryside" ($8.98), 10" h, has a weathervane motif with "jaunty rooster" top ornament. Sweep second hand on easy-to-read dial. Choice of "Turkey Red" (No. 25317), White (No. 25325), Woodtone (No. 25327), or Avocado (No. 25329) finish. Still in production in 1970. Two new colors—Blue (No. 25395) and Harvest (No. 25393) added in the 1969-70 catalog. (Photo: 1968-69 catalog) **($20-25)**

Introduced in the 1968-69 catalog, the "Dorena" ($9.98), 10" w, has a hexagonal shape with original hand-painted floral design. Sweep second hand. Choice of White with ivy finish (No. 25351) or Avocado with Dutch Tulip finish (No. 25353). (Photo: 1968-69 catalog) **($20-25)**

Introduced in the 1969-70 catalog, the "Spindle" ($9.98), 6-3/8" h x 9-5/8" w, features Early American styling with open frame spindle ends. Antique-style off-white dial. Choice of Woodtone (No. 25381), Harvest (No. 25383), or Avocado (No. 25385) finish. Self-starting electric movement. (Photo: 1969-70 catalog) **($15-20)**

Introduced in the 1968-69 catalog, the "Quincy" ($8.98), 9-7/8" h, is an Early American-style wall clock with scroll design and gold color grille inserts. Round lighted dial with dual track. Sweep second hand. Choice of Woodtone (No. 25350), Avocado (No. 25352), or Antique White (No. 25354). Harvest (No. 25362) finish added to 1969-70 catalog. (Photo: 1968-69 catalog) **($20-25)**

Introduced in the 1969-70 catalog, the "Town Crier" ($14.95), 7-3/4" h x 9" w, counts the hours and strikes the half hours. Can be used as a shelf or wall clock. Choice of Avocado (No. 25375), Woodtone (No. 25377), or Harvest (No. 25379) finish. (Photo: 1969-70 catalog) **($15-20)**

Introduced in the 1970 catalog, the "Posey" ($6.98), 9-1/2" dia., has a petal design in choice of Avocado-tone (No. 26067) or Poppy-toned (No. 26081) finish. Textured dial with raised numerals. Shatterproof crystal. Front hand set. Self-starting electric movement. (Photo: 1970-71 catalog) **($20-25)**

Introduced in the 1967-68 catalog, the "Melody" ($4.98), 5-5/8" h, has bold, easy-to-read numerals and sweep second hand. Choice of White (No. 25337), Woodtone (No. 25339), or Yellow (No. 25341) plastic case. Still in production in 1970. Designed by Giacinto C. D'Ercoli and Roger L. Kelly (Des. 211,895, awarded August 6, 1968). (Photo: 1970 catalog) **($15-20)**

Alarm Clocks

A new "Sanford" alarm (No. 47015, $14.95), 4" x 5-1/8", was introduced in the January 1965 *Tick Talk*. Cameo White case with white linen-textured dial. Large Roman numerals. Gold color bezel. Operates on a single "C" cell battery. Positive battery life indicator. Introduces the new buzzer alarm. Dropped from the 1968-69 catalog. (Photo: 1966-67 catalog) **($15-20)**

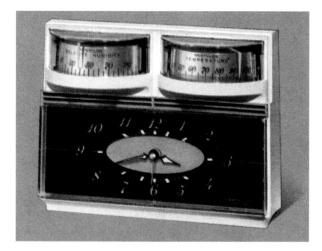

Introduced in the 1967-68 catalog, the "Comfort Alarm," 7-1/8" x 5-1/2", is a no-cord alarm clock combined with thermometer and hygrometer. The clock features pierced luminous hands and hour markers. The fire orange sweep alarm indicator matches the indicators on the thermometer and hygrometer. There is a temperature/humidity index on the back of the case. Choice of Beige (No. 83028, $25.00) or Wood Grain (No. 83030, $27.50) finish. Dropped from the 1969-70 catalog. (Photo: 1968-69 catalog) **($20-25)**

A second version of the new "Sanford" buzzer alarm (No. 47017, $15.95), 4" x 5-1/8", was introduced in the January 1965 *Tick Talk*. It has a walnut grain finish case and white linen-textured finish dial with Arabic numerals. No cord electric movement. Dropped from the 1968-69 catalog. (Photo: 1966-67 catalog) **($15-20)**

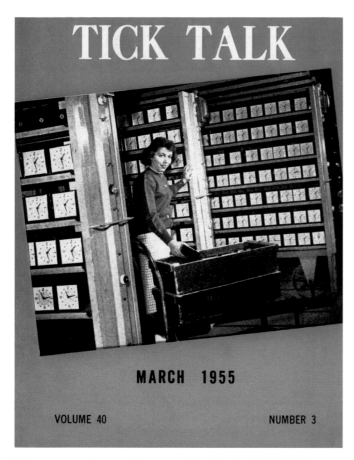

TICK TALK

MARCH 1955

VOLUME 40   NUMBER 3

The testing racks grace the cover of the March 1955 *Tick Talk* as Emma Jean Uranich places Country Clubs on the racks in the Four Inch Finishing Department.

Introduced in the 1969-70 catalog, the "Belfast" ($24.95), 4-1/2" x 5", has a mini-bell alarm with top indicator and on-off button. One-jewel battery movement. Luminous dial with embossed diamond cut markers. Sweep second hand. Choice of Ebony (No. 47128) or Woodtone (No. 47130) finish. (Photo: 1969-70 catalog) **($15-20)**

Introduced in the June 1966 *Tick Talk*, the "Woodbrook" ($18.95) is a battery-operated buzzer alarm with walnut finish. Sweep alarm indicator and shatterproof crystal. Luminous dial and pierced luminous hands. Available with either full or partial numeral dial. Choice of walnut finish with gold color trim (No. 47120) or walnut finish with silver color trim (No. 47122). Added to the 1967-68 catalog was the matching "Woodbrook Comfort Meter" with thermometer, hygrometer, and temperature/humidty index chart— Gold color trim (No. 83029); Silver-color trim (No. 83031). Dropped from the 1970 catalog. (Photo: 1967-68 catalog) **($30-35)**

Another of the safety cartoons making a frequent appearance in *Tick Talk*. (Photo: *Tick Talk*, March 1950)

Introduced in the 1969-70 catalog, the "Electrotone" ($18.95), 3-1/2" x 6-1/2", is a cordless alarm clock with lighted dial activated by a simple touch of the case top. Mellow "beep" alarm. Catalog notes that it is "American made." Choice of Antique White (No. 47124) or Woodtone (No. 47126) case. Dropped from the 1970 catalog. (Photo: 1969-70 catalog) **($20-25)**

General Time reported record sales and earnings during the first nine months of 1966. The earnings were the highest reported in fifteen years. (*Tick Talk*, November 1966)

Table clocks

Introduced in the April 1959 *Tick Talk*, "Isotron" (No. 260, $34.50), 4-1/2" x 6-3/8", marked Westclox's movement into the battery-operated electric clock field. It has a solid brass case with silver-plated panels. Modern style hands accent the brushed silver dial. It also features "exclusive automatic regulation for precision time." Silent operation on flashlight battery. Became Model No. 47001 in the 1962 catalog. Dropped from the 1963-64 catalog. (Photo: 1962 catalog) **($40-50)**

Introduced in the May 1963 *Tick Talk*, the "Award II Cordless" ($19.95), 4-1/2" h, is an occasional clock with traditional styling. Hand-rubbed wood grain finish. Cushioned base. Battery movement. Choice of walnut (No. 47003) or Mahogany (No. 47005) finish. A third finish, white with gold color (No. 47011) was added to the 1965-66 catalog. Dropped from the 1966-67 catalog. (Photo: 1965 catalog) **($25-30)**

4" high

Introduced in the June 1964 *Tick Talk*, the "Sanford" ($12.95), 4" x 5-1/8", is a classically styled occasional clock with spun aluminum dial framed by patterned silver color bezel. Rich hand-rubbed wood finish in choice of walnut (No. 47007) or mahogany (No. 47009). No cord electric movement. Dropped from the 1966-67 catalog. (Photo: 1965 catalog) **($25-30)**

Introduced in the October 1960 *Tick Talk*, the "Haywood" ($16.95), 16-3/4" h, was Westclox's first cordless electric wall clock. A flashlight battery was said to provide months of reliable service. A golden dial stands out against a wooden frame in choice of walnut (No. 46003) or mahogany (No. 46005) finish. Dropped from the 1963-64 catalog. (Photo: 1962-63 catalog) **($45-55)**

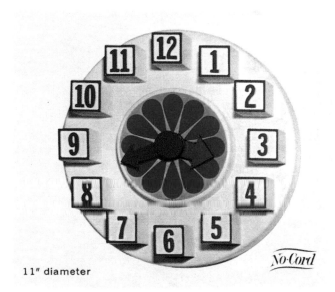

11" diameter

Introduced in the June 1966 *Tick Talk*, the "Block Clock" (No. 46099, $12.95), 11" dia., is a cordless children's clock with giant blocks forming the numerals. White case with bright yellow inner dial and orange tear-dropped markers. Dropped from the 1967-68 catalog. (Photo: 1966-67 catalog) **($65-75)**

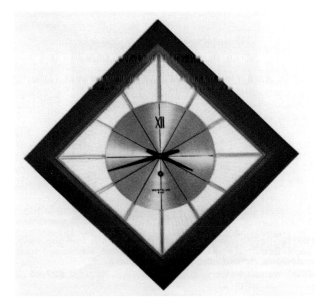

The 1962-64 "Embers" (No. 46001, $34.50), 19" h, is a cordless electric wall clock with golden spun dial and solid mahogany case. Also offered with 8-day keywound movement (No. 48009). Dropped from the 1964-65 catalog. (Photo: 1963-64 catalog) **($45-55)**

Introduced in the August 1962 *Tick Talk*, the "Variety" battery wall clock (No. 46017, $14.95), 9" square, has a distinct black case with satin center dial, and gold color trim. Roman numerals on a black pebble grain finish. Mounts flush against the wall. Remained in the catalog until 1970. (Photo: 1968-69 catalog) **($25-35)**

Introduced in the August 1962 *Tick Talk*, the "Meredith" (No. 46021, $27.95), 12" square, is a battery operated wall clock with a walnut finished solid hardwood case and spun finish metal dial. White leather textured dial, embossed sculptured corner designs, gold color top ornament. Hands and raised numerals are gold color. Dropped from the 1964-65 catalog. (Photo: 1963-64 catalog) **($30-35)**

Introduced in the August 1962 *Tick Talk*, the "Variety Mosaic," 9" square, was available in choice of self-starting electric movement (No. 26055, $12.95) or the new transistorized battery-operated movement (No. 46019, $17.95). The case features a mosaic pattern of hand-set ceramic tiles. Gold color embossed hour markers on a rich black dial. Black case with brilliant gold color trim. Front hand set and shatterproof crystal. The corded version was dropped from the 1965-66 catalog; the no-cord version from the 1968-69 catalog. (Photo: 1962-63 catalog) **($25-35)**

Introduced in the August 1962 *Tick Talk*, the "Stanton" (No. 46013, $12.95), 9" diameter, is a battery-operated wall clock with a metal case. The case has a tectone bronze finish with gold-color Federal-type design highlights and eagle at the top of the case. Roman numeral dial. Mounts flush against the wall. This initial version of the "Stanton" was dropped from the 1963-64 catalog as a variety of new finishes and dials were introduced. (Photo: 1962-63 catalog) **($25-35)**

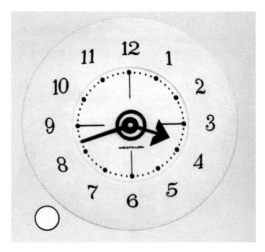

Four new styles of the no-cord "Stanton" were introduced in the May 1963 *Tick Talk*. The transistorized battery movement provides "Isotronic Accuracy." Metal cases. Left: Model No. 46033 ($10.95), charcoal finish. Right: Model No. 46043 ($9.95), Golden Maple finish. Dropped from the 1968-69 catalog. (Photo: 1963-64 catalog) **($45-55)**

Added to the "Stanton" line in the 1963-64 catalog, Model No. 46047 ($9.95) has black numerals on an Artic White case. Dropped from the 1968-69 catalog. (Photo: 1964-65 catalog) **($45-55)**

Two more models of the no-cord "Stanton": Left: Model 46039 ($9.95), Tile White with brown décor; Model 46031 ($10.95), Wedgwood finish. Not pictured: Model No. 46045 ($9.95), Pink; Model No. 46037 ($9.95), Tile White with Blue Décor. Model 46039 was dropped from the 1965-66 catalog; No. 46045 from the 1964-65 catalog; No. 46037 from the 1965-66 catalog; and No. 46031 from the 1968-69 catalog. (Photo: 1963-64 catalog) **($45-55)**

Introduced in the August 1962 *Tick Talk*, the "Wakefield" (No. 46023, $34.50), 22-1/2" high, has a solid maple case with nutmeg finish in Early American style. Polished gold color bezel with traditional black hands and Roman numerals. Transistorized battery movement. Dropped from the 1964-65 catalog. (Photo: 1963-64 catalog) **($25-35)**

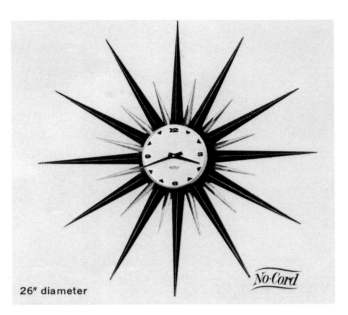

26" diameter

Introduced in the June 1964 *Tick Talk*, the "Waverly" (No. 46059, $17.95), 11-1/4" sq., has a circular brushed gold color dial accented by polished gold color bezel and mounted on an ivory leather textured background. Set in a gold-color antique-styled wood picture frame case. No cord electric movement. Still in production in 1970. (Photo: 1968-69 catalog) **($20-25)**

Introduced in the June 1964 *Tick Talk*, the "Granby" (No. 46051, $19.95), 26" dia., has contrasting black and gold color spikes and burnished brass finish dial. No cord electric movement. Dropped from the 1968-69 catalog. Originally offered with keywound movement (No. 48001). (Photo: 1966-67 catalog) **($25-30)**

Introduced in the 1963-64 catalog, the no-cord "Shadow Box" (No. 46029, $19.95), 12" x 10-3/4", has a black matte finish case with contrasting silver color trim. Spun metal dial. Designed by Jean Otis Reineke (Des. 197,433, awarded February 4, 1964). (Photo: 1968-69 catalog) **($55-65)**

View of the "new" Power & Light Department (Photo: *Tick Talk*, October 1950)

Introduced in the 1964-65 catalog, the no-cord version of the "Scroll" (No. 46055, $17.95), 22" h, has a white sculptured design with gold color highlights. No cord electric movement. Dropped from the 1970 catalog. (Photo: 1968-69 catalog) **($25-30)**

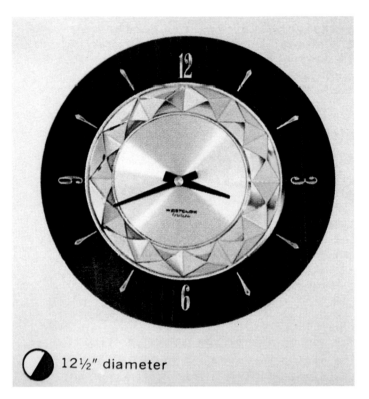

12½" diameter

Introduced in the June 1964 *Tick Talk*, the "Ardmore" (No. 46061, $15.95), 12-1/2" dia., has a wood-grained case with bright gold numerals. Spun gold color dial ornamented by faceted gold color center design. No cord electric movement. Remained in the catalog until at least 1970. (Photo: 1965 catalog) **($55-65)**

12" x 10¾"

Introduced in the June 1964 *Tick Talk*, the "Greenwich" (No. 46057, $17.95), 12" x 10-3/4", has a wood finish case in Early American style. Scalloped white dial with distinct block numerals and gold color trim. Hand-rubbed wood grain finish. No cord electric movement. Dropped from the 1967-68 catalog. (Photo: 1965 catalog) **($25-35)**

Introduced in the June 1964 *Tick Talk*, the "Medford" (No. 46053, $19.95), 16-1/2" x 13-1/2", has Victorian styling with a rich walnut finish frame and soft leather textured dial. No cord electric movement. Dropped from the 1970 catalog. (Photo: 1965 catalog) **($25-30)**

Westclox had an ongoing problem in trying to convince its employees to cross at the intersections. Obviously, the warnings had limited effect. (Photo: *Tick Talk*, April 1950)

Introduced in the June 1965 *Tick Talk*, the "Boston Lyre" (No. 46083, $19.95), 17-1/2" h, was another of the Early American series of battery operated decorator clocks. The gold color lyre shape case is topped by a gold color eagle. Dropped from the 1967-68 catalog. (Photo: 1965 catalog) **($25-35)**

Introduced in the June 1965 *Tick Talk*, the "Patriot" (No. 46081, $19.95), 14-1/2" h, was one of a series of cordless Early American decorator clocks. Octagon shaped case with white leather texture finish topped by eagle. Dropped from the 1967-68 catalog. (Photo: 1965 catalog) **($25-35)**

Introduced in the June 1965 *Tick Talk*, the "Cranbrook" (No. 46077, $19.95), 16-1/2" h, was part of the Early American series of battery operated clocks. It has an antique maple finish with Early American scene on the front. Gold color border on the dial. Dropped from the 1966-67 catalog. (Photo: 1965 catalog) **($25-35)**

Introduced in the June 1965 *Tick Talk*, the "Pennsylvania Spice Chest" (No. 46079, $19.95), 14 3/8" h, was part of the Early American Series of battery operated decorator clocks. It has a sculpted cherry wood finish with heart design on the dial. The shelf holds four spice bottles, flowers, or other décor. Two new finishes— Turkey Red (No. 46157) and Avocado (No. 46159) were added In the 1966-67 catalog. Dropped from the 1969-70 catalog. (Photo: 1965 catalog) **($25-35)**

Introduced in the 1965-66 catalog, the "Sturbridge" (No. 46085, $19.95), 13-1/2" h, was part of the Early American decorator's series. It has a warm antique walnut finish in a reproduction of an antique timepiece. Traditional eagle motif. Dropped from the 1967-68 catalog. (Photo: 1965 catalog) **($30-40)**

Introduced in the June 1965 *Tick Talk*, the "Connecticut Banjo" (No. 46075, $19.95), 17-1/2" h, was part of the Early American series of battery operated decorator clocks. This replica of a banjo clock has an antique maple finish and a harbor scene on the bottom panel. Dropped from the 1968-69 catalog. (Photo: 1965 catalog) **($25-35)**

Introduced in June 1965, the "Accent" ($11.95) features a "fresh cheerful design." Mounts flush to the wall and has front hand set. Available in white (No. 46065) or sandalwood (No. 46067). (Photo: 1965 catalog) **($20-25)**

Introduced in the June 1965 *Tick Talk*, the "Madrid" ($9.95), 9" dia., has a plastic case with "sophisticated Spanish motif" bordering the dial. Choice of white and brown (No. 46069) or white and charcoal (No. 46071) plastic case. Remained in the catalog through 1970. (Photo: 1968-69 catalog) **($20-25)**

This third version of the "Madrid" (No. 46117, $9.98) was in the catalog from 1967-1970. It has a white case with border flower motif. Metal dial. (Photo: 1968-69 catalog) **($20-25)**

Introduced in the June 1966 *Tick Talk*, the "Madrid" ($12.95), 9" dia., is a battery-operated wall clock that fits flush against the wall. Features bold numerals on a brushed dial with color accentuated hands. Choice of copper (No. 46113) or chrome (No. 46115) finish. Remained in the catalog through 1970. (Photo: 1968-69 catalog) **($30-40)**

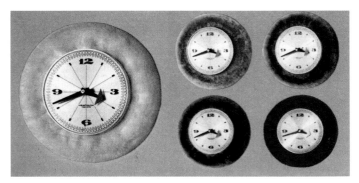

Introduced in the March 1966 *Tick Talk*, the "Powderette" ($12.95), 9-1/4" dia., features a circular case covered with acrylic fiber in choice of white, antique gold, or ice pink. The fiber band can be removed and machine laundered. Brushed silver metal dial highlighted by scroll tracing. Moisture resistant transistor movement runs for a year on a flashlight battery. Perhaps the tackiest clock Westclox ever produced. Initially offered in choice of White (No. 46093), Ice Pink (No. 46095) or Antique Gold (No. 46097). Ice Pink was dropped from the 1968-69 catalog and three new colors added—Bristol Blue (No. 46183), Avocado (No. 46185), and Hot Pink (No. 46187). (Photo: 1968-69 catalog) **($10-15)**

Introduced in the March 1966 *Tick Talk*, the "Bathmate" ($11.95) has easy to read black numerals and pierced metal scroll hands set on a brushed gold finish metal dial. The metal case has a semi-gloss finish in choice of white (No. 46087), verdian green (No. 46089), or peacock blue (No. 46091). Moisture resistant. Dropped from the 1969-70 catalog. (Photo: 1968-69 catalog) **($15-20)**

Introduced in the June 1966 *Tick Talk*, the "Brentwood" (No. 46107, $22.95), 12-7/8" x 13-3/4", is a battery-operated wall clock with "transitional style." Square, walnut finished frame on a brass grille insert. Full Roman numerals on a circular brushed gold color dial. Flush mount. Dropped from the 1970 catalog. (Photo: 1968-69 catalog) **($20-25)**

Introduced in the June 1966 *Tick Talk*, the "Rampart" (No. 46105, $18.95) is a battery-operated Early American style wall clock with basket weave textured case. Colonial cherry finish. Dial features full Roman numerals on a brushed gold color dial. Mounts flush to the wall. Dropped from the 1970 catalog. (Photo: 1968-69 catalog) **($20-25)**

Introduced in the June 1966 *Tick Talk*, the "Trenton" (No. 46101, $21.95), is a battery-operated wall clock with "unique double frame case." Walnut texture finish and "marbleized silver and gold color matte." Circular brushed brass finish dial with Roman numerals. Flush mount. Dropped from the 1969-70 catalog. Designed by Giacinto C. D'Ercoli (Des. 209,844, awarded January 9, 1968). (Photo: 1968-69 catalog) **($25-30)**

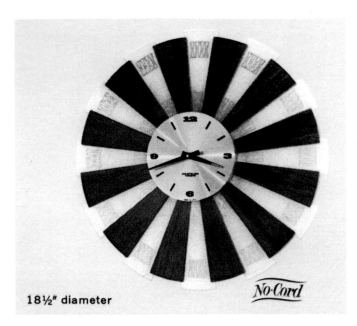

18½" diameter — No·Cord

Introduced in the June 1966 *Tick Talk*, the "Woodfair" (No. 46103, $24.95), 18-1/2" dia., is a battery-operated wall clock with alternating translucent plastic and walnut finished metal wedges radiating out from the dial. Embossed gold color design. Brushed gold color dial. Dropped from the 1968-69 catalog. Designed by Giacinto C. D'Ercoli and Roman J. Szalek (Des. 210,741, awarded April 9, 1968). (Photo: 1966-67 catalog) **($20-25)**

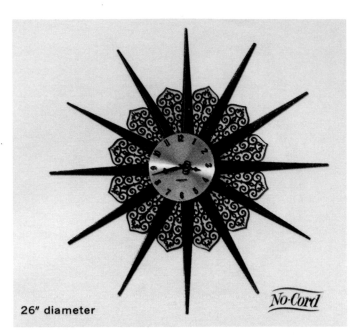

26" diameter — No·Cord

Introduced in the June 1966 *Tick Talk*, the "Seville" (No. 46111, $23.95), is a battery-operated wall clock with black satin finish spikes radiating from the brushed gold color dial. Interlaced between the spikes is gold color filigree. Flush mount. Dropped from the 1968-69 catalog. Designed by Roman J. Szalek (Des. 211,269, awarded June 4, 1968). (Photo: 1966-67 catalog) **($25-30)**

8⅝" high

Introduced in the March 1965 *Tick Talk*, the "No-Cord Woodbridge" (No. 46063, $12.95), 8-5/8" h, has a rich hand-rubbed woodtone finish. Hexagonal design with white metal dial finish. Runs for a year on one flashlight battery. The "Woodbridge Electric" (No. 25199, $8.98) has the same Colonial styling but has a self-starting electric movement with sweep second hand. The corded version was dropped from the 1967-68 catalog, but the no cord version continued in production through 1970. (Photo: 1965 catalog) **($25-30)**

The 1967-70 "Athenian" (No. 46123, $29.95), 27" dia., features diamond-shaped walnut veneer panels alternating with brass spheres. Brushed gold-color dial with geometric design. Battery movement. Designed by Ellworth R. Danz (Des. 212,029, awarded August 20, 1968). (Photo: 1968-69 catalog) **($25-30)**

Introduced in the 1967-68 catalog, the no-cord "Woodview" (No. 46147, $24.95), 9-3/16" x 21-5/8", has a solid walnut case with waffle-textured front panel. A diamond-shaped applique adorns the center of the panel. Antique-type distressed wood case. Brushed brass finish dial. Dropped from the 1970 catalog. Designed by David W. Miley (Des. 213,795, awarded April 8, 1969). (Photo: 1968-69 catalog) **($25-35)**

Introduced in the 1967-68 catalog, the no-cord "Vermillion" ($24.95), 13" x 14-1/2", has a wood frame case with gold color filigree design on a leatherette front panel inset. Circular brushed gold color dial with bezel, Roman numerals, and pierced scroll hands. Choice of Black (No. 46141), White (No. 46143), or Walnut (No. 46145) finish. Dropped from the 1970 catalog. (Photo: 1968-69 catalog). **($25-35)**

Hickory-Dickory Dock makes the cover of the June 1965 *Tick Talk*.

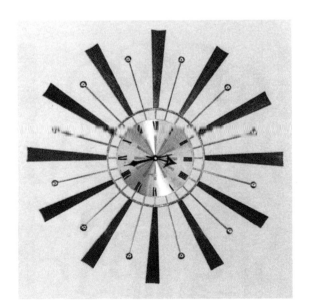

Introduced in the 1967-68 catalog, the no-cord "Triune" (No. 46121, $27.95), 22-1/2" dia., has alternating solid walnut wedges and brass finish spheres. Full Roman numerals on brushed gold color dial. Dropped from the 1970 catalog. (Photo: 1968-69 catalog) **($25-35)**

145

Introduced in the 1967-68 catalog, the no-cord "Carvwood" (No. 46155, $29.95), 22-3/4" h, has a diamond-shaped frame with antique walnut finish. Hand-carved look. Bold numerals and hands. Dropped from the 1969-70 catalog. (Photo: 1968-69 catalog) **($25-35)**

Introduced in the 1967-68 catalog, the no-cord "Capricorn" (No. 46139, $29.95), 9-7/8" x 17", was part of a line of custom decorator clocks. It features a walnut finish wood case with brushed gold color dial. The gold color horizontal stripes accent a brushed aluminum background. The disc at the top says "Tempus Fugit," a sophisticated way to say "time flies." Companion weather station available (No. 83035). Dropped from the 1969-70 catalog. Designed by Giacinto C. D'Ercoli (Des. 213,799, awarded April 8, 1969). (Photo: 1968-69 catalog) **($25-35)**

Introduced in the 1967-68 catalog, the no-cord "Parthenon" (No. 46119, $27.95), 26" dia., features walnut veneer "petals" alternating with walnut finish spheres. Circular brushed gold finish dial. Dropped from the 1969-70 catalog. Designed by Ellworth R. Danz (Des. 212,031, awarded August 20, 1968). (Photo: 1968-69 catalog) **($25-35)**

Introduced in the 1967-68 catalog, the no-cord "Normandy" (No. 46137, $29.95), 19-1/2" dia., was part of the custom decorator series. It features a black wrought iron case in geometric pattern. Brushed brass finish dial with Roman numerals. Decorative brass "tacks." (Photo: 1968-69 catalog) **($30-40)**

Introduced in the 1968-69 catalog, the no-cord "Ramada" ($35.00), 17-1/2" x 19-1/2", has a sculptured walnut finish with choice of red (No. 46189) or green (No. 46181) velvet background. Circular brushed gold-color dial with Roman numerals. Still in production in 1970. (Photo: 1968-69 catalog) **($25-35)**

Introduced in the 1967-68 catalog, the no-cord "Taurus" (No. 83037, $40.00), 13" x 17", has a walnut finish picture frame wood case. Brass grille insert and brushed gold color dial. Thermometer and hygrometer with protective glass cover. Dropped from the 1970 catalog. (Photo: 1968-69 catalog) **($25-35)**

Introduced in the 1968-69 catalog, the no-cord "Park-way" (No. 46165, $40.00), 16" x 27", has a diamond-shaped solid walnut case with horizontal brushed gold-color dial. Available with matching thermometer and hygrometer. Renamed the "Penthouse" in the 1969-70 catalog. (Photo: 1968-69 catalog) **($25-35)**

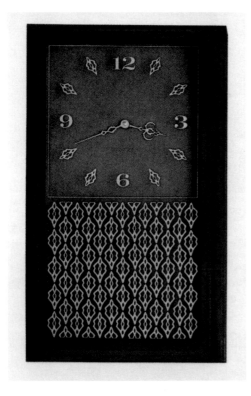

Introduced in the 1968-69 catalog, the "Parlia-ment" (No. 46175, $45.00), 10-3/4" x 22", has a picture frame case, the rectangular base of which has a gold-color grille. Walnut wood finish and gold-color numerals. Transistorized battery movement. (Photo: 1968-69 catalog) **($25-35)**

Introduced in the 1968-69 catalog, the "Newbury" ($45.00), 11-1/2" x 19-3/4", has a rectangular walnut wood case with velvet background and tempered glass cover. Gold filigree markers coordinate with lower panel. Transistorized battery movement. Choice of walnut with red (No. 46177) or green (No. 46179) background. (Photo: 1968-69 catalog) **($35-45)**

No. 46203 Avocado . . . . **$14.95**   **No. 46205** Harvest . . . . . **$14.95**   **No. 46207** Coppertone. **$14.95**   **No. 46209** Flame **$14.95**

Introduced in the 1969-70 catalog, the "Appliance-Mate" ($14.95), 9-1/4" dia., has a spun chrome face with easy-to-read numerals and sweep second hand. The case was offered in decorator tones to match kitchen appliances—Avocado (No. 46203), Harvest (No. 46205), Coppertone (No. 46207), and Flame (No. 46209). (Photo: 1969-70 catalog) **($20-25)**

Introduced in the 1969-70 catalog, the "Amesbury" (No. 46213, $50.00), 19-3/4" x 11-1/2", has a rectangular wood case that encloses wood paneling in a depressed maple finish. Round, porcelain-type, dial with full numerals and outside minute/hour track reminiscent of school clocks. Oval, porcelain-type eagle plaque. Fully transistorized battery movement. Dropped from the 1970 catalog. (Photo: 1969-70 catalog) **($40-50)**

Introduced in the 1969-70 catalog, the "Bainbridge" (No. 46227, $100.00), 32" x 10-1/2", has a solid maple case with Early American styling. Brass side rails. The lower portion of the case contains a thermometer and hygrometer. (Photo: 1969-70 catalog) **($30-35)**

Introduced in the 1968-69 catalog, the no-cord "Countryside" ($12.95), 10" h, has a weathervane motif with jaunty rooster on top. Shatterproof crystal. Available in White (No. 46129), Turkey Red (No. 46131), Avocado (No. 46133), and Woodtone (No. 46135). Still in the 1970 catalog. (Photo: 1968-69 catalog) **($20-25)**

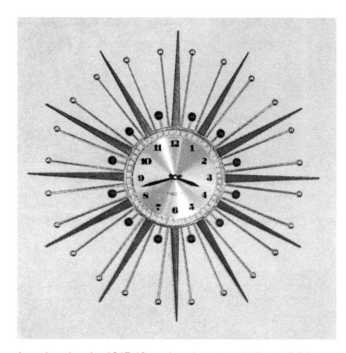

Introduced in the 1967-68 catalog, the no-cord "Drama" (No. 46125, $24.95), 22" dia., has brass and walnut finished spheres in varying sizes alternating with walnut veneer spokes. Features a circular brushed gold finish dial. Still in production in 1970. Designed by Ellworth R. Danz (Des. 212,027, awarded August 20, 1968). (Photo: 1968-69 catalog) **($25-35)**

Introduced in the 1968-69 catalog, the "Stanford" ($10.95), 9" x 7", has a rectangular case with silver-color border and checkerboard pattern panel. Bold numerals. Battery movement. Choice of White (No. 46167), Avocado (No. 46169), or Pineapple (No. 46171) plastic case. Still in the 1970 catalog. (Photo: 1968-69 catalog) **($20-25)**

Introduced in the 1968-69 catalog, the no-cord "Rutledge" (No. 46173, $50.00), 18" x 21", has a double-mounted case with cove-like corners. Raised Roman numerals with brushed gold-color dial center. Antique avocado finish. Still in production in 1970. The case appears to be based roughly on a design by Harold D. Fetty (Des. 192,524, awarded April 3, 1962) (Photo: 1968-69 catalog). **($25-35)**

Cover to *Tick Talk*'s December 1953 issue.

Introduced in the 1969-70 catalog, the "Calais" ($35.00), 20" h x 16-1/4" w, has a traditional French Provincial-style case with antique wood-grain texture. Gold outlined border and gold floral design below the dial. White porcelain-type dial with Roman numerals; pierced hands. No-cord fully transistorized movement. Choice of finishes—Antique White (No. 46215), Avocado (No. 46217), Fruitwood (No. 46219). Still in production in 1970 but only with Arabic numerals.. (Photo: 1969-70 catalog) **($25-30)**

Tick Talk occasionally featured its young bachelors. "Girls, here's something new for your scrapbook. His name is James 'Red' Shinski and he works in the Tool" reads the *Tick Talk* caption to this photo. (Photo: *Tick Talk*, March 1952)

Introduced in the 1969-70 catalog, the "Regal Arch" (No. 46229, $45.00), 24-3/4" h x 15" w, has traditional seventeenth century English styling. The rectangular arch-topped case is framed by ornate molding and ball ornaments. Ornate scrollwork surrounds the gold-color dial. (Photo: 1969-70 catalog) **($35-45)**

Introduced in the 1969-70 catalog, the "Camden" ($24.95), 12" dia., has a satin finish solid walnut plate design case. Gold color stick (No. 46241) or Arabic (No. 46243) numerals/markers. Tapered hands. Still in production in 1970. (Photo: 1969-70 catalog) **($40-50)**

Introduced in the 1969-70 catalog, the no-cord "Spindle" ($15.95) has the same case and dial design as the corded model and was offered in the same finishes—Woodtone (No. 46221), Harvest (No. 46223), and Avocado (No. 46225). (Photo: 1969-70 catalog) **($20-30)**

Introduced in the 1967-68 catalog, the "Westgate" (No. 46149, $24.95), 9-3/16" x 21-3/4", has a solid walnut case with brushed gold-color dial set against a wood-grained background accented by decorative pins. The lower panel has an amber-tone patterned bottle-glass effect. Designed by David W. Miley and Ellworth R. Danz (Des. 212,030, awarded August 20, 1968). (Photo: 1968-69 catalog) **($35-45)**

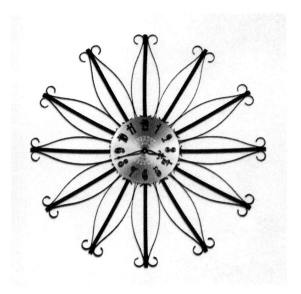

Introduced in the 1969-70 catalog, the "Flamenco" (No. 46211, $35.00), 24-1/2" dia., has Mediterranean styling with a black wrought iron case in a geometric sunburst design. Polished brass finish dial with white scroll filigree design. Ornamental scroll numerals and hands. (Photo: 1969-70 catalog) **($25-30)**

Introduced in the 1969-70 catalog, the "Cutting Board" ($19.95), 12" h x 7-1/2" w, has Early American styling with decorative tile face. Wood-grain finish case in choice of Avocado (No. 46191) or wood grain (No. 46193). Plain dial. Battery movement. (Photo: 1969-70 catalog) **($20-35)**

Although Westclox did not make tall case clocks, some owners incorporated Westclox into their own creations. Here a Westclox cordless has been incorporated into a grandfather clock. (Photo: *Tick Talk*, April 1964)

VACATIONITIS

Verdant hills

And bubbling streams

Call anon and stir up dreams—

Aimless dreams with buried thrills

Tingling free to fly and soar

Into space for evermore

Over mountains, over seas,

Nor be numbed by place or time—

Independence true, sublime!

Tarry not, time, if you please;

Itchy feet just yearn to roam

Somewhere, anywhere, from home!

Office Poet.

This poem, attributed simply to "Office Poet" appeared periodically in *Tick Talk* as vacation time approached. (Photo: *Tick Talk*, June 1951)

No. 84004
No. 84004
No. 46261

Introduced in the 1970 catalog, the "Candella" (No. 46261, $35.00), 25-1/4" dia., has an eighteenth century Chippendale floral design. Finished in antique metal gold-color. The round dial is accented in two-tone gold-color with black Roman numerals. Sweep second hand. Matching two-candle sconces (No. 84004, $19.95 pr.). (Photo: 1970 catalog) **($45-55)**

No. 46275
No. 84006

Introduced in the 1970 catalog, the "Espana" ($35.00), 24" x 24", has a Mediterranean-style case with the appearance of hand-carved wood. Wood grain finish. The dial features gold color accents with black Roman numerals. Sweep second hand. No-cord battery movement. Available in Antique Avocado (No. 46307) and Spanish Walnut Grain (No. 46309). (Photo: c.1971 No-Cord Decorator Clock catalog) **($45-55)**

Introduced around 1970, the battery-operated "Sonnet" ($24.95), 12" x 12", has no similarity to the corded "Sonnet" produced from 1962-69. It has a gold-finish diamond-shaped frame accented in red (No. 46273) or black (No. 46275) velvet. Dial features raised gold color numerals and sweep second hand. Sets of four assorted decorative wall plaques in red velvet (No. 84005, $14.95) or black velvet (No. 84006, $14.95) were offered to complete the wall display. (Photo: c. 1971 No-Cord Decorator Clock catalog) **($35-45)**

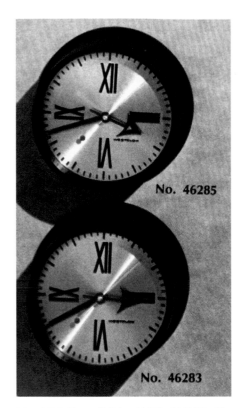

No. 46285

No. 46283

The 1970 "Aspen" (No. 46283, $17.95), 8" dia., no-cord wall clock has bold Roman numerals and markers on a brushed aluminum or gold-color circular dial. Woodtone case. Full sweep second hand. Battery movement. Also offered with a black case (No. 46285). (Photo: 1970 catalog) **($25-30)**

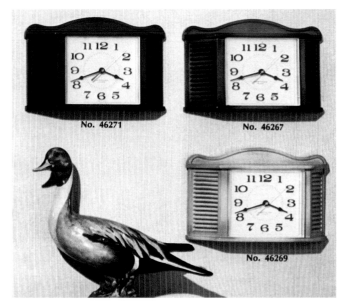

No. 46271

No. 46267

No. 46269

Introduced in the 1970 catalog, the "Ridgemont" ($15.95), 7" h x 10-1/2" w, has traditional Early American styling with side "shutters." White dial with large Arabic numerals and sweep second hand. Choice of Avocado (No. 46267) or Woodtone (No. 46271) finish. (Photo: 1970 catalog) **($25-35)**

No. 46279

No. 46277

No. 46281

Introduced in the 1970 catalog, the "Frolic" ($14.95), 8-3/4" dia., has a "bold, modern design colorfully accented." Full sweep second hand. Battery movement. Choice of Merry Gold (No. 46277) or Jolly Green (No. 46279) finish. (Photo: 1970 catalog) **($20-25)**

The circa 1970 "Zodiac Signs" ($19.95), 12" dia., features the 12 Zodiac signs raised on a colorful ceramic disc. In the center is a brushed brass dial with "sunface" motif. Sweep second hand. Battery movement. Choice of Green Goldstone (No. 46257) or Golden Harvest (No. 46259) finish. (Photo: 1970 catalog) **($25-35)**

July is vacation month at Westclox. *Tick Talk* cover art by Ben Thompson. (Photo: *Tick Talk*, July 1966)

The circa 1971 "Apothecary" ($29.95), 11-1/2" x 5", is a wood case apothecary style table clock with oval, full numeral dial. Full sweep second hand. Center dial design is also accented on the sides. The top, with ornamental ball, is removable. Glass crystal. Offered in Avocado (No. 47131), Tangerine (No. 47133), and Citrus Yellow (No. 47135). (Photo: c. 1971 No-Cord Decorator Clock catalog) **($20-25)**

The "Alhambra" name reappeared around 1971 on a "no cord" Mediterranean-style wall clock. The case of the new "Alhambra" ($24.95), 15-1/4" x 13-1/2", has a hand-carved appearance with rectangular, decorated leather textured dial. Gold-colored hands with bold Roman numerals and markers. Full sweep second hand. Offered in choice of Antique Avocado (No. 46289) and Walnut Grain (No. 46291). (Photo: 1970-71 catalog) **($25-35)**

The 1973 "Frontiersman" (No. 46623, $29.95), 18-1/4" x 15-1/2" x 2-1/4", has a weathered oak finish that "will recall stories of Jeb Stuart, Wild Bill Hickok, Wyatt Earp...with an authentic 'six-gun' resting on the pegs next to a marksmanship medal." The clock dial is painted on as a target. While Hickok and Earp were Western legends, Jeb Stuart was a Confederate Civil War hero. (Photo: 1973 catalog) **($25-35)**

No. 46621

The 1973 "Barrel 'n Spigot" (No. 46621, $27.95), 13" dia. x 4-3/4" deep, is "reminiscent of Clipper Ship days, Appalachian mountain men, cask laden wagon trains." Bold numerals give the appearance that they were burned into the antique oak finished plastic barrelhead. Sweep second hand. Operates on one "C" cell battery. (Photo: Promotional literature) **($25-35)**

Introduced in the August 1927 *Tick Talk* with additional details provided in the October 1927 issue, the "Auto Clock" ($2.50, plain dial or $3.50, luminous dial) has a nickel finish and is designed to be "...mounted on the instrument board where it can be a neighbour to the speedometer, or on the upper windshield frame near the rear vision mirror...." (Photo: *Tick Talk*, August 5, 1927) **($115-135)**

This Sterling electric automobile clock was designed for mounting above the windshield. (Photo: *Tick Talk*, July 20, 1929) **($65-75)**

Although most Sterling electric automobile clocks were sold directly to manufacturers, in August 1929 three new models were introduced for sale directly to the public. The clocks were intended to be mounted on the dash (shown), on the steering column, or above the windshield. A wire would be run from the clock to one of the ammeter posts to supply power to the clock. The clocks used about as much "juice" in one year as an ordinary dash light would use in two hours. (Photo: *Tick Talk*, July 20, 1929) **($65-75)**

This Sterling electric automobile clock was designed for mounting on the steering column. (Photo: *Tick Talk*, July 20, 1929) **($65-75)**

April 1930 saw the introduction of this new auto clock intended for mounting either in the dash or above the windshield. It has a butler nickel finish with trim metal dial. (Photo: *Tick Talk*, April 20, 1930) **($55-65)**

This Sterling Auto Clock was introduced in September 1930. It has a satin chrome finish with polished steel hands and etched silvered dial. Modernistic in design, it has a jeweled electric movement built in Westclox's Electric Clock Department. The clock is intended for mounting above the windshield near the rear view mirror. **($145-175)**

A Sterling "panel" model clock was also introduced in September 1930. Installation of the small round clock required drilling a one inch hole in the dashboard. The electric movement, which runs off the battery, uses less electricity in a year than a dash light uses in two hours. (Photo: *Tick Talk*, September 20, 1930) **($115-135)**

This Westclox auto clock was introduced in February 1931. It has a Butler-finished case "designed to harmonize with the fittings in the finest cars." It has luminous features and was intended for mounting above the windshield. It uses the same windup movement as previous Westclox auto clocks. (Photo: *Tick Talk*, February 5, 1931) **($55-65)**

"I might say, that those of you who drive a Cadillac may very well have a Westclox on your dashboard—we have made all of the clocks for Cadillac since the 1951 model year was introduced. If you have an Oldsmobile, a Ford, or a Chevrolet, the chances are very good that you're telling time with a Westclox, because we supply a major part of the clocks for those cars, too."

From a speech given before the Athens, Georgia, Chamber of Commerce by Donald J. Hawthorne, President of General Time Corporation, in February 1954.

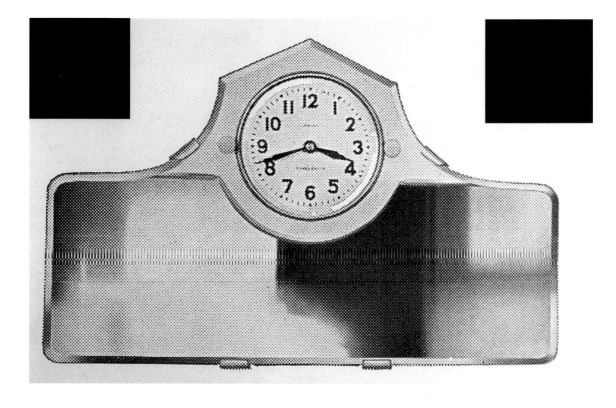

The Sterling Clock Company introduced this mirror clock in 1931. It was intended to replace the standard rear view mirror and was available in non-glare, gold, and silver finish. (Photo: *Tick Talk*, April 20, 1931) **($115-130)**

Introduced in 1931, this "Westclox Auto Mirror Clock" is intended to replace the standard rear view mirror. The mirror is non-glare and has beveled edges. (Photo: *Tick Talk*, May 20, 1931) **($175-200)**

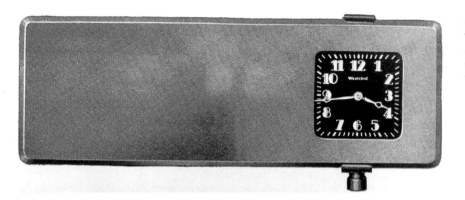

In March 1934, Westclox introduced a new Pull Wind Auto Mirror Clock (No. 763, $2.95). Three or four pulls of the knob and the clock was fully wound. One-day movement. It was assembled in the Watch Department. Discontinued in January 1938. (Photo: *Tick Talk*, March 1934) **($175-200)**

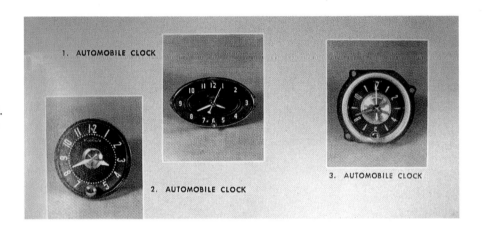

Three Westclox automobile clocks circa 1956. (Photo: 1956 Westclox open house program)

Connie Anderson regulates electric automobile clocks on the cover of the March 1956 *Tick Talk*.

Tick Talk "cover girl" Clara Szymovicz works on automobile clock dials. (Photo: *Tick Talk*, July 1947)

Weather Instruments

Introduced in the 1966-67 catalog, the "Weather Station" ($12.95), 10-5/8" x 3-3/8", combines the three individual "Weather-Mates" on a dual purpose desk stand and wall bracket. Choice of Brown (No. 83009) or Black (No. 83011) finish. Dropped from the 1969-70 catalog. (Photo: 1968-69 catalog) **($15-20)**

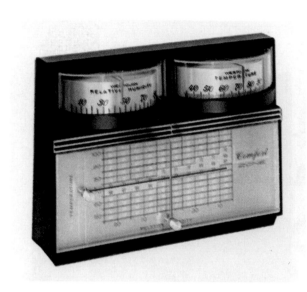

Introduced in the 1966-67 catalog, the "Comfort Meter" ($9.98), 7-1/8" x 5-1/2", is a combination thermometer and hygrometer in one case. The temperature/humidity index chart determines the "comfort zone." Can be used on a desk or mounted on a wall. Choice of Brown (No. 83025) or Black (No. 83027) plastic case. Dropped from the 1969-70 catalog. (Photo: 1968-69 catalog) **($15-20)**

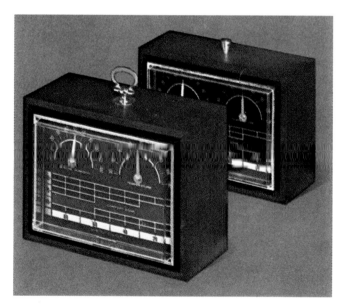

Introduced in the 1967-68 catalog, the "Woodbrook Comfort Meter" ($14.95), 4" h, has a walnut finish wood case. Combines thermometer, hygrometer, and temperature/humidity index chart with luminous features. Choice of gold color (No. 83029) or silver color (No. 83031) trim. Dropped from the 1969-70 catalog. (Photo: 1968-69 catalog) **($20-25)**

Introduced in the 1966-67 catalog, the "Weather-Mates," 3" h, have plastic cases with brushed aluminum aeronautical style dials. Special change indicators allow user to determine amount and direction of changes at a glance. Can be used on a desk or hung on a wall. From left: Thermometer in choice of brown (No. 83013) or black (No. 83015); Hygrometer in choice of brown (No. 83017) or black (No. 83019); Barometer in choice of brown (No. 83021) or black (No. 83023). Designed by Ellworth Danz, David Miley, and Ralph Preiser (Des. 207,422, awarded April 11, 1967). (Photo: 1968-69 catalog) **($15-20)**

Introduced in the 1967-68 catalog, the "Gemini" (No. 83033, $27.95), 10-3/4" x 12", has a walnut finish wood case with gold color bezel. The case, which mounts flush to the wall, contains a thermometer, hygrometer, and barometer behind a protective glass cover. Dropped from the 1969-70 catalog. (Photo: 1968-69 catalog) **($25-30)**

Introduced in the 1968-69 catalog, the "All-Temp" (No. 83061, $4.98), 2" h, is a swivel mounted thermometer with shatterproof crystal. Magnetic base for mounting on the dashboard, in the refrigerator, or on an outside window. (Photo: 1970 catalog) **($5-10)**

Introduced in the 1967-68 catalog, the "Capricorn" Weather Station (No. 83035, $29.95), 9-7/8" x 17", is a companion for the no-cord clock shown on the right. It combines a thermometer, hygrometer, and barometer in a walnut finish wood case. Protective glass cover. Both clock and weather station were dropped from the 1969-70 catalog. Designed by Giacinto C. D'Ercoli. (Photo: 1968-69 catalog) **($20-25)**

Introduced in the 1968-69 catalog, the "Weather-Tec Comfort Guide" (No. 83059, $9.98), 6" dia., is a combination hygrometer/thermometer in a brass finish wall-mount case. (Photo: 1968-69 catalog) **($10-15)**

Introduced in the 1968-69 catalog, the "Weather-Tec Barometer" (No. 83057, $10.95), 6" dia., has a brass finish case that mounts flush against the wall. (Photo: 1968-69 catalog) **($10-15)**

Introduced in the 1968-69 catalog, the "Guidex Combination" (No. 83063, $12.95), 6-7/8" x 3-1/2", combines the thermometer and barometer on a walnut finish desk stand. Brushed brass cases. (Photo: 1968-69 catalog) **($10-15)**

Introduced in the 1968-69 catalog, the "Guidex Weather-Mates," 3-1/4" h, have brushed brass cases with round dials. Bold, easy-to-read numerals. L to R: "Guidex Thermometer" (No. 83051, $6.98); "Guidex Hygrometer, No. 83053, $7.98); "Guidex Hygrometer" (No. 83049, $8.98). Still in production in 1970. (Photo: 1968-69 catalog) **($10-15)**

Introduced in the 1968-69 catalog, the "Guidex Weather Station" (No. 83055, $21.95), 10-1/4" x 3-1/2", combines all three Guidex Weather-Mates on a walnut finish stand. (Photo: 1968-69 catalog) **($15-20)**

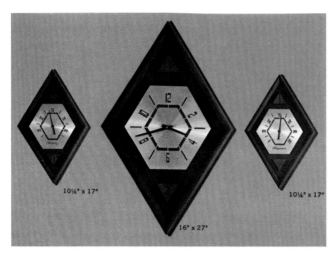

10¼" x 17"   16" x 27"   10¼" x 17"

The 1968-69 "Parkway Weathermates" consisting of hygrometer (No. 83045, $21.00); clock (No. 46165, $40.00); and Thermometer (No. 83047, $21.00). The solid walnut diamond-shaped cases for the thermometer and hygrometer are 10-1/4" x 17". Renamed "Penthouse" in the 1969-70 catalog. (Photo: 1968-69 catalog) **($40-50, set)**

Introduced in the 1969-70 catalog, the "Weather-Tyme" (No. 83034, $19.95), 2-13/16" x 5-1/8", features matching solid brass cases on a single base. Diamond-cut polished embossed numerals on the clock and thermometer. Luminous dials. (Photo: 1969-70 catalog) **($20-25)**

Timers

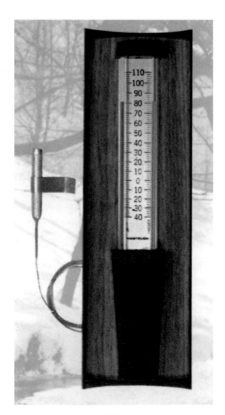

Introduced in the 1970 catalog, the "Indoor-Outdoor Thermometer" (No. 83041, $7.98), 11-5/8" h x 3-1/2" w, is a twin thermometer on a recessed wood grain finish panel. Remote sensing element with four foot capillary lead. (Photo: 1970 catalog) **($5-10)**

Introduced in the August 1948 *Tick Talk*, the "Switch Clock" (No. 980, $12.50), 4-7/8" h, is designed to turn appliances on and off at desired intervals. Ivory finish metal case with gold color trim. A radio, percolator, or other appliance could be plugged into the outlet in the back of the clock. The "on" and "off" switches are then set to the desired times and the "Pull" switch is set. After the appliance has been turned on, the timing device automatically shuts off to prevent repeating the same operation. A switch on the back of the clock permits operation of the appliance in the usual manner without unplugging it from the back of the clock. Self-starting electric movement. **($20-25)**

Introduced in August 1954, the "Lookout Portable Timer" ($3.95), 3-1/2" h, was available in choice of white (No. 140), red (No. 141), yellow (No. 142), green (No. 143), or copper (No. 145) finished metal case. It could be set on a table or mounted on the wall. Only red, white, and copper cases offered after 1957. New model numbers assigned after 1960—red (No. 50001), white (No. 50003), and copper (No. 50005). A new chrome version (No. 50017) was added to the 1964-65 catalog and the red case was dropped. The "Lookout Timer" was dropped from the 1966-67 catalog and replaced by two new models. Based on a 1949 design by Max Schlenker (Des. 158,016, awarded April 4, 1950). (Photo: 1957 catalog) **($15-20)**

In 1970, a newly restyled "24-Hour Switch Timer" ($9.98) was introduced with trapezoidal case accentuated with walnut color front. Repeats automatically every 24 hours with no resetting required. Choice of White (No. 52007), Avocado (No. 52009), or Woodtone (No. 52011) case. (Photo: 1970 catalog) **($5-10)**

Introduced in 1967, the "24-Hour Switch Timer" ($10.95), 3-1/2" h, has easy-to-read day-night hour periods with orange-tipped time indicator hand. Turns appliances up to 1800 watts or lights up to 840 watts on and off automatically every 24 hours without resetting. Choice of Woodtone (No. 52001) or Antique White (No. 52003) finish. Gold color spun dial. (Photo: 1968-69 catalog) **($5-10)**

Introduced in the January 1965 *Tick Talk*, the "Lookout Jr. Timer" ($3.98), 2-7/16" h, has a cylindrical design with time settings up to one hour. Choice of combination black and white (No. 50019) or all white (No. 50021) case. Remained in the catalog for the remainder of the 1960s. (Photo: 1968-69 catalog) **($5-10)**

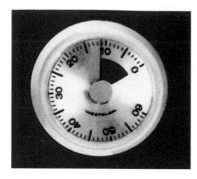

Introduced in the June 1966 *Tick Talk*, the "Lookout Deluxe Timer" ($4.98), 2" h, has a "fire orange" flag indicator that shows the time remaining. The modern cylindrical design permits optional wall mounting. Choice of White (No. 50031), Charcoal (No. 50033), or Woodtone (No. 50035) plastic case. Remained in the catalog for the remainder of the 1960s. (Photo: 1968-69 catalog). **($5-10)**

Introduced in the 1968-69 catalog, the restyled "Time-N-Temp" ($5.98), 2" h, has the same basic case design as the Lookout Deluxe, but adds an indoor/outdoor thermometer to the center of the dial. Orange flag indicator shows time remaining. Sixty minute timer. Choice of White (No. 50037) or Avocado (No. 50039) plastic case. (Photo: 1968-69 catalog) **($5-10)**

Introduced in the 1967-68 catalog, the "Lookout Switch Timer" ($5.98), 3-7/16" h, can be used either as a 60-minute interval timer or as an automatic timer to turn appliances and lights off. Fire orange indicator shows time remaining. Choice of White (No. 50025), Avocado (No. 50027), or Woodtone (No. 50029) plastic case. Still offered in the 1969-70 catalog. Designed by David W. Miley (Des. 210,474, awarded March 12, 1968). (Photo: 1968-69 catalog). **($5-10)**

Introduced in the 1969-70 catalog, the "Long-Ring Timer" ($5.98), 3-3/4" h x 4-1/4" w, has a plastic case in choice of White (No. 50041), Avocado (No. 50043), or Harvest (No. 50045). Times up to 60 minutes. (Photo: 1969-70 catalog) **($5-10)**

Other Westclox Products

Introduced in October 1960, the "Travelaire" was described as "A New Kind of Radio," combining a six transistor battery operated radio with a keywound clock. The use of a keywound clock was intended to prevent the clock from draining the battery. The "Travelaire" was made in "his" and "hers" finishes. "His" is oxford gray with ivory trim while "hers" is turquoise with ivory trim. Shock resistant case and shatterproof crystal. Leather carrying cases were offered for both models—gray cowhide for "his" and light tan for "hers." Earphones and battery were included. (Photo: *Tick Talk*, October 1960) **($30-40)**

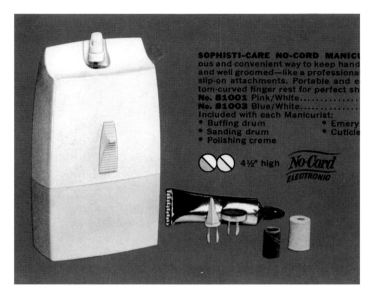

Introduced in the 1965-66 catalog, the "Sophisti-Care No-Cord Manicurist" ($7.98), 4-1/2" h, was one of Westclox's first ventures outside of timekeeping. Included in the set was a buffing drum, sanding drum, polishing crème, emery disks, and cuticle remover. Available in choice of Pink/White (No. 81001) or Blue/White (No. 81003). Dropped from the 1968-69 catalog. Designed by Austin H. Munson and Roman J. Szalek (Des. 206,040, awarded October 18, 1966). (Photo: 1967-68 catalog) **($5-10)**

Wake to Music

In 1925, *Tick Talk* reported the invention of what may have been the first musical alarm. After removing the gong from a Big Ben alarm, S. D. Snavely tied one end of a piece of thread to the winding key and the other end to the starting lever of his phonograph. He then set the alarm as usual. At the appointed hour, the alarm-winding key began turning. As the thread was wound around the key, the phonograph's starting lever was released and the record began playing.

(Author's Note: the story does not mention the tune on the gramophone. Hopefully, it was Irving Berlin's "Oh How I Hate to Get Up In the Morning.")

Wake to music as Big Ben starts the gramophone. (Photo: *Tick Talk*, February 1925)

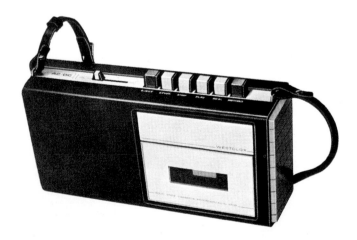

A Westclox portable AC/battery-operated solid-state cassette recorder (No. 80055, $59.95). Complete with shoulder strap and microphone with remote control switch. (Photo: Undated sales flyer, circa 1973) **($5-10)**

Pre-1930

This Big Ben Christmas poster was provided free on request to any jeweler. Black background with orange lettering, green fir boughs, and red candle. (*Tick Talk*, Dec. 1916) **($45-55)**

This 1916 poster uses the original "baby Ben" trademark with the small "b." (*Tick Talk*, December 1916) **($75-85)**

Big Ben has a prominent role in The Serenaders Banjo Orchestra, a New York group. The giant Big Ben cutout is equipped with a battery-operated gong. The drummer operates the gong through use of a foot petal. (*Tick Talk*, March 1917)

This 1917 Packard advertisement is a remake of the Westclox ad that appeared in the *Saturday Evening Post* on February 17, 1917. Packard established a "Big Ben Club" as part of a sales promotion. The clubs met at 8 o'clock every morning to lay out the day's sales campaign. Prior to establishment of the Big Ben Clubs, automobile dealerships typically began the work day at 10 AM. *Tick Talk* noted that the Western Clock Company's largest stockholder owned two Packards. (*Tick Talk*, June 1917)

This large cut-out, 21-1/2-inches high and 27-inches wide, was printed in eight colors and mounted on heavy board. It features Big Ben, America, Sleep-Meter, and Baby Ben. It was provided free to any dealer handling the four models. (*Tick Talk*, January 1920) **($150-175)**

This 1918 Big Ben cut-out, 17-inches high, was provided free to dealers upon request. *Tick Talk* notes that the cutout is unusual in that the clock is not prominently featured in order the show that Big Ben belongs in refined company. (*Tick Talk*, September 1918) **($75-90)**

This 1921 Pocket Ben Display Stand was provided free to dealers purchasing an assortment of twelve Pocket Ben and Glo Ben watches. The stand is constructed of American walnut left in its natural finish. It has a gold line border with red ornaments at the corners and center. "Westclox" is in maize bordered in black. The words "Pocket Ben" and "Glo Ben" are in gold. (*Tick Talk*, April 1921) **($85-100)**

Pocket Ben Display

In 1922, dealers ordering two dozen Pocket Ben's received this free lithographed display, 21" h x 54" w. (Photo: *Tick Talk*, March 1922) **($90-105)**

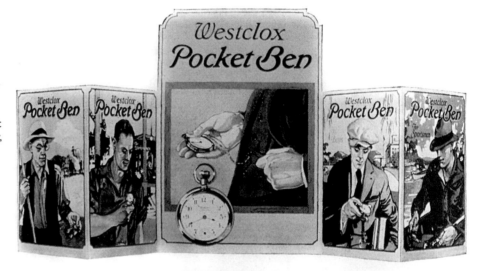

This 1921 Pocket Ben display is lithographed on cardboard and has an easel back. The bull's-eye surrounding the Pocket Ben is in shades of green while the tag is in its natural colors. The panel on the right is deep blue with black and yellow border. The words "Pocket Ben" are white. (*Tick Talk*, July 1921) **($75-90)**

What looks like a giant Pocket Ben in this store window is actually a giant cutout surrounded by a display of actual Pocket Ben and Glo-Ben models. The giant display was part of a set of five displays provided free to dealers. The other four displays, shaped like the Westclox tag, have scenes of a school boy, farmer, mechanic, and sportsman. (Photo: *Tick Talk*, June 1922) **($105-120)**

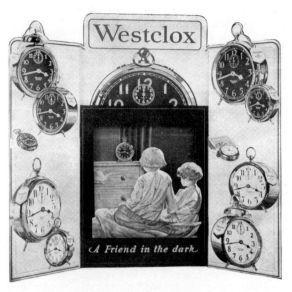

Westclox By Night

"Westclox By Night" is the theme of this lithographed display, Westclox's first luminous display. An electric light glows through the large half dial in the center. The display is 30-inches high and 32-inches wide. Provided free to dealers upon request. (Photo: *Tick Talk*, September 1926) **($375-425)**

Big Ben, Baby Ben, Blackbird, Bunkie;
Sleep-Meter, Jack o'Lantern, Big Ben Lummie;
Pocket Ben, Glo-Ben, Amer-i-ca.
Bluebird, Baby Ben Lum-i-na;
Now is the time for a Ha! Ha! Ha!
      Westclox!   Westclox!
            Rah!

This cheer was developed by a porter for William J. Miller Jewelers of Baltimore. The porter, responsible for keeping the Westclox stock complete, developed the cheer to help check inventory without use of stock sheets. (Photo: *Tick Talk*, April 1925)

This special Christmas display was sent to dealers in late November 1926. The display is heavy cardboard finished in holiday colors. **($75-90)**

This small, six color, "Sunrise" display, 13" h x 12" w, can accomodate as many as five Westclox—either the standard or deluxe models of Big Ben and Baby Ben and two Pocket Bens. (Photo: *Tick Talk*, July 1928) **($75-90)**

The central section of this 1927 Pocket Ben window display stands 21-inches high and features a giant hand tinted in natural flesh color. Two smaller side pieces feature Pocket Ben and Glo-Ben. The display was furnished to dealers purchasing an assortment of twelve watches. (Photo: *Tick Talk*, June 1927) **($155-175)**

The 1928 "Westclox in Color" display, 14" h x 23" w, is elaborately colored. It is intended for use in either a window or counter display and accommodates the entire line of Westclox in colors. (Photo: *Tick Talk*, October 1928) **($175-225)**

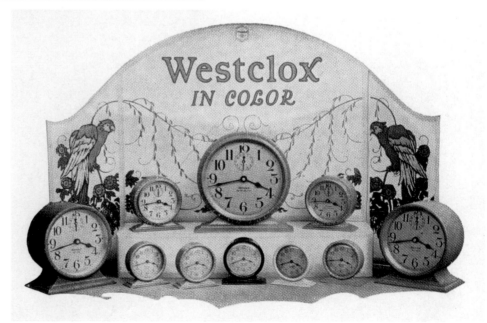

This 1928 four clock display, 19" l, is finished in black with a velvet top. It accommodates one of each color model. (Photo: *Tick Talk*, October 1928) **($60-75)**

An array of advertising aids were included in the "Pocket Ben Selling Kit" announced in the September 5, 1921, *Tick Talk*. The kit included a Pocket Ben show card on which is stitched a clock pocket, four window posters, 200 imitation watch cutouts, 300 face-to-face holders, an eight color display stand, and a set of four postcards. (Photo: *Tick Talk*, September 5, 1921) **($175-225)**

In 1929, the Western Clock Company acquired this new fire truck, replacing the old horse drawn model. (Photo: *Tick Talk*, July 20, 1929)

Westclox 1928 Christmas display. This full-color display could be used with either color or nickel models. (Photo: *Tick Talk*, November 1928) **($65-80)**

Tick Talk

TRADE MARK REG. U. S. PAT. OFF.

All set for Christmas morning

"Tiny Tim" is featured on this 1929 poster display card. (Photo: *Tick Talk*, May 1929) **($45-55)**

This cover of the December 1928 *Tick Talk*.

"Were You On Time This Morning?" is the simple question posed by this 1929 window display, 13" h x 26" l, free to dealers upon request. (Photo: *Tick Talk*, January 1929) **($175-200)**

The 1929 "Good Night Display," 24" h x 19" w, is lithographed in eight colors. The same image was used in the October 1929 *Saturday Evening Post* advertisement. (Photo: *Tick Talk*, July 1929) **($125-175)**

The 1929 "Velvet Stand" is a countertop display finished in imitation alligator hide and velvet. (Photo: *Tick Talk*, July 1929) **($65-75)**

The 1929 Westclox Auto Clock stand, 14" h x 19" w, displays the actual clock against a colorful background. (Photo: *Tick Talk*, July 1929) **($115-130)**

A 1929 Pocket Ben display, 19" w x 15" h, and finished in eleven colors. A smaller display (not pictured), 12" h x 10" w, was also offered to dealers free of charge. **($115-130)**

This ad appeared in the August 8, 1925, *Saturday Evening Post* and subsequently in a number of other magazines and farm journals. (Photo: *Tick Talk*, August 5, 1925)

Advertisements appearing in the *Saturday Evening Post* and other major publications in June 1920 featured the "big four"—Big Ben, America, Sleep-Meter, and Baby Ben. (Photo: *Tick Talk*, May 1920)

In 1927, the "girls" were treated to a Beau Brummel contest featuring a dozen of Westclox's most eligible bachelors. (Photo: *Tick Talk*, May 5, 1927)

Big Ben was featured in Westclox's July 1920 advertising. (Photo: *Tick Talk*, June 1920)

The best call for breakfast

FOR an earlier break-fast—two Big Bens, one for the cook and one for yourself.

Hers set for an hour earlier, yours for a slow cup of coffee, the cream off the news and—another cup if you please

Each presenting two ways of getting up early: on the *installment*

plan by coaxing you at half minute intervals for all of ten minutes—on the *let's have it over* plan by settling it for good with one straight five minute ring.

Each prepared to do it as you choose and ready to *ring off* in the middle of his call whenever you please.—Each 7 inches tall, pleasing to wind, pleasing to read and pleasing to hear.

Each $2.50 anywhere in the States, $3.00 anywhere in Canada. Each *made in La Salle, Illinois, by Westclox.*

This advertisement appeared on page one of the *Saturday Evening Post*, November 29, 1913. (Photo: *Tick Talk*, December 1913)

He Flags the Sleeper

AT three-fifteen the call boy comes, to wake the railroad man. Big Ben was on the job *first.*—He started the day at *three.* He is right on the minute when there's an early run.

The railroad boys all like Big Ben. He helps them make the grade. He calls, "All aboard!"—they're out of bed—plenty of time and a grin—signals set against a grouch—all cheery clear ahead.

Big Ben will run *your* day on schedule time—he'll sidetrack the Sandman whenever you say.

You'll like Big Ben face to face. He's seven inches tall, spunky, neighborly—downright good all through. He rings two ways—ten half-minute calls or steadily for five minutes.

Big Ben is six times factory tested. At your jeweler's, $2.50 in the States, $3.00 in Canada Sent prepaid on receipt of price if your jeweler doesn't stock him.

Westclox folk build more than three million alarms a year—and build them well. All wheels are assembled by a special process—patented, of course. Result—accuracy, less friction, long life.

La Salle, Ill., U.S.A.   **Western Clock Co.**   Makers of *Westclox*

The Westclox advertisement appeared in the *Saturday Evening Post* October 21, 1916. (Photo: *Tick Talk*, October 1916)

A good windup for any day

FOR that broken shoe-string, that rebellious necktie and that blocked street car line

For that flying start on Monday morning's mail and that *all-cleaned-up* feeling on Saturday noon

For that early ride back home, that change

before dinner, that hit with *her,* with the kids, and—that smile from the cook

Big Ben—the best wind-up for any day—two splendid clocks in one. A rousing good alarm to get up with, a rattling good reminder for the down-town desk.

Seven inches tall—easy to wind, easy to read and pleasing to hear—$2.50 anywhere in the States—$3.00 anywhere in Canada. Made in La Salle, Illinois, by Westclox.

This advertisement appeared on page one of the *Saturday Evening Post*, October 25, 1913. (Photo: *Tick Talk*, November 1913)

A Westclox display at the 1921 Petersborough Industrial Exhibition. (Photo: *Tick Talk*, October 5, 1921)

This 1923 pressed steel counter display, 7" x 19-1/2" was offered to dealers for $3.00. Three sides of the display are glass providing maximum exposure. (Photo: *Tick Talk*, November 1923) **($115-130)**

Dealers purchasing an assortment of twelve Pocket Ben watches in 1929 received this free counter display. It is 21-inches high and both the center and side displays hold real pocket watches. (Photo: *Tick Talk*, September 1929) **($95-110)**

This 1926 counter display was offered to dealers to help promote the new DeLuxe models. The display is 15-inches long. (Photo: *Tick Talk*, August 1927) **($85-100)**

A swimming hole was featured on the cover of this June 1935 vacation issue of *Tick Talk*.

This special 1929 store display was provided free to dealers purchasing an assortment of three Baby Ben De Luxe alarms in color. (Photo: *Tick Talk*, June 1929) **($125-140)**

This compact 1928 "Pocket Ben" display, 13" x 4-1/2", of permanent composition material was offered free to dealers. It is richly colored in gilt and orange with raised lettering. (Photo: *Tick Talk*, February 1928) **($55-70)**

This 1928 "Sun Cutout" window display, 29" x 24", "makes Westclox sing 'Good Morning' in your window—the sun rays of blue and yellow harmonize beautifully with the rich orange border." (Photo: *Tick Talk*, February 1928) **($155-170)**

View of the north end of the lounge in the Foremen's Club, February 1920. The furniture is dark oak with leather upholstery. (Photo: *Tick Talk*, February 1920)

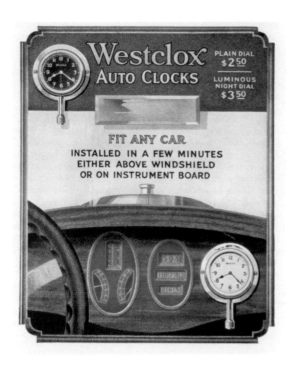

This 1928 Christmas display, 12-1/2" x 13-1/2", was intended for either window or counter display. It has a "soft starry blue sky…[and] life-like, red, burning candles…[that] together with the holly, make a richly colored combination." (Photo: *Tick Talk*, November 1928) **($75-90)**

This 1927 shelf display, 14" h, was shipped free to dealers purchasing an assortment of six or more Auto Clocks. Although the display holds actual clocks, the clocks are also lithographed on the display. (Photo: *Tick Talk*, October 1927) **($65-75)**

Santa approaches the Westclox "chimneys." (Photo: *Tick Talk*, December 20, 1929)

Color cover to the July 20, 1927, *Tick Talk*. The factory traditionally closed in July for vacation.

A 1930s metal display stand, 20-1/2" x 17-3/4" x 4-1/4", with strong Art Deco styling. **($250-300)**

April showers bring May Westclox sales. This Spring 1929 "Blue Bird" window display, 26" high x 24" wide, is finished in eight colors and displays eight clocks. *Tick Talk* notes that "a distinct idea is back of it all—the rising sun is suggestive of early morning—the beautiful blue birds, just as life-like as can be, provide a note of action that adds to attention getting value—the whole idea ties up nicely with alarm clocks." (Photo: *Tick Talk*, April 1929) **($275-325)**

1930-1949

This 1939 Christmas display was provided to dealers at no cost. It consists of a centerpiece with space to accommodate Big Ben and other clocks in front of a big red candle. On the left are "slip over" cards to fit Big Ben, Baby Ben, and Travalarm. On the right is a special display for Wrist Ben, Rocket, and Judge. (Photo: *Tick Talk*, October1939) **($215-240)**

A 1930s metal display, 27" x 20" x 3-3/4", with styling reminiscent of the Trilon and Perisphere from the 1939 New York World's Fair. **($250-300)**

A 1930 store display stand for the La Salle series clocks. (Photo: *Saturday Evening Post*, October 18, 1930) **($75-90)**

$6.00

A 1938 Westclox display with Big Ben front and center. **($175-200)**

Clock display for the newly introduced 1938 "Spur" (Photo: *Tick Talk*, January 25, 1938) **($125-140)**

Special 1938 "Wrist Ben" watch display card provided to jewelry dealers purchasing two strap and two bracelet models. Three of the models are mounted on the display, which is finished in gray, gold, black, and red. (Photo: *Tick Talk*, April 25, 1938) **($65-75)**

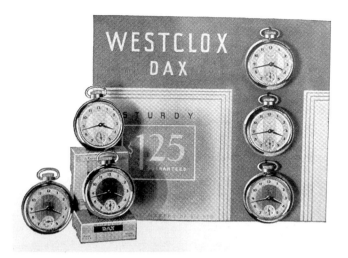

Special 1938 "Dax" watch display card provided to jewelers purchasing six watches. Three of the watches are mounted on the display card, which is finished in orange, green, and gray. (Photo: *Tick Talk*, April 25, 1938) **($55-65)**

This special 1938 "Pocket Ben" watch display card was provided to jewelers purchasing six watches. Three of the watches are mounted on the display which is finished in orange, green, and gray. (Photo: *Tick Talk*, April 25, 1938) **($55-65)**

In 1938, Westclox introduced a special gift display for June graduations, weddings, and other special occasions. The display, which consists of a centerpiece and two side cards, is ivory with purple and green accents. (Photo: *Tick Talk*, April 25, 1938) **($250-275)**

Special window display prepared for use during the 1938 "Westclox Week" promotion. The centerpiece is 33-inches wide and 27-inches high. The side cards are 15-inches by 13-inches. It is printed in red, blue, gray, and black. (Photo: *Tick Talk*, August 5, 1938) **($575-625)**

The special Christmas 1938 Westclox display provided free to dealers. (Photo: *Tick Talk*, September 15, 1938) **($150-170)**

This colorful and impressive display was offered to dealers carrying Pocket Ben and Dax. This 1939 display is 31-inches wide and 29-inches high and has six Pocket Ben and six Dax watches attached. (Photo: *Tick Talk*, March 28, 1939) **($675-750)**

The display provided dealers for "Westclox Week"—October 7-14, 1939. (Photo: *Tick Talk*, August 1939) **($475-525)**

The special display provided dealers for the 1940 "Westclox Week." The three piece display in red, blue, and gray, was provided free to dealers who ordered twelve or more clocks. The display was made to accommodate a flasher unit. (Photo: *Tick Talk*, August 1940) **($750-825)**

The window display created for the 1941 "Westclox Week." Provided free to dealers who ordered twelve or more Westclox, the display is constructed to permit dealers to adjust the dimensions to fit their showroom window. In association with Westclox Week, a $500 prize was offered to the dealer with the best window display. (Photo: *Tick Talk*, July 1941) **($750-825)**

The testing racks grace *Tick Talk's* October 1947 cover.

A 1955 Pocket Ben display. (Photo: *Tick Talk*, February 1955) **($45-55)**

A 1955 Westclox display. (Photo: *Tick Talk*, February 1955) **($65-75)**

This impressive three-piece display was introduced in the July 1952 *Tick Talk* and features the new "Sphinx" on the side units. (Photo: *Tick Talk*, July 1952) **($450-500)**

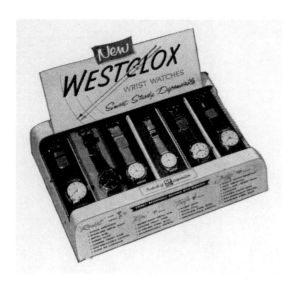

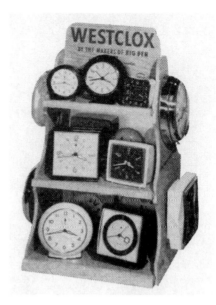

A 1955 dealer display for Westclox wrist watches. (Photo: *Tick Talk*, February 1955) **($35-45)**

A 1955 dealer display for Westclox electric wall clocks. (Photo: *Tick Talk*, February 1955) **($45-55)**

In addition to the seasonal, disposable displays provided free to dealers, Westclox, in 1956, made available to dealers floor cases designed specifically for selling clocks and watches. The cases were available in three widths—30-inches, 48-inches, and 72-inches (shown)—and had a standard blond oak finish. Dealers could special order other finishes to match their store's décor. The display cases came complete with fluorescent lighting and an outlet to demonstrate electric clocks. Storage space was included in the rear of the case. (Photo: *Tick Talk*, September 1956) **($175-225)**

This 1957 display was provided dealers purchasing Assortment No. 320A containing fourteen Big and Baby Bens in assorted finishes. (Photo: 1957 catalog) **($75-90)**

This 1959 "Woody Woodpecker" display was provided free to dealers purchasing an assortment of the Woody Wood-pecker children's clocks. (Photo: 1959-60 catalog) **($145-160)**

The 1958 "Four Ben Assortment" (No. 275) came with this handy display shipper. The assortment included two Baby Bens and two Big Bens. (Photo: 1958 catalog) **($55-65)**

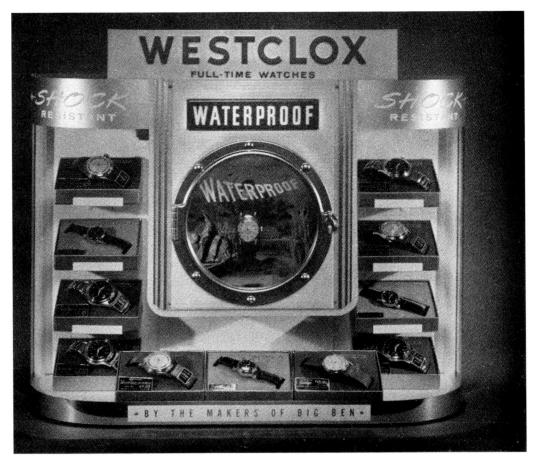

This display was provided free to dealers who purchased the "88" assortment of twelve Westclox wrist-watches. The assortment consisted of one #770 Automatic Waterproof; one #713 Waterproof; two #683 Judge Waterproof; three #688 Wrist Ben Waterproof with Strap; two #698 Wrist Ben Waterproof with Metal Expansion Band; and three #658 Coquette Waterproof. The display is lighted in such a way that the watch in the middle appears to be underwater. (Photo: *Tick Talk*, March 1958) **($65-75)**

The 1958 "Traveler Assortment" (No. 445) came with this free display. The assortment included three Travalarms and three Travettes. (Photo: 1958 catalog) **($65-75)**

Dealers purchasing the 1957-58 "America Assortment" (No. 2940) received this free display. The assortment contained twelve clocks, four of each color. (Photo: 1958 catalog) **($45-55)**

This display was provided free with purchase of the 1958 "Calico Horse Assortment" (No. 530). The assortment consisted of six clocks, two of each color. (Photo: 1958 catalog) **($175-215)**

Provided free with purchase of the 1958 "Sailor Assortment" (No. 505) was this handy window or counter display. The assortment included two of each color. (Photo: 1958 catalog) **($85-100)**

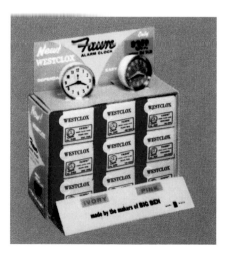

Dealers purchasing the 1957-58 "Fawn Assortment" (No. 2052) received this free display. The assortment included nine clocks. (Photo: 1958 catalog) **($45-55)**

This motion display was provided free with the purchase of the 1958 "Automatic Watch Assortment" (No. 769). The assortment included four watches, two in gold color and two in chrome. (Photo: 1958 catalog) **($45-55)**

Dealers purchasing the 1958 "Electric Wall Clock Assortment" (No. 811) received this free display. Included in the assortment were Orbit White, Frill Wrought Iron, Snowflake Charcoal, Spice Copper, Frolic Yellow, Glendale Turquoise, Wallmate White, and Wallmate Red. (Photo: 1958 catalog) **($105-120)**

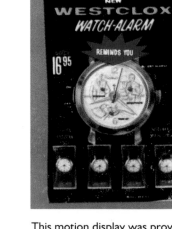

Dealers purchasing the 1958 "Two-Way Wall Clock Assortment" (No. 1610) received this free display. The assortment included the Glendale in red and turquoise and the Frolic in white and yellow. (Photo: 1958 catalog) **($60-70)**

Dealers purchasing the 1958 "Electric Alarm Assortment" (No. 555), 13-1/2" x 12-3/4" x 4", received this free countertop display. Included in the assortment were the Lace Pink Luminous, Lace Antique White Plain, Fortune Gray Luminous, and Tide Ivory Plain. (Photo: 1958 catalog) **($50-60)**

This motion display was provided free to dealers purchasing the 1958 "Watchlarm Assortment" (No. 795) consisting of two Watchlarms with leather straps and two with metal band. Became "Watchlarm Assortment No. 7950" in the 1960 watch catalog. (Photo: 1958 catalog) **($65-75)**

Dealers purchasing the 1958 "Coquette Assortment" (No. 665) received this free display. The assortment included two Coquette Square and two Coquette Diamond watches. (Photo: 1958 catalog) **($55-65)**

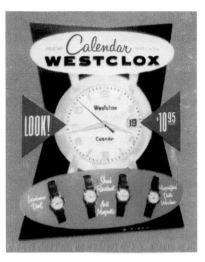

Dealers purchasing the 1957-58 "Calendar Watch Assortment" (No. 2920) received this free display. The assortment consisted of four calendar watches. (Photo: 1958 catalog) **($45-55)**

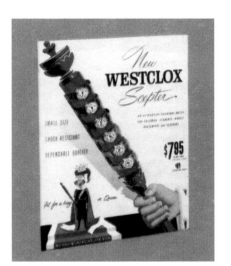

Dealers purchasing the 1957-58 "Scepter Assortment No. 677" consisting of six watches, three No. 667 with leather strap and three No. 668 with metal band, received this free display. The same display was offered in the 1960 watch catalog as "Scepter Assortment No. 6770." (Photo: 1958 catalog) **($45-55)**

Dealers purchasing the 1958 "Scepter Assortment No. 695" consisting of six watches, three No. 669 with leather strap and three No. 670 with metal band, received this free display. (Photo: 1958 catalog) **($45-55)**

Dealers purchasing the 1958 "Shadow Thin Assortment" (No. 4981) received this free display. The assortment included four watches, two No. 729 with metal band and two No. 728 with strap. (Photo: 1958 catalog) **($40-50)**

Dealers purchasing the 1958 "Dax Pocket Watch Assortment" (No. 685) received this free counter display. Included in the assortment were six watches. Became No. 6850 in the 1959 watch catalog. (Photo: 1958 catalog) **($45-55)**

Dealers purchasing the 1958 "Scotty Assortment" (No. 603) of six watches received this free counter display. Became No. 6030 in the 1959 watch catalog. Not shown: "Scotty Assortment No. 6040" consisted of six Scotty Model No. 616 with gold color case. (Photo: 1958 catalog) **($45-55)**

Dealers purchasing the 1957 "Pocket Ben Assortment" (No. 644) received this free countertop display. The assortment consisted of four plain and two luminous models. (Photo: 1957 catalog) **($45-55)**

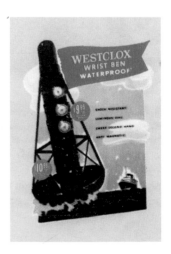

Dealers purchasing the 1958 "Pocket Ben Assortment" (No. 644) received this free countertop display. The assortment consisted of four plain and two luminous models. Became No. 6440 in the 1959 watch catalog. (Photo: 1958 catalog) **($45-55)**

This 1957 display was provided to dealers purchasing the "Wrist Ben Waterproof Assortment No. 675." (Photo: 1957 catalog) **($50-60)**

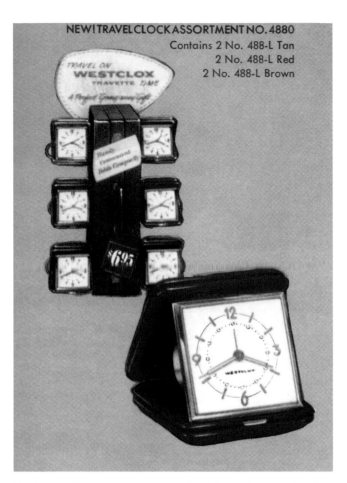

NEW! TRAVEL CLOCK ASSORTMENT NO. 4880

Contains 2 No. 488-L Tan
2 No. 488-L Red
2 No. 488-L Brown

Dealers purchasing an assortment of six Travette's, two of each color, received this free 1959-60 display (No. 4880). (Photo: 1959-60 catalog) **($145-160)**

Dealers purchasing the 1959-60 "Colt-Walltone Assortment" No. 8989 received this free countertop display. The assortment contained two Walltones and two Colts. (Photo: 1959-60 catalog) **($50-60)**

Dealers purchasing the 1959-60 "Gift Exclusives Assortment" (No. 8008) received this free display. The assortment contained Nos. 707, 803-L, 470-L, and 425-L. (Photo: 1959-60 catalog) **($85-100)**

Dealers purchasing the 1959-60 "Drowse Assortment" (No. 8000) received this free full color display. The assortment included two No. 800 and two No. 800-L. (Photo: 1959-60 catalog) **($65-75)**

Dealers purchasing the 1959-60 "Children's Clock Assortment" (No. 5100) received this free display. The assortment included one each of the "Calico Horse" in red, yellow, and blue and "Sailor" in red, cocoa, and blue. (Photo: 1959-60 catalog) **($125-140)**

Dealers purchasing the 1959 "Torch Assortment" (No. 6720) received this free display. The assortment contained six No. 671-L, three with black strap and one each with pink, white, and blue strap. (Photo: 1959 Watch Catalog) **($40-50)**

Dealers purchasing the 1959 "Coquette Assortment" No. 6590 received this free display. The assortment included one each of model Nos. 659, 660-B, 661, 662, and 663. (Photo: 1959 Watch Catalog) **($40-50)**

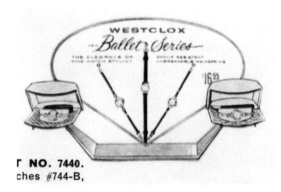

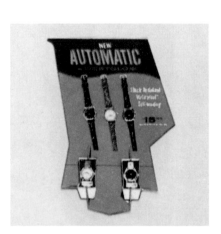

Dealers purchasing the 1959 "Ballet Assortment" (No. 7440) received this free display. The assortment contained one each of Nos. 744-B, 744-C, 745-B, 745-C, and 746. (Photo: 1959 Watch Catalog) **($65-80)**

Dealers purchasing the 1959 "Waterproof Automatic Lancer Assortment" No. 7790 received this free display. The assortment contained two No. 781-L and two No. 782-L watches. (Photo: 1959 Watch Catalog) **($40-50)**

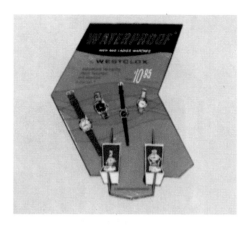

Dealers purchasing the 1959 "Waterproof Watch Assortment" No. 6580 received this free display. The assortment included one each of model Nos. 658-L, 740-L, 740-LB, 688-L, 688-LB, and 683-LB. (Photo: 1959 Watch Catalog) **($40-50)**

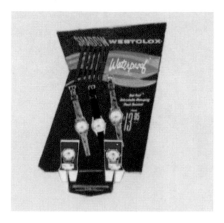

Dealers purchasing the 1959 "Shadow Thin Assortment" No. 7550 received this free display. The assortment included two #755, one #755-B, one #757, and one #757-B. (Photo: 1959 Watch Catalog) **($40-50)**

1960-1970

Dealers purchasing the 1959 "Wrist Ban Assortment" No. 6220 received this free display. The assortment included four #687 and two #687-L. (Photo: 1959 Watch Catalog) **($45-55)**

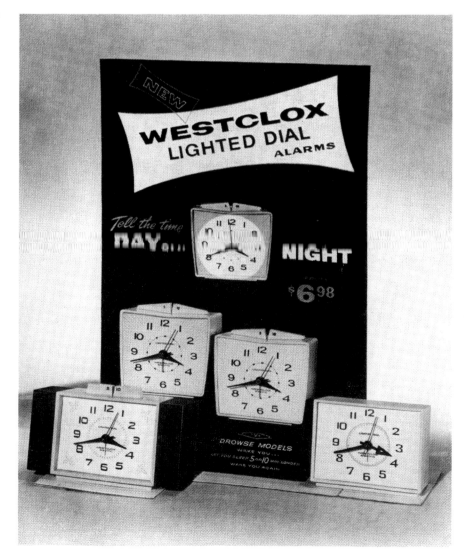

In 1961, Westclox offered this free display to dealers who purchased an assortment of the new "Dialite" models. These models have a light source behind the dial that is estimated to last eighteen years and provide a "pleasant pink light." (Photo: *Tick Talk*, June-July 1961) **($35-45)**

Dealers purchasing an assortment of Keywound Automatic Drowse alarm clocks in 1964 received this free counter display. (Photo: *Tick Talk*, January 1964) **($75-90)**

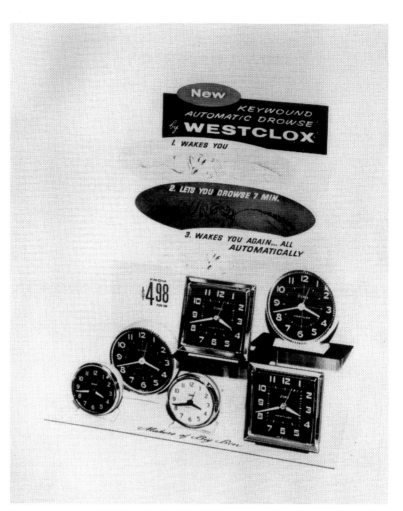

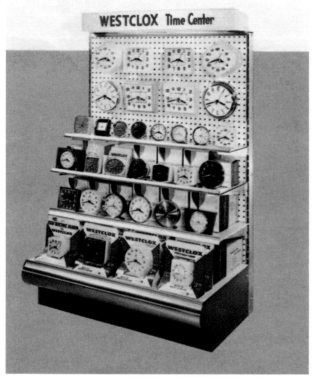

The 1962 "Westclox Illuminated Time Center" (No. 19014) was provided to dealers purchasing a large assortment of timepieces. Purchasers received six Baby Bens and six Big Bens free to offset the cost of the display. (Photo: 1962 catalog) **($175-200)**

This 1965 display was offered to dealers purchasing six of Westclox's lower priced alarm clocks. (Photo: *Tick Talk*, March 1965) **($40-50)**

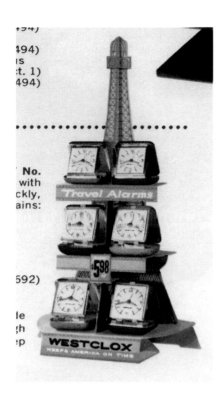

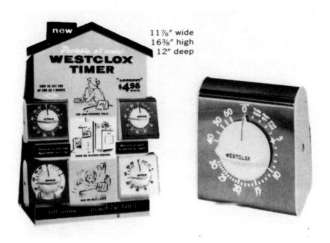

This 1962-64 display, 16-1/8" x 11-7/8" x 12", was provided free to dealers purchasing the Lookout Timer Assortment No. 19018. The assortment included two #50005, and one each of #50001 and #50003. (Photo: 1963-64 catalog) **($40-50)**

The 1963-64 "6-Pack Travel Clock Display" No. 19065, 28" h, has a "continental flair." It was provided to dealers purchasing four Touralarms and four Travette IIs. (Photo: 1963-64 catalog) **($135-150)**

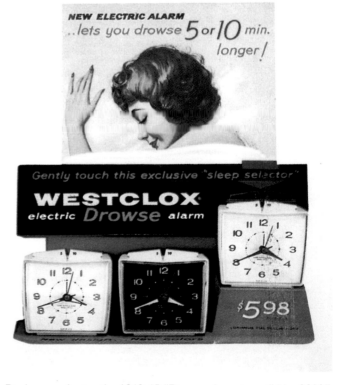

The 1963-64 "12-Pack Illuminated Travel Clock Display" (No. 19067) was provided free to dealers purchasing an assortment of twelve travel alarms. (Photo: 1963-64 catalog) **($55-65)**

Dealers purchasing the 1962-65 "Drowse Assortment" No. 29007 received this free display. The assortment contained four Drowse alarms. (Photo: 1962 catalog) **($50-60)**

Dealers purchasing the 1962-64 Dialite Display Assortment No. 29010 or No. 29011 received this free display. Assortment No. 29010 contained two No. 20076 Dunbar and two No. 20106 Drowse alarms. Assortment No. 20911 contained two No. 20106 Drowse and one each of No. 21038 Drowsewood and No. 20076 Dunbar. (Photo: 1962 catalog) **($60-70)**

The 1962-63 Westclox Illuminated Time Center, No. 19034 (30" w) and No. 19035 (36" w), has an illuminated sign that lights the entire display. The locking top unit accomodates watches and travel clocks. Both units are 63-inches tall. Not pictured: The Standard Time Center, No. 19036 (30" w) and No. 19037 (36" w) has the same features as above but has a nonilluminated plastic sign and is 55-inches high. (Photo: 1962-63 catalog) **($175-200)**

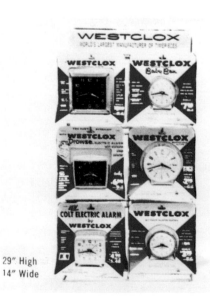

Dealers purchasing the 1962-63 No. 19006 Assortment received this countertop display, 29" x 14", that requires less than one square foot of counter space. The assortment included two each of #12525 (Fawn), #15535 (Bingo), #15534 (Spur), #20581 (Colt), and #20602 (Drowse) and one each of #11503 (Baby Ben) and #11504 (Baby Ben). (Photo: 1962-63 catalog) **($25-35)**

Dealers purchasing the 1962-63 "4-Pack Travel Clock Assortment" No. 19048 received this counter or window display, 13-1/2" x 10" x 5-1/2". Included in the assortment were two Travettes and two Travalarms. (Photo: 1962-63 catalog) **($125-150)**

Dealers purchasing the "Illuminated Travel Clock Assortment" No. 19049 received this display, 16" x 17" x 4-3/4". The assortment included three Travettes, three Travalarms, one Travette Deluxe, and one Travalarm Deluxe. (Photo: 1962-63 catalog) **($95-115)**

Dealers purchasing the 1962-63 "Big and Baby Ben Assortment" No. 19053 received this countertop display, 19-1/2" x 10-5/8" x 12-7/8". The assortment included four Baby Bens and two Big Bens in various finishes. (Photo: 1962-63 catalog) **($50-60)**

Dealers purchasing the "Quick Profit Pack" No. 19050 received this display, 27" x 14" x 12". The assortment included one each of the following keywound models: Bingo, Hustler, Fawn, America, Spur, and Crest. (Photo: 1962-63 catalog) **($40-50)**

This 1962-64 revolving display, 15" x 14", was provided free to dealers purchasing the Dunbar 8-pack assortment No. 29016. (Photo: 1963-64 catalog) **($60-70)**

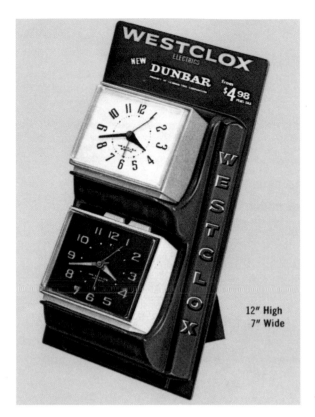

12" High
7" Wide

Dealers purchasing a 4-pack assortment of Dunbars in 1962-63 received this easel back display (No. 29015), 12" x 7". (Photo: 1962-63 catalog). **($35-45)**

Dealers purchasing the "Ladies Shock Resistant Watch Display" No. 39040, 15" x 8" x 3-1/2", received six models: #35121, #35041, #35043, #32061, #32063, and #30021. Not Shown: "Men's Shock Resistant Watch Display" No. 39041, same display containing the following models: #35121, #35156, #35158, #34001, #36011, and #36013. (Photo: 1962-63 catalog) **($25-35)**

Big Ben is front and center in this 1964 display. On the right side of the display are special tie clasps and bow pins featuring the new oval-shaped Big Bens. (Photo: *Tick Talk*, March 1964) **($115-130)**

Dealers purchasing the 1962 "Moonbeam Assortment" No. 29004 received this flashing light display. (Photo: 1962 catalog) **($65-75)**

Dealers purchasing the 1962 "Scotty Display Assortment" No. 39002 received this display and six watches. (Photo: 1962 catalog) **($40-50)**

Dealers purchasing the 1962 "Dash-Colt Assortment" No. 29005 received this store display and four clocks, two of each model. (Photo: 1962 catalog) **($40-50)**

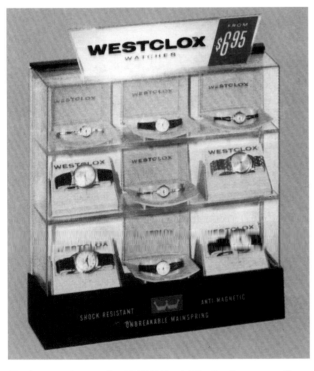

Dealers purchasing the 1962 "Watch Display Assortment" No. 39023 received this permanent pilfer-proof watch display. The assortment contained twelve assorted watches. (Photo: 1962 catalog) **($40-50)**

The 1963-64 "Custom II Illuminated Time Center" No. 19057 ($603.24), 36" x 63" x 18", has a locking top unit for watches and travel clocks, an electric outlet for testing clocks, an illuminated sign that lights the entire unit, a motorized revolving unit to display wall clocks, and a bottom storage compartment. Free Bens were provided to offset the cost. Not Pictured: The 1963-64 "Deluxe Time Center" No. 19060 (30" w) and No. 19061 (36" w) are similar to the Custom II but lack the revolving unit. Not Pictured: The 1964-65 Time Center No. 19059 appears identical to No. 19057. Not Pictured: The 1964-65 "Deluxe Time Center" No. 19092 (30" w) and No. 19093 (36" w) are similar to No. 19057 but lack the revolving unit. (Photo: 1963-64 catalog) **($175-250)**

Dealers purchasing the 1964-65 Assortment No. 19071 received this handy blister pack display, 14-1/4" x 32-1/8" x 7-3/4". The assortment contained a variety of Bingo, Hustler, Fawn, Spur, and Crest models. Taking up less than 3/4 square foot of counter space, Westclox estimated dealer profit from this display at $78.10 per square foot. (Photo: 1964-65 catalog) **($25-35)**

The 1963-64 "Revolving Counter Display" No. 29025, 12-1/4" x 37", was provided free to dealers purchasing eleven clocks at dealer cost and one at consumer price. Estimated profit per square foot for this display was $149.09 per year. (Photo: 1963-64 catalog) **($150-175)**

Dealers purchasing the 1963-65 Best Seller Assortment No. 19070 received this countertop display, 14-1/2" x 27" x 7-1/2". Models included in the assortment were: #15032, #12025, #12031, #12038, #15055, and #15056. Estimated profit per square foot generted by this display was $39.05 per year. (Photo: 1963-64 catalog) **($75-90)**

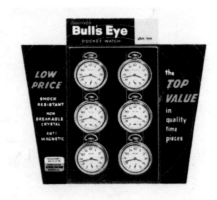

A new display card was included with the Bull's Eye Assortment (No. 39001) in 1962-63. (Photo: 1962-63 catalog) **($35-45)**

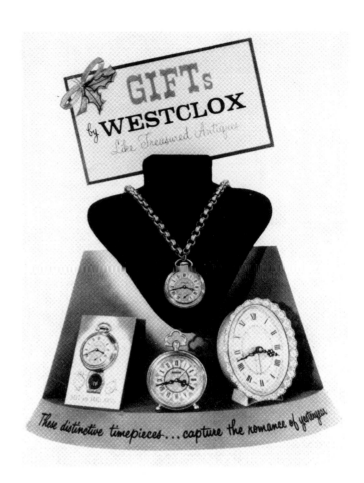

Westclox offered this display to coincide with the introduction of its new "Antique Style" clocks and watches. (Photo: *Tick Talk*, June 1965) **($45-55)**

17⅜" wide
22¾" high
8¼" deep

Dealers purchasing the 1962 "Bull's Eye Display Assortment" No. 39001 received this easel back display and six watches. (Photo: 1962 catalog) **($35-45)**

Dealers purchasing the 1963-65 "Electric Wall Clock Assortment" (No. 29031) received this counter display, 17-3/8" x 22-3/4" x 8-1/4". The assortment contained five models. (Photo: 1963-64 catalog) **($115-130)**

16" wide
15½" high
6" deep

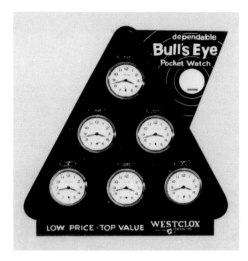

The display card for Bull's Eye Assortment (No. 39001) was updated in the 1966-67 catalog. (Photo: 1966-67 catalog) **($35-45)**

Dealers purchasing the 1963-64 "Award II Assortment No. 29030" received this distinctive display, 16" x 15-1/2" x 6". The assortment contained four models, including two corded and two no-cord. The same display was offered in the 1964-65 catalog with purchase of the "Award II Assortment No. 29033." (Photo: 1963-64 catalog) **($115-130)**

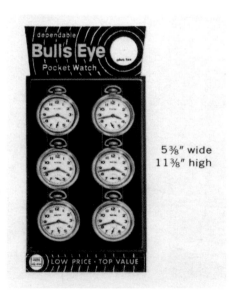

5⅜" wide
11⅜" high

The display card, 5-3/8" x 11-3/8", for the Bull's Eye Assortment (No. 39001) was again updated in the 1963-64 catalog. It remained unchanged through 1965. (Photo: 1963-64 catalog) **($35-45)**

wide
high
deep

The 1967-68 display card for the Bull's Eye Assortment (No. 39001). (Photo: 1967-68 catalog) **($35-45)**

This 1968-69 "Bull's Eye" display (No. 39001) was provided to dealers purchasing six Bull's Eye pocket watches. Remained unchanged in the 1969-70 catalog. (Photo: 1968-69 catalog) **($30-40)**

Another new display card was introduced for the "Pocket Ben Assortment" (No. 39004) in the 1963-64 catalog. The card remained unchanged through the 1965 catalog. **($35-45)**

5 3/8" wide
11 3/8" high

Dealers purchasing "Pocket Ben Assortment No. 39004" in 1962-63 received six Pocket Bens and this easel back display, 10" x 11". (Photo: 1962-63 catalog) **($35-45)**

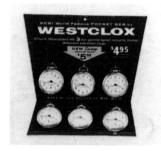

Dealers purchasing "Pocket Ben Assortment No. 39004" from the 1962 catalog received six pocket watches and this display. (Photo: 1962 catalog) **($35-45)**

The 1966-67 catalog introduced a new display card for the Pocket Ben Assortment (No. 39004). (Photo: 1966-67 catalog) **($35-45)**

A new Pocket Ben Assortment (No. 39093) containing six watches was introduced in the 1967-68 catalog. With it came another new display card, 9-1/4" x 9-7/8" x 3". (Photo: 1967-68 catalog) **($35-45)**

9¼" wide
9⅞" high
3" deep

This 1962-63 display was provided to dealers purchasing the "Scotty Assortment" (No. 39036) containing four plain and two luminous models. (Photo: 1962-63 catalog) **($35-45)**

This 1968-70 "Pocket Ben" display (No. 39093) was provided to dealers purchasing two each of the three Pocket Ben models. It remained unchanged in the 1969-70 catalog. (Photo: 1968-69 catalog) **($35-45)**

A new display, 5-3/8" x 11-3/8", was included with purchase of the Scotty Assortment (No. 39036) in the 1963-64 catalog. Remained unchanged through 1965. **($35-45)**

5⅜" wide
11⅜" high

This 1966 "product-in-use" counter display was provided to dealers purchasing an assortment of three "Twin Face" electric alarms. The *Tick Talk* copy notes that the "product-in-use" display helps dealers sell the clock to the "almost 40 million twin-bed users". (Photo: *Tick Talk*, March 1966) **($45-55)**

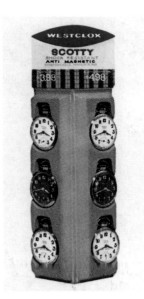

The 1967-68 catalog reveals yet another new display for the "Scotty Assortment" (No. 39036). **($35-45)**

This 1968 "Scotty" display (No. 39036) was provided to dealers purchasing an assortment consisting of four plain and four luminous models. Remained unchanged in the 1969-70 catalog. (Photo: 1968-69 catalog) **($45-55)**

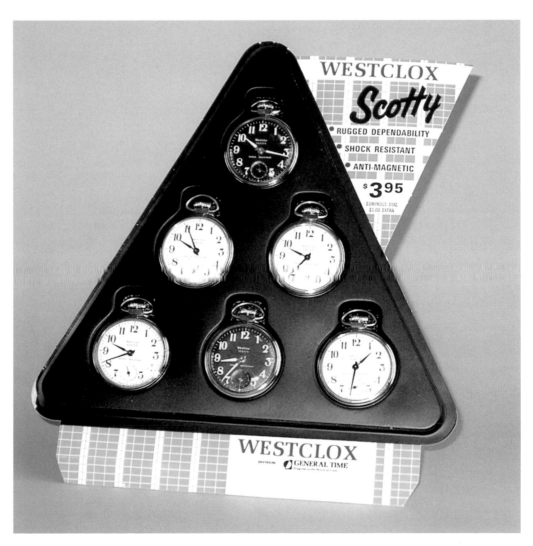

A newly restyled display was included with purchase of the Scotty Assortment (No. 39036) in the 1966-67 catalog. **($35-45 display only; $250-300 display with watches)**

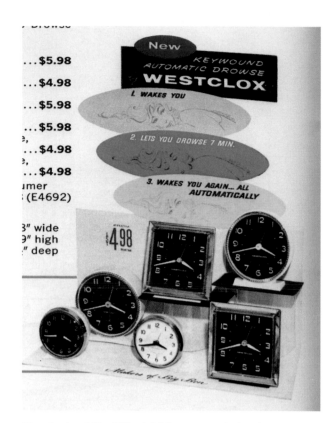

This distinctive display, 20" x 24" x 9", was provided free with purchase of the 1964-65 "Ben Assortment" No. 19079. The display promotes the modern new oval design of the Bens. Included are six clocks. (Photo: 1964-65 catalog) **($105-120)**

This display, 18" x 19" x 6-1/2", was provided with purchase of the 1964-65 "Keywound Automatic Drowse Assortment" No. 19077. The assortment includes two Fawn, two Spur, and two Hustler models. (Photo: 1964-65 catalog) **($85-95)**

Dealers purchasing the 1964-65 "Clock Shoppe" Assortment No. 19080 received this free display, 21" x 22" x 9-1/2". The assortment includes six keywound alarms, four electric alarms, and two electric wall clocks. (Photo: 1964-65 catalog) **($125-140)**

No. 19086

This display, 16" x 22" x 5-1/2", was provided to dealers purchasing the 1964-65 "Keywound/Electric Drowse Assortment" No. 19086. The assortment included one each of the "Fawn Drowse Keywound," "Spur Drowse Keywound," "Drowse Electric" Sandalwood, and "Drowse Electric" Antique White. (Photo: 1964-65 catalog) **($75-85)**

No. 29050

This display, 13" x 21-1/2" x 10", was provided to dealers purchasing the "Lighted Dial Wall Clock Assortment" No. 29050. The assortment included one "Lighted Dial" in each color. (Photo: 1964-65 catalog) **($75-85)**

No. 19090

This 1964-65 display, 14-1/4" x 15-1/2" x 4-1/2", was provided to dealers purchasing the "Lookout Timer Assortment" No. 19090. Included in the assortment were two chrome, one white, and one copper timer. (Photo: 1964-65 catalog) **($55-65)**

No. 29032

This display, 20" x 17-1/4" x 6-1/2", was provided to dealers purchasing the 1964-65 "Electric Wall and Alarm Clock Assortment" No. 29032. The assortment included the "Tide" in Antique White, "Dunbar" in Sandalwood, and "Pert" in White and Sandalwood. (Photo: 1964-65 catalog) **($85-95)**

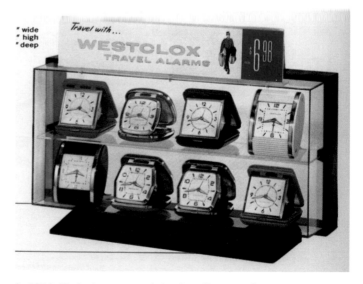

In 1964-65, dealers received this free illuminated permanent display, 17" x 12" x 5", with purchase of the "8-Pack Assortment" of eight travel alarms (No. 19076). (Photo: 1964-65 catalog) **($55-65)**

This display, 12" x 15", was provided to dealers purchasing the 1964-65 "Pocket Watch Assortment" No. 39057. The assortment includes eight Scotty and four Pocket Ben models. (Photo: 1964-65 catalog) **($45-55)**

Dealers purchasing the 1964-65 "Stanton No-Cord Assortment" No. 59003 received this free display, 17" x 22-1/2" x 5-3/4". The assortment contains four Stanton models. (Photo: 1964-65 catalog) **($55-65)**

This 1964-67 display, 8-1/2" x 12" x 4", was provided to dealers purchasing the "Magnet Watch Assortment" No. 39060. The one-piece display contains a steel surface to demonstrate the holding power of the magnet. The assortment includes three each of the plain and luminous models. (Photo: 1964-65 catalog) **($35-45)**

7⅜" Wide 18¼" High 5" Deep

This 1964-67 display, 7-3/8" x 18-1/4" x 5", was provided to dealers purchasing "Pocket Watch Assortment No. 39500." The assortment includes twelve watches in blister packs: three each of Pocket Ben (No. 40502), Pocket Ben Sweep (No. 40504), Scotty (No. 40505), and Scotty Black Dial (No. 40506). (Photo: 1964-65 catalog) **($35-45)**

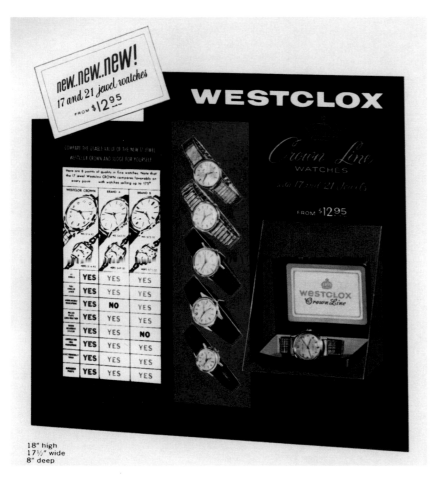

18" high
17½" wide
8" deep

No. 39066

This display, 10-1/4" x 15-1/2" x 7-1/2", was provided free to dealers purchasing the 1965 Pocket Watch Assortment No. 39066 consisting of eight Scotty and eight Pocket Ben models. (Photo: 1965 catalog) **($55-65)**

This 1964-65 display, 18" x 17-1/2" x 8", was provided to dealers purchasing the Men's Wrist Watch Assortment No. 39061. The assortment includes six watches, one of which is highlighted by reflected light. The other eight models are mounted on a clear plastic panel. Not Pictured: The Ladies' Wrist Watch Assortment No. 39062 has the same features and dimensions. (Photo: 1964-65 catalog) **($55-65)**

12½" wide
27" high
12½" deep

This 1965-67 display, 12" x 26-1/2" x 12", was provided to dealers purchasing the Johnny Zero Assortment No. 39072. The assortment included three each of the Pro-sport, Air Force style, Combat, and Frontiersman. (Photo: 1966-67 catalog) **($75-85)**

16" wide
51" high
16" deep

This revolving display, 16" x 51" x 16", was provided to dealers purchasing the 1964-65 "Wee Winkie Assortment No. 19113." The three-sided display holds the Little Red Barn, See-Saw, Jumbo Alarm, Circus Parade, and Hickory-Dickory Dock. (Photo: 1965 catalog) **($175-200)**

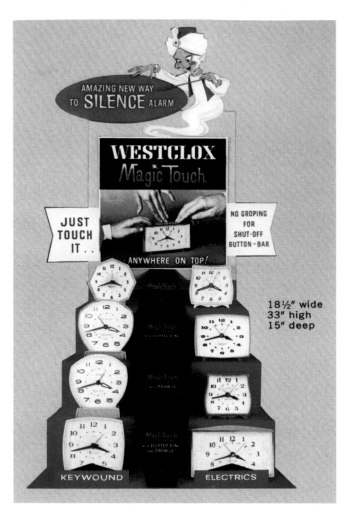

The 1966-67 rotating "Decorator Clock Time Center," 42" x 81" x 42". The time center was provided to dealers purchasing Assortment No. 29042 containing ten electric wall clocks and eighteen no-cord wall clocks. Two free clocks were provided to offset the cost of the display. (Photo: 1966-67 catalog) **($75-85)**

This display, 18-1/2" x 33" x 15", was provided to dealers purchasing the 1966-67 "Magic Touch Assortment" No. 19131. The assortment contains eight Magic Touch models. (Photo: 1966-67 catalog) **($55-65)**

Dealers purchasing the 1966-67 Assortment No. 19147 received this counter display, 11-1/4" x 14" x 8-1/2". The assortment contained six timers, two Lookout Jr., and three Lookout Deluxe. (Photo: 1966-67 catalog) **($45-55)**

The 1966-67 rotating "Decorator Clock Counter Time Center," 27-1/2" x 33" x 27-1/2", was provided to dealers purchasing Assortment No. 29043 containing nine electric decorator clocks and seven no-cord decorator clocks. Two additional clocks were provided free to offset the cost of the display. (Photo: 1966-67 catalog) **($65-75)**

26" wide
32½" high
23½" deep

This "Custom Decorator Clock Center" was provided to dealers purchasing Assortment No. 29044 containing fifteen decorator clocks. One additional clock was provided free to offset the cost of the display. The double hinged display is 72" high with 24" center panel and 18" side panels. It can be used as a freestanding floor display or mounted on a wall. Also offered in the 1967-68 catalog with purchase of Assortment No. 59012. (Photo: 1966-67 catalog) **($85-100)**

This 1966-68 "Wee Winkie" display, 26" x 32-1/2" x 23-1/2", was provided free to dealers purchasing Assortment No. 19144 containing five clocks—Circus Parade, Jumbo alarm, Hickory-Dickory Dock, Little Red Barn, and Block Clock. (Photo: 1966-67 catalog) **($115-140)**

24" wide
41" high
8½" deep

14" wide
21" high
6½" deep

This "Wee Winkie" rotating display, 24" x 41" x 8-1/2", was provided free to dealers purchasing the 1966-68 Assortment No. 19143 containing all eight Wee Winkie models. (Photo: 1966-67 catalog) **($145-160)**

This "Johnny Zero" easel back display, 14" x 21" x 6-1/2", was provided free to dealers purchasing Assortment No. 39086 containing three each of the "Cycle Watch" and "Secret Agent." (Photo: 1966-67 catalog) **($35-45)**

Circa 1965 Christmas display and gift boxes. Because the boxes do not mention Westclox, they have little value. **($5-10)**

A Westclox holiday display. (Photo: *Tick Talk*, September 1966) **($65-80)**

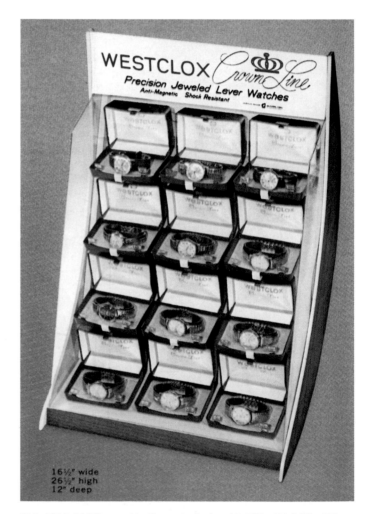

16½" wide
26½" high
12" deep

16¾" wide
8¾" high
6¾" deep

This 1966-68 countertop display, 16-3/4" x 8-3/4" x 6-3/4", was provided free to dealers purchasing the "Man-Time Assortment" No. 39084. The assortment contained six watches, one of each style and finish. (Photo: 1967-68 catalog) **($25-35)**

This 1966-67 "Crown Line" watch display, 16-1/2" x 26-1/2" x 12", was provided to dealers purchasing either "Men's Wrist Watch Assortment No. 39094," "Ladies Wrist Watch Assortment No. 39085," or "Best Seller Wrist Watch Assortment No. 39096." The cases have tilt-down clear plastic front with padlock. Each assortment contains eleven watches. Dealers were given one additional watch to defray the cost of the display. (Photo: 1966-67 catalog) **($25-30)**

This Johnny Zero display, 14" x 21" x 6-1/2", was provided to dealers purchasing Assortment No. 39098 containing two Cycle watches, two Combat watches, one Pro-Sport watch, and one Secret Agent watch. (Photo: 1967-68 catalog) **($45-55)**

The 1967-68 "Wall Clock Time Center," 27-1/2" x 33" x 27-1/2", (No. 29057) was provided to dealers purchasing an assortment of sixteen wall clocks. Dealers were given two free clocks to offset the cost of the display. The display has five rotating pegboard panels. (Photo: 1967-68 catalog) **($65-75)**

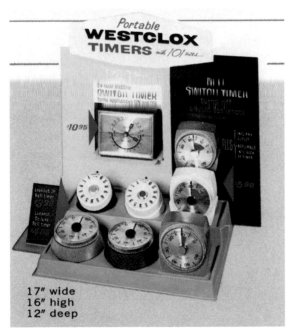

This 1967-68 Timer display, 7" x 16" x 12", was provided to dealers purchasing "Timer Assortment No. 19175" containing eight timers. (Photo: 1967-68 catalog) **($45-55)**

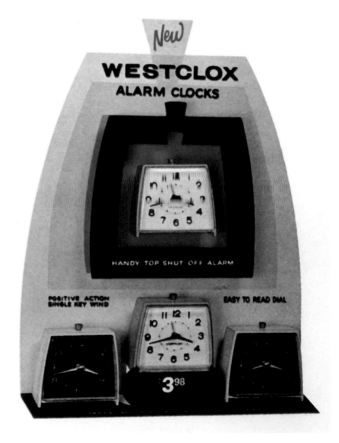

This free 1965 display, 13" x 18" x 7-1/2", was provided to dealers purchasing the "Fayette Assortment" No. 19104 containing four clocks. (Photo: 1965 catalog) **($55-65)**

This free 1965 display, 13-3/4" x 18-1/4" x 6", was provided to dealers purchasing the "Fayette Lighted Dial Assortment" No. 19108 containing four clocks. (Photo: 1965 catalog) **($55-65)**

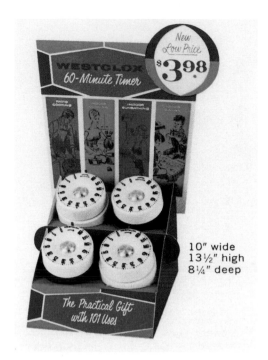

Dealers purchasing the 1965 "Lookout Jr. Timer Assortment" No. 19103 received this free display, 10" x 13-1/2" x 8-1/4". The assortment contained four timers. (Photo: 1965 catalog) **($35-45)**

This 1965 display, 17-1/2" x 18" x 10", was provided free to dealers purchasing "Contessa Assortment No. 29034" containing six clocks. (Photo: 1965 catalog) **($85-100)**

Dealers purchasing the 1965 "Sanford No-Cord Alarm Assortment" No. 59004 received this distinctive motion display, 16-1/2" x 19" x 4-1/2". The assortment contained three clocks. (Photo: 1965 catalog) **($45-55)**

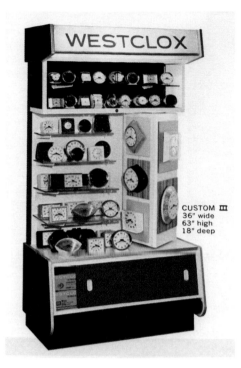

CUSTOM III
36" wide
63" high
18" deep

This countertop version of the "Money Tree" display was provided with purchase of Assortment No. 29036 containing thirteen clocks. Three free clocks were provided to offset the cost of the display. (Photo: 1965 catalog) **($135-150)**

Introduced in the 1965 catalog, the "Custom III Illuminated Time Center" (No. 19115), 36" x 63" x 18", offered fifty-one percent more space in the top locking compartment and thirteen percent more spinner area than the Custom II. It also has a larger electric sign illuminating the display. A real trend setter, the display offered the "walnut plastic laminate" that was to sweep the nation in the late 1960s and 1970s. Not Pictured: Deluxe Time Center No. 19116 (30" w) and No. 19117 (36" w) have the same features as the Custom III except the revolving display unit. (Photo: 1965 catalog) **($175-200)**

32" wide
75" high
24" deep

Introduced in the 1965 catalog, the "Money Tree" display (No. 29035), 82" high and 44" diameter, holds thirty-two wall clocks in only three square feet of floor space. The clocks rotate on two independent levels. Coppertone finish. Assortment No. 29035 included sixteen No-Cord®, fourteen electric, and four Lighted Dial® models. Dealers were provided two free clocks to offset the cost of the display. (Photo: 1965 catalog) **($175-200)**

82" high
44" dia.

This 1964-65 "Early American Decorator Clock" display, 32" x 75" x 24", was provided free to dealers buying Assortment No. 59006 consisting of twelve clocks. (Photo: 1965 catalog) **($125-140)**

The "Early American
Decorator Clock"
display, 32" x 75" x
24", was restyled in
the 1966-67 catalog
and provided free to
dealers purchasing
Assortment No.
59009 containing
twelve clocks. Note
the new "rich Early
American design"
legs. (Photo: 1966-
67 catalog) **($110-
125)**

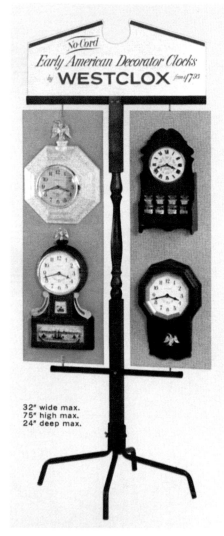

32" wide max.
75" high max.
24" deep max.

This "lighted suitcase" display, 17-3/4" x 16-1/2" x 7-1/2", was
provided to dealers purchasing the 1966-70 "Travel Clock
Display Assortment" No. 19136. The assortment included
twelve models. The same display was provided in the 1967-68
catalog with purchase of the "Permanent Lighted Travel Clock
Display" No. 19177. Dealers now purchased the display and
were given a free Travel Ben to offset its cost. (Photo: 1966-67
catalog) **($150-165)**

23" wide
25" high
8" deep

This free travel clock suitcase display, 23" x 25" x 8", was provided to
dealers purchasing the 1965 Travel Assortment No. 19107 containing
eighteen travel clocks. (Photo: 1965 catalog) **($125-140)**

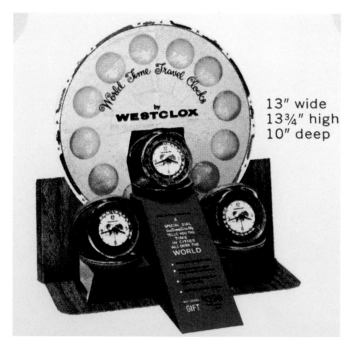

13" wide
13¾" high
10" deep

Dealers purchasing the 1965 "World Time Travel Clock Assortment" No. 19105 received this free counter display, 13" x 13-3/4"
x 10". The assortment contained three clocks. (Photo: 1965
catalog) **($65-75)**

This 1968 Standard Counter Time Center (No. 19209), 28" x 12-1/2" x 6", is reversible for front or rear opening. Each section locks independently. The assortment purchased with the display included five keywound models, one travel alarm, and six electric models. Two free Baby Bens were included to offset the cost of the display. Also offered in the 1967-68 catalog with purchase of Assortment No. 19158. (Photo: 1968-69 catalog) **($45-55)**

This 1965 countertop display, 10-1/2" x 16-1/2" x 4-1/2", was provided to dealers purchasing "Travel Ben Assortment" No. 19114. The assortment includes three Travel Bens, one in each color. (Photo: 1965 catalog) **($45-55)**

The 1968-70 timer display (No. 29071), 16" x 17" x 12", was provided free to dealers purchasing an assortment consisting of the following model Nos. 50019, 50021, 50033, 50035, 50025, 50027, 50037, and 52001. (Photo: 1968-69 catalog) **($45-55)**

This 1968 Wee Winkie easel back display (No. 19210), 24" x 41" x 8-1/2", was provided free to dealers purchasing two each of "Circus Parade" and "Little Red Barn" and one "Jumbo Alarm." (Photo: 1968-69 catalog) **($110-125)**

The 1969-70 "Standard pilfer-proof Time Center" (No. 19253), 30" x 60" x 18". (Photo: 1969-70 catalog) **($175-200)**

17⅜" wide
22¾" high
8¼" deep

This 1963-64 display, 17-3/8" x 22-3/4" x 8-1/4", was provided to dealers purchasing Stanton Assortment No. 59001 consisting of four Stanton models. (Photo: 1963-64 catalog) **($45-55)**

This 1969-70 display, 15-1/2" x 14-1/2" x 5-1/2", was provided to dealers purchasing either the "Men's and Ladies' 9-Pack Assortment No. 39145," "Ladies 9-Pack Assortment No. 39144," "Crown Jewel 9-Pack Assortment No. 39146," or "Men's 9-Pack Assortment No. 39143." (Photo: 1969-70 catalog) **($55-65)**

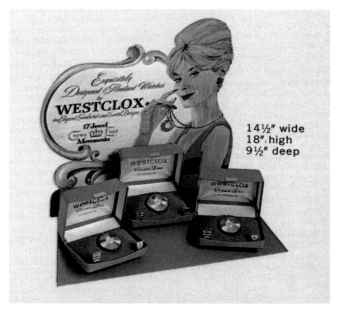

14½" wide
18" high
9½" deep

Dealers purchasing the 1966-67 "Ladies Pendant Watch Assortment" No. 39076 received this free display, 14-1/2" x 18" x 9-1/2". The assortment contained three watches. (Photo: 1966-67 catalog) **($45-55)**

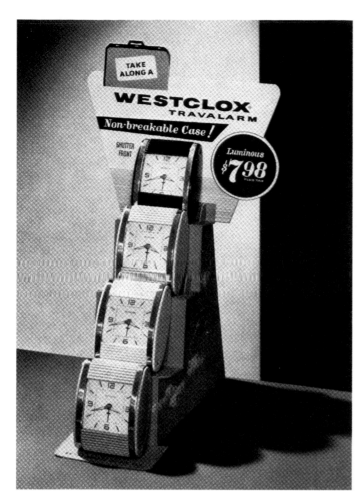

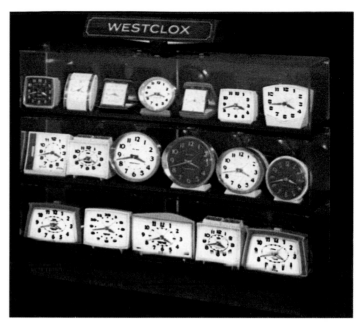

This 1968 Deluxe Illuminated Counter Time Center (No. 19208), 28" x 23" x 6", is reversible for front or rear opening. Each section locks independently. Included in the assortment were six keywound models, three travel alarms, and nine electric models. Three free Baby Bens were included to offset the cost of the display. Also offered in the 1967-68 catalog with purchase of Assortment No. 19156. (Photo: 1968-69 catalog) **($65-75)**

To mark the 1961 introduction of Travalarm in two new colors—Seafoam Green and Danube Blue—this free counter display was provided dealers purchasing Travalarm Assortment No. 19022 containing one of each color. (Photo: *Tick Talk*, March 1961) **($45-55)**

FREE counter-top display.

This 1962-63 Permanent Watch Case (No. 39050), 25-13/4" x 18" x 5", was provided to dealers purchasing an assortment of sixteen watches. It is illuminated and has an ebony wood finish. Pilfer-proof doors open from the rear. (Photo: 1962-63 catalog) **($65-75)**

The 1968 Wall Clock Counter Time Center (No. 29069), 32" x 31" x 8", consists of a pegboard display complete with a header. Included with the display are nine models: Quincy in woodtone, avocado, and antique white; Monitor in desert tan; Countryside in turkey red; Dorena in white and avocado; and Stanford no-cord in avocado and pineapple. Not Pictured: A similar display (No. 29094) was offered in the 1969-70 catalog with purchase of an assortment of nine different wall clocks. (Photo: 1969-70 catalog) **($85-100)**

The Standard Time Center No. 19203, 30" x 60" x 18", features see through adjustable glass shelves, an electrical test outlet, storage base with sliding doors, and pilfer-proof top cabinet. It came with an assorment of fourteen keywound alarms, ten electric alarms, four electric wall clocks, two timers, four travel clocks, and two No-Cord decorator wall clocks. Fourteen free Bens were included to offset the price of the display. Also offered in the 1969-70 catalog with purchase of a different assortment (No. 19252). (Photo: 1968-69 catalog) **($175-200)**

The Custom pilfer-proof Time Center No. 19205, 36" x 72" x 18", is completely enclosed and pilfer-resistant. The entire display is illuminated. It came with an assortment consisting of thirty-eight keywound alarms, thirty electric alarms, nine electric wall clocks, five timers, ten travel clocks, and four No-Cord decorator wall clocks. Twenty-two free Bens were included to offset the cost of the display. Also offered in the 1969-70 catalog with a different assortment (No. 19255). (Photo: 1968-69 catalog) **($225-250)**

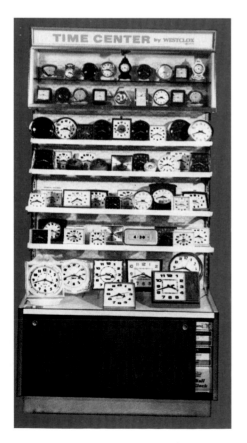

The Deluxe Time Center No. 19204, 36" x 72" x 18", features adjustable glass shelves, electrical test outlet, storage base with sliding doors, and a large pilfer-proof top cabinet. It came with an assortment consisting of twenty-nine keywound alarms, twenty-one electric alarms, seven electric wall clocks, four timers, eight travel clocks, and three No-Cord decorator wall clocks. Eighteen free Bens were included to offset the cost of the display. Also offered in the 1969-70 catalog with purchase of a different assortment (No. 19256) (Photo: 1968-69 catalog) **($175-200)**

Dealers purchasing three All-Temp (No. 83061) thermometers received this free countertop display (No. 19218), 8-1/2" x 7-1/2" x 4". In the 1969-70 catalog the same display was provided with purchase of six All-Temps under a new catalog number (No. 19243). (Photo: 1968-69 catalog) **($35-45)**

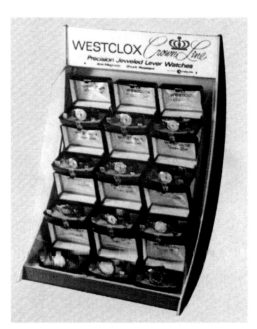

This 1968 countertop display, 16-1/2" x 24-1/2" x 13", was provided to dealers purchasing either the Men's 12-Pack Assortment (No. 39119) or Ladies 12-Pack Assortment (No. 39120). (Photo: 1968-69 catalog) **($55-65)**

The 1968 Time Centers have illuminated displays, "decorator" clear plastic divider, adjustable glass shelves, plastic shelf edging, storage base with sliding doors, and electrical test outlet. Shown is the "Super Store Profit Center I (No. 19206), 48" x 54" x 48", which came with an assortment of clocks and timers with a retail value of over $1,163. Not Pictured: "Super Store Profit Center II (No. 19207), 96" x 54" x 48", which came with an assortment of clocks and timers with a retail value of over $2,300. The same displays were offered with purchase of different assortments in the 1969-70 catalog (Nos. 19257 and 19258, respectively). (Photo: 1968-69 catalog) **($175-200)**

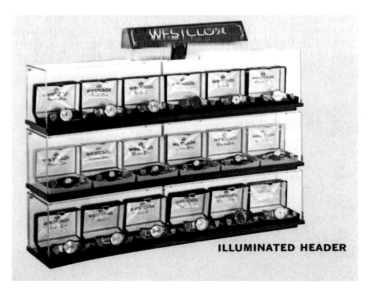

ILLUMINATED HEADER

This 1968 watch display cabinet, 28" x 8-3/4" x 6", was provided with purchase of either the Crown Jewel Wrist Watch Assortment (No. 39122), Men's 6-Pack Assortment (No. 39123), or Ladies 6-Pack Assortment (No. 39124). (Photo: 1968-69 catalog) **($45-55)**

This 1968 display, 28" x 23" x 6", was provided to dealers purchasing "Best Seller Wrist Watch" Assortment No. 39121. The display has an illuminated header. A free watch was included to offset the cost of the display. (Photo: 1968-69 catalog) **($65-75)**

The 1968 "Permanent Pocket Watch Assortment" display (No. 39118), 9-3/4" x 19-3/4" x 7", was available to dealers purchasing nine pocket watches and three stop watches. A Pocket Ben Lighted Dial was provided free to offset the cost of the display. (Photo: 1968-69 catalog) **($65-75)**

The 1967-70 "Magnet Watch Assortment" (No. 39092) display, 8-1/2" x 10-1/4" x 5-1/2", contains six watches. (Photo: 1968-69 catalog) **($35-45)**

The 1968 Pocket Watch Assortment display (No. 39108), 8-1/2" x 15" x 8-1/2", is a revolving display that holds one display card each of Pocket Ben, Bull's Eye, Scotty, and Pocket Watch Thongs (No. 39107). (Photo: 1968-69 catalog) **($55-65)**

The 1969 Deluxe Counter Time Center (No. 19251), 28" x 23" x 6", was provided to dealers purchasing an assortment consisting of six keywound alarms, three travel alarms, and nine electric alarms. Three free Baby Bens were included to offset the cost of the display. (Photo: 1969-70 catalog) **($85-95)**

The 1969 Boutique Alarm Assortment (No. 19241) display, 15-1/2" x 14-1/2" x 5-1/2", was provided to dealers purchasing two each of the following models: Nos. 12090, 12096, 12092, 12098, 12100, and 12102. (Photo: 1969-70 catalog) **($65-75)**

This countertop display (No. 19247), 15-1/2" x 14-1/2" x 5-1/2", was provided free to dealers purchasing an assortment of twelve travel alarms. (Photo: 1969-70 catalog) **($65-75)**

The "Permanent Lighted Travel Clock Display" (No. 19234), 17-3/4" x 16-1/2" x 7-1/2", was provided to dealers purchasing an assortment of twelve travel alarms. (Photo: 1969-70 catalog) **($145-170)**

Part Five: After Hours
Selected Bibliography

Books

Ball, Charlotte, ed. *Who's Who in American Art: Vol. III for the Years 1940-1941*. Washington, D.C.: The American Federation of Arts, 1940.

Byars, Mel. *The Design Encyclopedia*. New York: John Wiley & Sons, Inc., 1994.

Collins, Philip. *Pastime: Telling Time From 1879 to 1969*. San Francisco: Chronicle Books, 1993.

Crum, Elmer G. and William F. Keller, ed. *150 Years of Electric Horology*. Exhibit prepared for the 1992 Chicago Convention of the National Association of Watch and Clock Collectors.

Flinchum, Russell. *Henry Dreyfuss, Industrial Designer: The Man in the Brown Suit*. New York: Cooper-Hewitt, National Design Museum, Smithsonian Institution & Rizzoli, 1997.

Genauer, Emily. *Modern Interiors: Today and Tomorrow*. New York: Illustrated Editions Company, Inc., 1939.

Linz, Jim. *Art Deco Chrome*. Atglen, PA: Schiffer Publishing Ltd., 1999.

Linz, Jim. *Electrifying Time: Telechron and G.E. Clocks, 1925-1955*. Atglen, PA: Schiffer Publishing Ltd., 2001.

McDermott, Kathleen. *Timex: A Company and Its Community 1954-1998*. Middlebury, CT: Timex Corporation, 1998.

Meikle, Jeffrey L. *Twentieth Century Limited: Industrial Design in America: 1925-1939*. Philadelphia: Temple University Press, 1979.

Stein, Mark V. *The Collector's Guide to Twentieth Century Modern Clocks: Desk, Shelf, and Decorative*. Baltimore: Radiomania Books, 2002.

Wilson, Richard Guy, Dianne H. Pilgrim, and Dickran Tashjian. *The Machine Age in America 1918-1941*. New York: The Brooklyn Museum in association with Harry N. Abrams, Inc., 1986.

Articles

Boehm, Lisa Krissoff. 1998. "Industrial Relations at Westclox Corporation, Peru, Illinois 1887-1980." *NAWCC Bulletin*, February, 26-30.

Krissoff, Lisa Beth. 1992. "Industrial Relations at Westclox Corporation, Peru, Illinois 1887-1980." Unpublished paper, portions of which were incorporated into the article published in the *NAWCC Bulletin* of February 1998.

"Peruvian, Oldest Westclocker, Tells of Plant's Growth in Half Century." *The Daily Post-Tribune*, La Salle, Illinois, December 12, 1936. p. 7.

Tjarks, Richard C. and William S. Stoddard. 1983. "Introduction to Westclox" *NAWCC Bulletin* No. 225, August, 446-463.

Tjarks, Richard C. and William S. Stoddard. 1984. *NAWCC Bulletin*, August, 473-475.

Archives

National Association of Watch and Clock Collectors. Columbia, Pennsylvania: Westclox catalogs, sales and promotional material, *Tick Talks*, photographs, wholesale jewelry catalogs, clippings.

Public Library. Peru, Illinois: clippings, *Tick Talks*, photographs, *Tales and Pictures of Peru, 1835-1985*.

Internet Resources

Westclox History at ClockHistory.com. This website is maintained by Bill Stoddard of Bill's Clockworks. ©2003

Appendix 1:
Designs Lost: Designs That Did Not Enter Production

The following pages illustrate some of the design patents awarded to the Western Clock Company and General Time that are not known to have entered production. Some of these designs, particularly those from 1910s where limited records are available, may have entered production. There are several clocks, such as the "Mermaid" and "Cupid" on a 1915 price list for which photographs were not located. If you have a production example of one of these clocks, please contact the author at

jimlinz@documenteddesign.com

so that it can be included in a future edition.

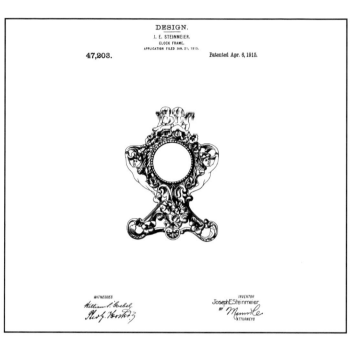

No production example of this 1915 design by Joseph E. Steinmeier was found in available records, but this could be the "Cupid" model listed in a 1915 price list. (Des. 47,203, awarded April 6, 1915)

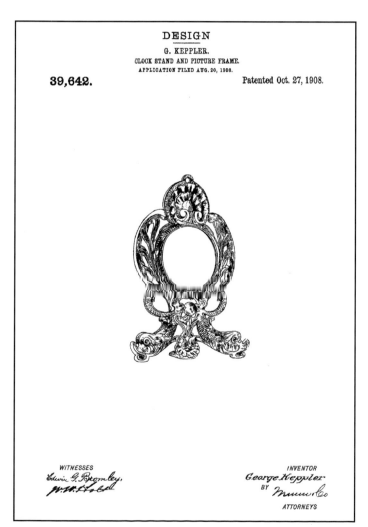

This 1908 design by George Keppler of New York was not found in available records, but may have entered production. Little information was available on models introduced between 1907 and 1920 other than Big Ben and Baby Ben. (Des. 39,642, awarded October 28, 1908)

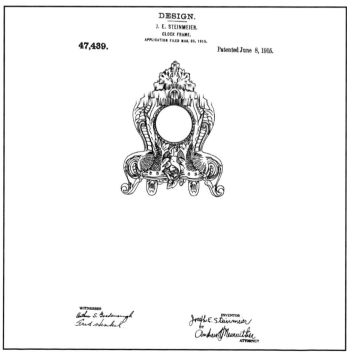

While no production example of this 1915 design by Joseph E. Steinmeyer was found, this is likely the design for the "Mermaid" model listed in a 1915 price list. (Des. 47,439, awarded June 8, 1915)

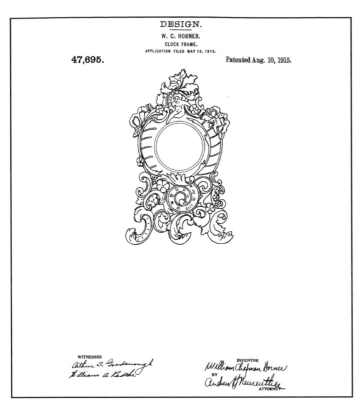

No production example of this 1915 design by William Chapman Horner of Indianapolis was found in the records reviewed, but there were several models listed in a 1915 price list for which photographs were not available. (Des. 47,695, awarded August 10, 1915)

This clock dial designed by George Graff has the shape of the dial on the Model 405, but is a different design. Rights were assigned to the Dura Company. (Des. 83,104, awarded January 20, 1931)

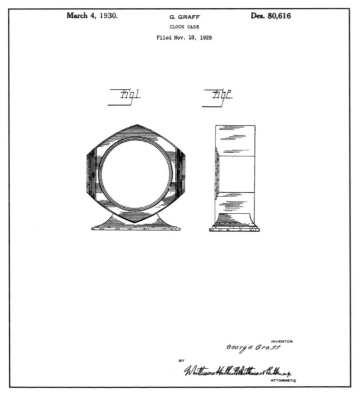

George Graff designed this case at the same time he designed the cases for the first three clocks in the La Salle series. Like those designs, rights to the patent were assigned to Dura. Westclox appears to have decided against production of this design. (Des. 80,616, awarded March 4, 1930)

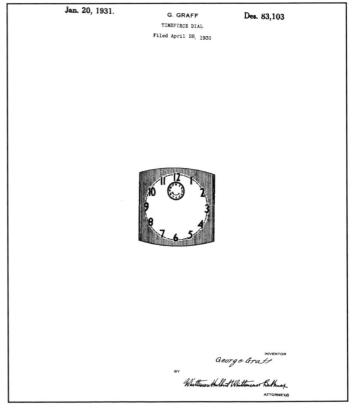

This clock dial designed by George Graff has the same shape as the dial on the Model 404 clock in the La Salle series, but differs from the dial used on the production model. Rights to the design were assigned to the Dura Company. (Des. 83,103, awarded January 20, 1931)

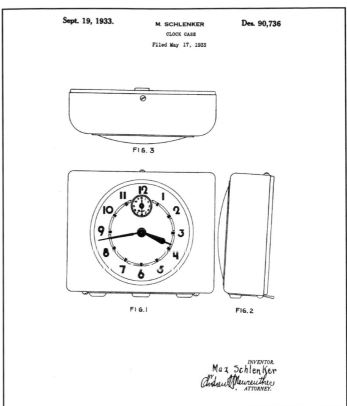

Henry J. Wagner of La Salle designed this special watch dial for the 1933 World's Fair. It is not clear whether the dial was applied to pocket watches sold at the Fair. (Des. 90,144, awarded June 13, 1933)

This 1933 design by Max Schlenker does not appear to have entered production. (Des. 90,736, awarded September 19, 1933)

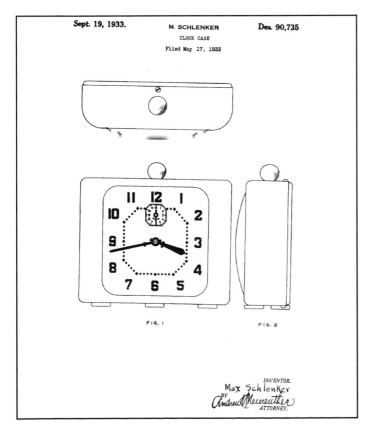

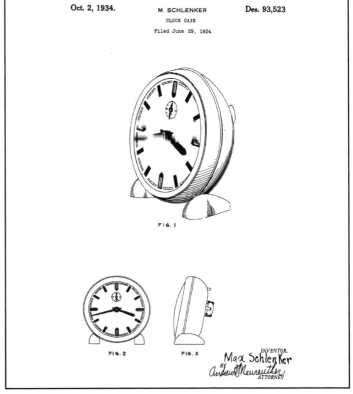

This 1933 design by Max Schlenker does not appear to have entered production. (Des. 90,735, awarded September 19, 1933)

This 1934 design by Max Schlenker with its pontoon feet would have been a real trend setter had it reached production. (Des. 93,523, awarded October 2, 1934)

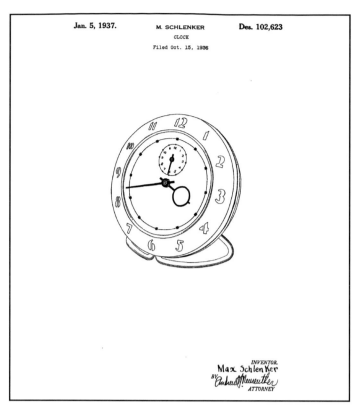

Jan. 5, 1937.   M. SCHLENKER   Des. 102,623
CLOCK
Filed Oct. 15, 1936

INVENTOR.
Max Schlenker
BY
ATTORNEY

Designed at the same time as the "Pittsfield" and using many of the same design elements, this Max Schlenker design did not reach production. (Des. 102,623, awarded January 5, 1937)

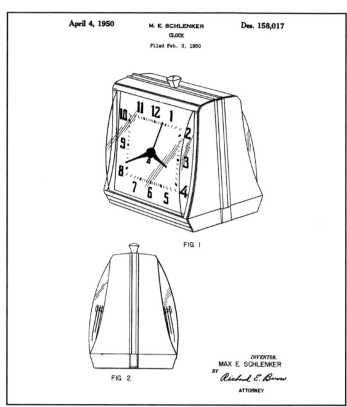

April 4, 1950   M. E. SCHLENKER   Des. 158,017
CLOCK
Filed Feb. 3, 1950

FIG. I

FIG. 2

INVENTOR.
MAX E. SCHLENKER
BY
Richard E. Burn
ATTORNEY

This 1950 Max Schlenker design for a "partners" clock does not appear to have entered production, but records from the early 1950s are incomplete. (Des. 158,017, awarded April 4, 1950)

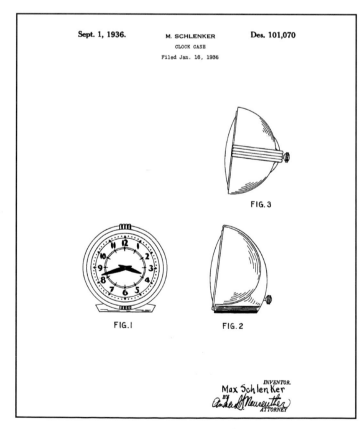

Sept. 1, 1936.   M. SCHLENKER   Des. 101,070
CLOCK CASE
Filed Jan. 16, 1936

FIG. 3

FIG. I   FIG. 2

INVENTOR.
Max Schlenker
BY
ATTORNEY

Another of the Max Schlenker designs of the 1930s that never reached production. (Des. 101,070, awarded September 1, 1936)

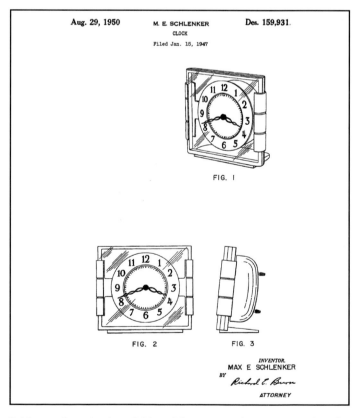

Aug. 29, 1950   M. E. SCHLENKER   Des. 159,931.
CLOCK
Filed Jan. 15, 1947

FIG. I

FIG. 2   FIG. 3

INVENTOR.
MAX E. SCHLENKER
BY
Richard E. Burn
ATTORNEY

Evidence of production of this stylish post-war design was not found, but records from the early 1950s are incomplete. (Des. 159,931, awarded August 29, 1950)

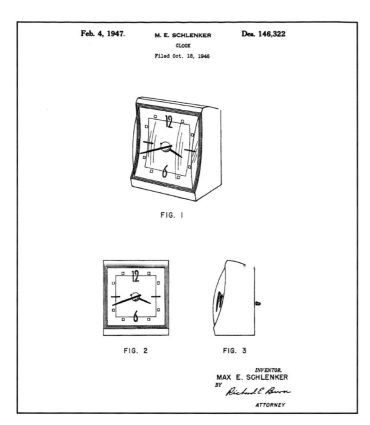

Feb. 4, 1947. M. E. SCHLENKER Des. 146,322
CLOCK
Filed Oct. 18, 1946

FIG. 1

FIG. 2 FIG. 3

INVENTOR.
MAX E. SCHLENKER
BY
Richard E. Burn
ATTORNEY

This post-war design by Max Schlenker does not appear to have entered production. (Des. 146,322, awarded February 4, 1947)

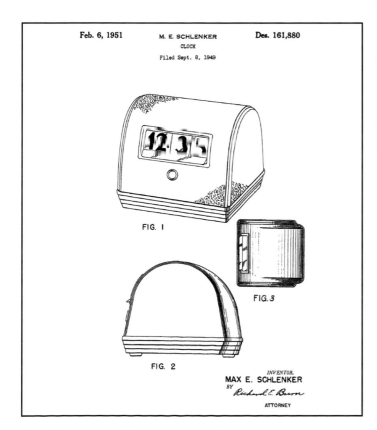

Feb. 6, 1951 M. E. SCHLENKER Des. 161,880
CLOCK
Filed Sept. 8, 1949

FIG. 1

FIG. 3

FIG. 2

INVENTOR.
MAX E. SCHLENKER
BY
Richard E. Burn
ATTORNEY

This 1949 design for a cyclometer clock does not appear to have entered production. (Des. 161,880, awarded February 6, 1951)

United States Patent Office Des. 210,548
Patented Mar. 19, 1968

210,548
CLOCK CASING
Giacinto C. D'Ercoli, Park Forest, Roger L. Kelly, Arlington Heights, and Ellworth R. Danz and Roman J. Szalek, La Salle, Ill., assignors to General Time Corporation, Stamford, Conn., a corporation of Delaware
Filed July 19, 1967, Ser. No. 7,885
Term of patent 14 years
(Cl. D42—7)

FIG. 1

This 1967 design, a joint effort by Giacinto C. D'Ercoli, Roger L. Kelly, Ellworth R. Danz, and Roman J. Szalek, had not entered production by 1970. (Des. 210,548, awarded March 19, 1968)

Appendix II: Factors That Affect Values

Many factors affect what sellers can expect to charge and what buyers can expect to pay for a clock or display. These include the location and venue in which the item is offered for sale, the condition of the clock or display both in terms of appearance and function, and the strength of the design. In setting prices, sellers also need to consider what they paid for the item and how long they are willing to keep it in inventory to obtain the "best" price. Individuals seeking to sell a clock or display to a dealer or at a garage sale should expect to get no more than thirty to fifty percent of its value. Dealers incur significant selling expenses and cannot afford to acquire inventory at prices approaching what they expect to charge for an item.

Neither the author nor the publisher accepts responsibility for any losses that might occur through use of this guide.

Location and Venue

Regional variation in prices seems to be declining, in part because of the widespread availability of price guides and the proliferation of antique shows that draw dealers from around the country. Still, prices are likely to be higher in antique shops in major metropolitan areas and in "trendy" shopping districts like Melrose Avenue in Los Angeles.

Prices within a community also vary depending on the type of store. Thrift stores and church bazaars have low selling expenses—the goods were donated and many of the staff are unpaid volunteers—and can afford to offer items for rock bottom prices. Real bargains can still be found, but it is hit or miss. It may take 100 visits to a thrift store to find a treasure. Competition for thrift store bargains is also intense as casual dealers increasingly seek inventory for on-line auctions such as ebay™.

Bargains can also be found at weekend garage sales. Homeowners running garage sales have culled out items that they no longer need or want and are often content to get a fraction of true value. What does not sell is often carted off the dump or donated to a thrift shop. Rarely do homeowners do the research to determine the true value of items that have been gathering dust in the attic for many years. The downside of garage sales is that you may have to wade through tons of baby clothes and furniture to find anything of interest to a collector.

Garage sales are generally a better source of bargains than estate sales. Although estate sales must, like the garage sale, dispose of vast quantities of merchandise in a short period of time, they are increasingly run by professional estate agents having a better (but often inflated) idea of the value of items offered for sale. Expect prices to be much higher, sometimes exceeding what you might pay in a retail shop. Prices are almost invariably slashed by up to fifty percent on the final day of the sale, so bargains can still be found.

Auctions are another place to find bargains. Traditional estate auctions, such as those listed in *Antique Week* and any number of other antiques publications, provide the best opportunity to find bargains because they offer a wide array of merchandise and a limited number of competitors. Still, it takes only one other

bidder to quickly turn that bargain into a costly mistake. While this happens occasionally at estate auctions, it happens frequently at on-line auctions like ebay®. With millions of users able to view and bid on items, rare clocks and watches frequently sell for far more than what a dealer can expect to obtain for the same item in a retail shop. Conversely, however, ebay is a bargain hunter's paradise for common items with selling prices often well below retail values. When shipping costs are included, however, purchasing lower-priced items can quickly become more costly than buying the same item at an antique mall.

Among the dealers charging the highest prices are those in the mega-malls located in close proximity to an interstate highway or a resort area. Dealers have to charge higher prices in such malls because of high booth rental fees. In addition, some of the malls collect ten percent or more of the sale price. Most malls, however, will give a standard ten percent off posted prices with payment by check or cash. Employees do not routinely offer the discount; you have to ask if the dealer does better on prices.

Prices are also generally higher at clock and art deco shops, but here you get added value. The clock has almost always been cleaned and restored to good working condition. In the long run, paying a higher price for a restored clock may be appreciably less expensive than buying a non-working clock and paying to have it fixed.

Local weekend flea markets can also be a good source of bargains. Bargains can still be found at the larger, nationally advertised, markets like Renningers and Brimfield but they are increasingly populated by full-time dealers who travel from show to show with the same merchandise. Obviously, however, they are constantly adding new merchandise. While they avoid the high monthly rental of an antique mall, they still incur significant expenses for travel, lodging, and booth rental. Nothing, however, beats the ambiance and excitement of the early morning search for bargains at a flea market.

Condition

Values reflected in this guide are for clocks and displays in excellent condition. For a clock, this means:

—It is in good running condition and keeps accurate time. For alarm clocks, the alarm must work.

—The case, dial, and movement are original. If the dial or movement have been repaired or replaced, only new original stock or remanufactured parts have been used.

—The case shows minimal wear. The finish on wooden cases is sound, veneered surfaces are intact, and there are no scratches or gouges in the wood. Bakelite and other plastics are free of cracks, chips, burn marks, and uneven coloration. Plated surfaces are intact with no base metal showing through.

—The dial is free of oil or water stains, peeling paint, or other damage.

–The crystal is intact and free from clouding.

–Painted surfaces are intact and free of stains, peeling, and flaking.

For a display, this means:

–A cardboard display must be free of bends, discoloration, and water damage.

–Paint must be intact and free from peeling and scratching.

–Plated surfaces must be free of scratching and pitting.

–All portions of the display must be present and free of damage.

–Wood must be free of scratches and gouges.

–Lithographed tin and sheet metal signs and displays must be free of bends, discoloration, and flaking paint.

Because few clocks and displays meet these stringent requirements, both sellers and buyers should take into consideration the actual condition in determining value. The effect on value depends on the type(s) and number of defects and their effect on the appearance of the item. As a general rule, deduct:

–two to five percent if the cord is damaged but the clock works. Replacing the cord is among the easiest repairs and many owners are comfortable undertaking this "repair."

–five to twenty percent if the clock is not working properly. Although a clock that is not working has a lower value than does a clock in perfect working condition, in general, working condition is not as important as appearance in setting prices. Deduct less if the clock runs but is noisy or if some function, like the alarm, does not work.

–fifty to seventy-five percent if the clock has a replacement quartz movement. Substituting a quartz movement for the original movement essentially destroys the appeal of the clock to collectors.

–ten to thirty percent for a cracked or missing crystal. Cracked or missing crystals significantly lower value because the purchaser will incur cost in finding a replacement. If the crystal is flat glass it can often be replaced at a reasonable cost. The same is true for convex crystals as long as they are round. Deductions in the upper range apply to convex crystals in unusual shapes, which are virtually impossible to replace.

–twenty-five to sixty-five percent for chips or missing pieces of plastic cases. As a rule, the more visible the crack, chip, or gouge, the more it affects value. If there is significant damage to the case visible from the front or side, values drop at least fifty percent.

–ten to thirty percent if the dial is damaged. The dial is the focal point of the clock and any significant damage, including stains, flaking paint, and scrapes from improperly positioned hands has a major impact on appearance and value. Other than cleaning and touch up of minor scrapes, dial restoration requires the help of a professional and is likely to cost more than the clock.

–twenty-five to sixty percent if the wood has gouges, scratches, or missing parts. Numerous products are available to fill and cover scratches and such defects can often be minimized at little cost and effort. Gouges and missing parts, however, require more extensive repairs and have a significant effect on value. If the wooden case has peeling or missing veneer or missing parts, cut its value by thirty to forty percent.

–ten to twenty-five percent if ornamental trim is missing.

–ten to twenty-five percent if metal parts are dented, worn, or heavily scratched. Trim parts that are tarnished but otherwise in good condition do not significantly detract from value.

–five percent for each missing knob.

Under the above adjustments, clocks with multiple defects quickly lose most if not all of their value. Their value never, however, drops to zero. An insurer declares an automobile a total loss when the cost to repair the car exceeds its fair market value. Such cars, however, still have some salvage value. Similarly, clocks with multiple defects that would require more than a 100 percent adjustment can be sold for parts at five to twenty percent of value.

Similar deductions should be made in valuing displays.

Design and Designer

Clocks by big name designers like Henry Dreyfuss, Walter Dorwin Teague, Paul Frankl, and Russel Wright invariably bring higher prices than those by lesser know or anonymous designers. Some individuals focus their collections on the works of specific designers, like Russel Wright, rather than on a particular category of collectibles, like clocks. Expect clocks designed by Max Schlenker to soar in value as more is learned about the work of this extraordinary designer.

Ultimately, it is the quality of the design, not the name of the designer, that makes a clock or display collectible. In general, electric clocks with strong Art Deco and Mid-Century Modern designs are the most collectible and have higher values. Interpretations of period designs, particularly tambour style mantel clocks, are less collectible, and 1950s plastic alarm clocks have little current value.

Artistic merit is the most important factor to consider in placing a value on a clock or watch display. Displays with strong Art Nouveau or Art Deco styling have the greatest value, but modern designs of the 1950s and 1960s are increasingly popular. While industrial design largely took a back seat to cost-containment in the 1960s, as America tried to survive increasing foreign competition, graphic design continued to flourish.

Rarity

In general, the laws of supply and demand apply to clocks and displays, just as they do to other collectibles, but must not be applied in isolation. A clock that did not sell well when it was introduced because of a dull case design will not appeal to most collectors. Such clocks appeal to the small group of collectors whose collections are based on completeness more than aesthetics. Such collectors may be willing to pay a premium price for a bland but rare clock, but the clock may sit in inventory for months or years before the right collector comes along.

Where rarity has the greatest effect on value is when a clock with an exceptional design did not sell well because of some external force, such as the Great Depression or World War II.

Rarity does not necessarily lead to higher values. Because alarm clocks largely became disposable during the 1950s and 1960s, such clocks are much more difficult to find than clocks made in the 1930s and 1940s. During the 1960s, alarm clocks were typically thrown out rather than repaired, making those that survive rare. Although the better designs occasionally show up in antique shops, alarm clocks from the 1950s and 1960s are more likely to be found in thrift shops for a dollar or two. It appears unlikely that most will appreciably increase in value in the next twenty-five years because they lack that special ingredient—style—that makes a clock collectible.

Clock and watch displays, particularly those from the first half of the twentieth century, are exceedingly rare, adding to their value. Many of the displays were produced for special promotions, such as the annual "Westclox Week" promotions of the late 1930s, and were thrown away following the end of the promotion. Similarly, model-specific displays were typically discarded when the model was dropped or redesigned. Even the more permanent displays were often discarded as new displays were introduced.

Composition

Composition refers to the materials used in the manufacture of the clock case or display stand. For Art Deco-era clocks, plastic cases, whether constructed of Bakelite, Catalin, or Plaskon, are highly desirable because of the attractiveness of the plastic. Plastic cases had a look of quality and are among the most collectible, particularly those in bright colors or with "marbleized" effects. Cases of chrome and glass are also highly collectible from the Art Deco era. Less popular are wood cases and enameled metal cases.

By the 1950s and 1960s, however, new "improved" plastics were being used in clock cases. Although these cases are more impact resistant, they lack the depth and attractiveness of Bakelite. By and large they look cheap. Coupled with many less than stellar designs during the 1960s, plastic went from being a symbol of quality and permanence to the symbol of the disposable society that emerged in the 1960s and 1970s. Like any rule, however, there are exceptions. Plastic-cased clocks with strong designs, such as the "Coquette" and "Dynamic," are among the 1950s and 1960s clocks most likely to increase in value over the next twenty-five years.

In general, clocks of the 1960s with wood (not wood-grained), brass, or glass cases have retained their value much better than those with plastic cases and unimaginative designs.

Composition is also important for clock and watch displays, although not nearly as important as design. More permanent stands made of wood or metal have added value, whereas stands made of plastic (particularly wood-grained plastic) have somewhat lower values. Composition becomes less important, however, when functionality becomes the driving force behind demand. Whereas collectors may shy away from a wood-grained plastic counter-top clock case, an antique dealer looking for a secure way to display "smalls" is likely to pay less attention to the attractiveness of the case.

Functionality

Functionality is also an important factor to consider in determining the value of a clock and watch display. A display that can be used to accommodate a collection of clocks or watches has added value. What better way to show off a collection of Art Deco clocks that on an original 1930s store display stand.

Even a display that lacks artistic merit may have value if it has a secondary use. For example, the large "Time Centers" Westclox introduced in the 1960s do not have a strong artistic appeal, but nevertheless have value because they can be used as display cases in antique malls. In addition, they offer an effective way to present a collection. For example, displays provide a space-efficient way to show off a collection of wall clocks.

Similarly, smaller locking countertop displays are attractive to antique dealers as an effective means to display jewelry or other small items while preventing theft.

Beware of Fake "Black Memorabilia" and "World's Fair" Clocks

Because Black memorabilia is a hot area of collectibles, a few unscrupulous dealers are creating Black memorabilia by adding newly manufactured dials featuring such characters as "Black Popeye" and "Black Mickey" to old clocks. They then charge hundreds of dollars for what would otherwise be a $10 clock. One sure sign of a fake is a dial marked "©1938" on a Big Ben produced in the 1960s.

Similarly, dials featuring the General Electric pavilion at the 1939-40 New York Worlds Fair are increasingly showing up on Westclox and other clock makes. Would Westclox really create a clock that advertises one of its primary competitors? I think not.

Appendix III: Index to Model Names

Appendix IV: Index to Model Numbers